Aesthetics of Anxiety

SUNY series: Insinuations: Philosophy, Psychoanalysis, Literature

Charles Shepherdson, editor

Aesthetics of Anxiety

RUTH RONEN

SUNY PRESS

Cover image © 2008 Artists Rights Society (ARS), New York/ADAGP, Paris.
Max Ernst, "Hommage a Rimbaud."

Published by
State University of New York Press, Albany

Printed in the United States of America

For information, contact State University of New York Press, Albany, NY
www.sunypress.edu

Production by Eileen Meehan
Marketing by Michael Campochiaro

Library of Congress Cataloging-in-Publication Data

Ronen, Ruth.
Aesthetics of anxiety / Ruth Ronen.
p. cm. — (SUNY series, Insinuations)
Includes bibliographical references (p.) and index.
ISBN 978-0-7914-7667-3 (hardcover : alk. paper)
ISBN 978-0-7914-7668-0 (pbk. : alk. paper)
1. Psychology and philosophy. 2. Anxiety. 3. Aesthetics. I. Title.

BF41.R66 2009
111'.85—dc22 2008005672

10 9 8 7 6 5 4 3 2 1

To Gabriel

CONTENTS

LIST OF ILLUSTRATIONS

ACKNOWLEDGMENTS

Lacanian psychoanalysis and philosophical aesthetics constitute a terrain not much trodden by other academics, which is why I owe a real debt to those few who have supported and accompanied this project in various ways.

I would first like to thank Gabriel Dahan, without whom this world, of all possible worlds, would have remained out of reach. I thank him also for inaugurating my interest in Lacanian psychoanalysis and for contributing to my finding ways of turning "civilization and its discontents" into a productive rethinking of problems in aesthetics.

I am grateful to Ellie Ragland, Rodolphe Gasché, and Tierry de Duve, who read various parts of this work at earlier stages and whose responses encouraged me to continue in this vein of research.

I am much indebted to State University of New York Press for its cooperative and sympathetic attitude: to director James Peltz and to Charles Shepherdson, editor of the SUNY series *Insinuations: Philosophy, Psychoanalysis, Literature,* under which this book is being published. Shepherdson's persisting and unequivocal belief and support of my work have made this publication possible.

I am thankful to friends and colleagues who ventured with me into the psychoanalytic domain and helped me develop ways of thinking about psychoanalysis within philosophy that exceed simple application. Shirley Sharon-Zisser, Efrat Biberman, and Adam Tennenbaum have played an indispensable part in recent years' learning.

My gratitude also is due to my students, those whose work I have supervised and those who have participated in my graduate seminars. Their enthusiasm, infinite curiosity, and intellectual openness have always fueled my thought and will continue to assure me that my work has a place in this world.

I am grateful to my family for bearing with me patiently.

I thank Mical Raz for her careful and wise editing, which has substantially contributed to the final product, and my deep gratitude goes to Rona Cohen, my student and assistant, whose help, intelligence, and goodwill cannot be overstated.

Parts of three of the chapters in this book were previously published. An earlier version of the first chapter was published under the title "Art and Anxiety, or: Lacan with Joyce," *Return: A Journal of Lacanian Studies*, 2 (2005): 143–56.

An early version of chapter 2 was published in the electronic journal *Psyart*, "Look the Doll in the Eyes: The Uncanny in Contemporary Art" (2005).

An earlier version of the sixth chapter was published under the title "A Portrait of the Artist as a Vanishing Genius," *Literature and Aesthetics* 16:1 (2006): 37–58.

Work toward this book has been supported by the Israel Science Foundation (ISF).

Introduction

Aesthetics of Anxiety

> That which anxiety is profoundly anxious about is not *definite* kind of Being for Dasein.
>
> —Heidegger, *Being and Time*

How can anxiety be associated with the concerns of aesthetics? The aesthetics of anxiety aims to go beyond the idea that there is anxiety in aesthetics. It aims to structurally place anxiety at the very heart of aesthetic experience. The aesthetics of anxiety brings anxiety, as an affect that universalizes the human condition in psychoanalytic thought, into the picture of aesthetic theory and reveals this universal notion to be particularized in every work of art, in every act of creation. This project is carried out within the overall domain of aesthetic inquiry, planting the psychoanalytic idea of anxiety as interlacing the fundamental repertoire of questions, concepts, and problems with which the aesthetic discipline within philosophy is preoccupied.

Anxiety is universal, which is what justifies its philosophical relevance and our present attempt to articulate its place within the experience of art. Yet while anxiety can be taken as universal both in philosophical and in psychoanalytic contexts, its universalization as an aesthetic response is no trivial task. The first difficulty has to do with whether we can seriously contend that anxiety is involved in every aesthetic experience, both from the side of the creation and from that of the aesthetic judgment. Second, considering the Kantian aesthetic viewpoint, which locates the aesthetic in pleasure, and taking into account the Heideggerian reconsideration of art and its function in terms of the origin of an artwork, universalizing aesthetics around a negative affect produced by art may seem to be too limited on both counts. Anxiety as a central notion of aesthetics is, however, compatible with both orientations: it neither locates the *aesthetic* in an alternative, negative affect nor does it *aestheticize* art, reducing it to a kind of truth-indifferent affect. The aesthetics of anxiety pursued in this study, although following in many ways the outlines of Kantian aesthetics, also provides ways of reconsidering the truth of art by revealing anxiety as intimately linked to Being in the aesthetic mode. In this sense, the aesthetics of anxiety is not alien to Heidegger's philosophy of art either, although the latter only occupies a marginal, occasional place in this study.

As a post-Kantian aesthetics, the aesthetics of anxiety follows the Kantian idea that the universalization of pleasure could not have been attained by Kant without aesthetic pleasure being identified with a cognitive structure rather than having materialized in psychological or mental subjective states. We are pleased by art but at the same time we can entertain other modes of pleasure. One could feel pleasure because the object is taken to be beautiful, or because one owns it, or because we love watching the art of the great masters, or because this piece of art was created by a close friend. So subjective signs of pleasure are of little help when it comes to aesthetic pleasure and its universal status, nor do cognitive criteria for the presence of pleasure exhaust the universal dimension of the aesthetic. The same can be said about anxiety; its structuration involves more than addressing one's intuitions, whether emotional, cognitive, or ethical; it involves a definition of the structural cause of anxiety.

Anxiety is universal, and yet we do not all feel anxious under the same circumstances, or in view of the same artistic objects. We would not necessarily identify our feeling toward art as anxiety under all conditions. Nor is the supposition that the process of creation is imbued with anxiety expected to withstand an empirical test. And yet Alain Badiou has commented on Lacan's seminar on anxiety by saying that it is through anxiety that the subject, in his unary [single] trait, sees the light of day,[1] That is, subjectivity is constituted through anxiety. Along similar lines, it is claimed here that it is through anxiety that the subject inhabits the aesthetic domain, sees the light of art. Anxiety is hence claimed in this study to be universal, because it is located at the heart of the logic that determines the origin of art and of the aesthetic subject experiencing it. This latter tenet brings us into the heart of psychoanalytic thought where anxiety is shown to be connected to the very cause of human desire. Anxiety, in its psychoanalytical determination, is hence in line with both philosophical orientations to art (the Kantian and the Heideggerian). By associating anxiety with an aesthetic query, we hope to ground the universal dimension of psychic reality to which anxiety refers, within philosophical thought.

DISPLEASURE IN AESTHETICS

The history of aesthetics, especially of aesthetics in the analytic tradition, has been extensively occupied with the nature of aesthetic pleasure, and with the possibility of distinguishing *aesthetic* pleasure from other kinds of pleasure.

Anxiety, proposed here as an aesthetic notion, immediately touches on the place of negative pleasure, that is, of displeasure, in aesthetic considerations. The idea of displeasure in the context of aesthetics appears to stem from the concept of aesthetic pleasure as its natural opposite but also divulges its problematic limit, raising the question of whether displeasure also can be part of aesthetic experience. While displeasure may be considered to lie outside of aesthetic considerations when the latter focus on pleasing affects, negative affects do form part of aesthetic experience, as attested to, for instance, by the ancient notion of *catharsis.* Catharsis distinguishes the experience elicited by tragedy as a pleasing relief of the negative sentiments of pity and fear. Aristotelian catharsis already touches on two crucial aspects of displeasure in the context of aesthetic experience: (1) the affinity between aesthetic affects and ethical considerations (as catharsis refers to a pleasure produced by a representation of the suffering of others); (2) the need to distinguish aesthetic *sentiments* (both positive and negative) from aesthetic *affects* (the latter overstepping the positive-negative straightforward divide of sentiments).

Displeasure cannot be easily untied from pleasure not only in Aristotle but also in Kant, who had secured a distinct place for aesthetics in terms of the mental powers of pleasure and displeasure.[2] Displeasure, for Kant, also assumes a central place in what concerns the distinct aesthetic judgment of the sublime. For Kant, displeasure also is present in relation to the possibility of negative judgments of taste (of what is deemed ugly or repulsive), a negativity that can yet be properly aesthetic.

It is no coincidence that aesthetics cannot be argumentatively "purified" of displeasure; displeasure has a structural role in the very delimitation of the domain of pleasure. It appears that displeasure looms paradoxically in the very insistence on the specifically "aesthetic" nature of pleasure: displeasure cannot be posited as the limit of aesthetic pleasure without it being functional in the very consolidation of pleasure as aesthetic. Moreover, following recent decisive attempts to reveal the crucial place of reason and the experience of freedom in Kant's aesthetics (proposed, for instance, by Gasché, and by Guyer), will reveal that disengaging displeasure from the aesthetic domain is problematic. One consequence of the shift in emphasis can be that of assigning a different place to displeasure within aesthetics, the latter no longer viewed as distinctly separate from broader epistemic and ethical considerations. That is, once we grasp aesthetic responses as being somehow subservient to purposes of morality, even when the freedom of the aesthetic remains intact, this place assigned to practical reason cannot leave out the possibility of aesthetic displeasure. We should mention by way of illustration that for Kant the lower faculty of desire is based on the pleasure the subject feels in the reality of the object, a desire that determines the relation to an object according to the extent of gratification it actually supplies. However, the higher faculty of desire, the one associated with pure reason, "must be able to determine the will by the mere form of a practical rule without presupposing any feeling and hence without any representation of the agreeable or disagreeable as the matter of the faculty of desire."[3] The intervening role of the practical law of reason in aesthetic considerations hence necessarily entails a transcendence of the pleasure/displeasure distinction.

KANT'S AESTHETICS AND MODERNIST UPHEAVALS

The primacy of pleasure in aesthetic experience is generally taken to be constituted by the aesthetics of Kant. Kant's *Critique of Judgment*, which in many respects created the field of aesthetics, has subsisted throughout the years, contributing momentously to the history of aesthetics. Kant also enjoys a striking presence in the aftermath of his theories, and his presence is still felt in the most recent resurgence of aesthetic theory. This enduring popularity, even if sometimes embodied in criticism, appears to lose nothing of its intensity, despite radical modernist and postmodernist changes in art-producing practices. Many of these practices seem to counter, in their very foundations, the idea of a distinct mode of aesthetic expression caused by beauty and producing pleasure of an aesthetic kind. And yet the current philosophy of art is profoundly influenced by Kantian conceptions and preoccupations, a striking fact primarily because Kant's aesthetics is primarily about nature and not about art at all, let alone modernist art. Kant enjoys a constant presence in current aesthetics that is no longer an aesthetic of nature and that considers art forms that are distant from anything Kant had in mind. Aesthetic discourse still reacts to Kantian notions in productive ways, and not just by interpreting or criticizing him (see the works of de Duve, Derrida, Foster, Danto), an ongoing relevance that may suggest, among other things, that Kant's thought goes beyond an aesthetic of nature and is not as obverse of displeasing art and of negative aesthetic values as traditionally believed.

While the attempt to define pleasure as well as beauty positively (in cognitive or epistemological terms) is hardly compatible with art after Duchamp, giving up on these notions (as vague, redundant, indeterminate, or even "politically correct or incorrect") would mean giving up on the very project of aesthetics, it being, since the eighteenth century guided by the belief that the philosophy of art presents a distinct, well-differentiated domain within philosophy. The distinctness of the aesthetic is essential not only for the Kantian aesthetic paradigm but also for the Hegelian death of art and for Heidegger's idea that truth happens in the artwork as "beauty is a fateful gift of the essence of truth."[4] Thus being able to define the object called art (the beautiful or sublime object), and the effect specific to art (aesthetic pleasure), is naturally taken as stipulating the very foundations of aesthetics as a distinct philosophical domain.[5] Without these specifically aesthetic concepts that serve to describe the practice of art, either aesthetic concepts would become applicable to all avenues of life (e.g., one can draw aesthetic pleasure from horror or evil events; a poet, a scientist, or a philosopher can equally be described as "creative," etc.) or art would lose its particularity as a distinct mode of signification or as a distinct site of truth-happening. It is against this kind of aesthetic drift, propagated by the notions that everything could be aesthetic, that there is nothing outside of the aesthetic, and that everyone is an artist, that the present study locates itself.

The ongoing presence of eighteenth-century aesthetic concepts in current discourse on art, however, does not always entail keeping with the rudiments of traditional aesthetic theory. In the face of modernist artistic practices and their disparagement of aesthetic values, some philosophers of art have solved this predicament with subversive moves. Some have recommended a reconsideration of the very idea of an aesthetic domain (Dickie, Coleman). Others have suggested possibilities such as the replacement of the beautiful with the artistic (Kieran) or the ethical (Norton). Another move vis-à-vis Kantian aesthetics, mentioned earlier, is a move that also may seem subversive of Kant's primary aims but in fact unearths a whole dimension, hitherto scarcely discussed, by Kant's analytic commentators: the ethical dimension in the aesthetic. While Kant states in §59 that beauty is the symbol of the morally good and refers to ideas of reason as part of the solution to problems posed by aesthetic judgments, a cursory glance at analytic approaches to Kant shows that the relevance of problems of taste to Kant's moral philosophy has either been overlooked or downplayed at least until the 1980s. This is partly related to the fact that analytic aestheticians have, for many years, considered Kant's aesthetics an early version of formalism, hence outside the concerns of any ethics. Recent commentaries suggest, however, that Kantian aesthetics goes beyond its traditional analytic reading and cannot be sharply distinguished from Kantian ethics, as the case of the sublime or of the intellectual interest in the beautiful, within the limits of aesthetics, indicates (see Gasché, Guyer, Danto).[6] This move of countering a kind of autism of the aesthetic canonically attributed to Kant is not, however, to be considered subversive of the very idea of the aesthetic. It does not dilute or undermine the distinctive nature of an aesthetic kind of experience. This book will introduce the central notion of anxiety and displeasure as distinctly aesthetic experiences, although their ethical implications cannot be overlooked.[7]

DISPLEASURE AND ANXIETY IN AESTHETIC EXPERIENCE

What kind of pleasure can be immanent to art? Is there a pleasure that is raised by art but is irrelevant to other human contexts (that is, a singular kind of pleasure)? The question of immanence and singularity vis-à-vis art, to use Badiou's terms,[8] requires going beyond the Kantian idea that aesthetic pleasure is attributed primarily to natural objects, and that all pleasure is of the same kind. As noted earlier, Kant's aesthetics is not primarily an aesthetics of art and, furthermore, Kant implies that we cannot differentiate aesthetic pleasure from other pleasures just by the properties of the pleasure itself. Pleasure for Kant is always the same pleasure, and it is through the cognitive state that is conditioning it that pleasure in the beautiful can be differentiated from pleasure in the agreeable. Guyer, probably the most prominent commentator and interpreter of Kant, indeed claims in his first book on Kant's aesthetics that "pleasure [is] a feeling, which Kant's entire argument makes clear is a single psychological state phenomenologically identical in all of its occurrences."[9]

That is, even in relation to Kant, the forerunner of modern aesthetics, securing the singularity of aesthetic pleasure and its immanence to art demands some considerable interpretative effort. It requires a specifically aesthetic pleasure to be carved as distinct from other modes of pleasure, even if pleasure itself is always the same, and this carving allows us to view Kant's aesthetics as an aesthetics of art. It is precisely in this context of reconsidering the idea of an immanent, singular aesthetic experience that the notion of anxiety introduces itself. To propose an aesthetics of anxiety is not a way of encroaching upon aesthetic pleasure replacing it with displeasure, nor is it a proposal to reconsider the place of displeasure within traditional aesthetics. Rather, the aesthetics of anxiety requires a radical rethinking of aesthetics, as anxiety depends on an understanding of aesthetic pleasure as *superseding the distinction between positive pleasure and negative displeasure.* Aesthetic experience requires a notion that exceeds the confines of pleasure and the conception of the aesthetic as formally self-sustaining without compromising the singular satisfaction we draw from art and the immanence of this satisfaction to distinct objects of appreciation. In this junction of what may appear to be almost impossible demands, we propose the idea of anxiety as a vista through which a rereading of Kant becomes possible and a singular and immanent notion of the aesthetic can be articulated. How is this aesthetic agenda to benefit from the idea of anxiety in psychoanalysis?

Anxiety, as this book will demonstrate, is raised within the structure that relates the subject to its object of desire, and the object of desire is accessible only as an object of lack. Human desire can never be satisfied or fully gratified. Thus the psychoanalytic notion of desire, unlike the Kantian desire, is not strictly on the side of pleasure and happiness, and the anxiety related to desire necessarily goes beyond the pleasure principle. Lacan claims in one of his seminars that "pleasure limits the scope of human possibility—the pleasure principle is a principle of homeostasis. Desire, on the other hand, finds its boundary, its strict relation, its limit, and it is in the relation to this limit that it is sustained as such, crossing the threshold imposed by the pleasure principle."[10] Desire is where the relation to the object exceeds the question of pleasure and yet still has a limit; desire crosses the threshold of pleasure, because its object is not the object in reality (the object in reality functioning as a substitute that satisfies only partially). While the object in reality is the one that actually gives pleasure, desire encounters its object at the limit where the pleasure from the object is lost. At this limit, where one comes across the lost object, desire stops, thus producing anxiety.

Desire has to do with the relations between what is given to the subject's demand for pleasure and the object that causes desire, which is an object of real loss always rendering the satisfaction attained partial and "not it." Anxiety in its fundamental relation to desire is raised on a somewhat paradoxical account: that of the possibility of the object of desire not being encountered in the image actually present and, at the same time, that of the possibility of coming too close to the object that is the cause of desire. The former is the possibility that the object encountered as the object of satisfaction will fail to stand for the subject's lack, will fail to appear as a lacking substitute for another, primordial, real object (it will fail to embody the *object-a*, to use Lacan's term). The latter possibility is that what is actually represented will fail to screen out the object that causes desire, that is, the object that caused the appearance of a pleasing substitute in the first place.

In these preliminary terms, I introduce through the concept of anxiety the idea of a "higher" desire, which prevents the subject of aesthetic experience from entering a homeostatic pleasure. Anxiety, in assuring the relation of the subject to what aesthetically grips her or his faculties, yet "reminding" her or him of an immanent loss in relation to which the artistic object is judged, can help us address the question of aesthetic affect. Anxiety marks the limit of the principle of pleasure, thus marking the possibility of the desiring subject to "desire highly," just as displeasure serves as the limit of pleasure, thus marking the possibility of the subject of judgment to judge aesthetically.

PSYCHOANALYSIS AND AESTHETICS

The phrase "the aesthetics of anxiety" poses a challenge before aesthetic tradition by singling out displeasure as being a significant aesthetic concern. Nevertheless, anxiety in aesthetics involves a displeasure that transcends the pleasure principle and is not simply to be perceived as the opposite of pleasure. Hence, anxiety relates to a displeasure intimately tied to possibilities of satisfaction and enjoyment. Furthermore, by indicating that the anxiety fundamental to psychic experience constitutes the basis of *aesthetic experience*, the aesthetics of anxiety views aesthetic experience as being a distinct kind of experience to which human subjects are given. This should be stressed especially since the psychoanalytic conception of art may appear detached from aesthetic concerns, as its applicability exceeds the limits of the aesthetic in its philosophical determination. This incommensurability can be described in the following terms: while aesthetics, at least in the analytic tradition, addresses the question of the relations between beauty in the object and pleasure in the subject, psychoanalysis interests itself in art insofar as art gives rise to unconscious formations that are *displeasurable* to the subject as much as they attract or appeal to her or him. When Freud writes about the relations between psychoanalysis and aesthetics, he seems indeed to endorse the distance between them. In introducing the notion of the *uncanny*, he refers to it as being outside the concerns of aesthetics, a domain that interests itself in what is beautiful, attractive, and sublime and in feelings of a positive nature. Aesthetics chooses not to address affects often produced by art, such as the affects of anxiety, distress, and repulsion. For Freud, the role of psychoanalysis in this context is to examine these very questions that aesthetics avoids, or is prevented by its inherent interests from addressing.[11]

Yet Freud does not suggest two sets of questions, one addressed by philosophical aesthetics and one by psychoanalysis, in relation to art. Rather, the significant implication to be drawn from the psychoanalytic interest in art is that the repertoire of classic aesthetic concepts is permeated by unconscious formations that point to the fact that aesthetic experience is not to be simply defined by the positive side of things. Beauty, for instance, from a psychoanalytic perspective, can be regarded as a type of *sublimation*, which is a formation transforming the fact of repression into a socially acceptable image. In other words, beauty in art is understood by psychoanalysis to be a product of culture associated with the frustration, deprivation, and castration (as prototypical forms of lack) that civilization imposes on the hypothetically free movement of the drives. Hence, beauty in art elicits enjoyment, but this enjoyment has to do with displeasing, even painful, effects. Psychoanalysis, through its interest in art, reveals that pleasure and displeasure in aesthetic experience are not straightforwardly correlated with positive or negative sentiments.

But before pointing to what is beyond the pleasure principle, the psychoanalytic notions of anxiety and the uncanny introduce a preliminary way of countering the alleged aesthetic dominance of pleasure in relation to aesthetic experience. Freud, in his essay on the uncanny, refers to anxiety as being embodied in literary experience, showing how its manifestations take many and varied forms. Objects not clearly defined as human or inhuman, occurrences of doubles, omnipotence of thought—these and others elicit anxiety. The uncanny has to do with uncertainty, hesitation, and animation, and with the compulsion to repeat—a repertoire of almost unlimited possibilities of formation. The embodiment of anxiety-ridden experiences is extensive in art, and with this singular intensity, the uncanny constitutes an aesthetic experience that cannot be correlated with positive sentiments, nor simply equated with extra-artistic experience.

Freud, who developed in three major essays the notion of anxiety as being beyond the pleasure principle,[12] already thought of anxiety as a *particular affect of a universal structure* rather than as a subjective reaction to a specific theme, object, or sense-stimulus (which could characterize the psychological approach to anxiety). Anxiety, just as Kantian pleasure, is not to be located in a specific feature of the object causing it, nor understood as automatically raised in every subject facing that object. Lacan would later say that when one faces a picture by Zurbaran presenting to us Lucy with her eyes on a plate or Agatha with her breasts so placed, it is not the signification of this picture that troubles the spectator.[13] These images present to us "the object of our desire," yet in no way do they introduce us, in themselves, to the order of anxiety. That is, anxiety is there yet not as a given but as something it is necessary to seek out. So the key to understanding the pictures is anxiety, says Lacan, yet the place of anxiety is not determined by the nature of the objects depicted nor by the masochistic subject assumed in them. Zurbaran presents in these images subjects reduced to the position of an object of enjoyment, which is the masochistic gesture of positing herself or himself in the function of human rag, a poor scrap separated from the body.[14] Lacan correlates the anxiety raised by a particular artistic scene with the universal psychic structure of perversion by claiming that the anxiety raised by this artwork has to do with the way art makes us see the subject reduced to the *object a*, to the very object marking the lack in one's satisfaction. However, it is only through the neurotic *Erlebnis*, which transforms the masochistic position depicted in the image into a reference to something beyond, that anxiety is produced. The observer of art facing the image of the pervert with her or his object of enjoyment bluntly exposed will be affected by anxiety. Lacan had indeed associated on various occasions the anxiety raised by art and the pervert psychic structure in terms of which the work of art maintains its relation to its observer/reader. This is not the exclusive structure within which anxiety is raised, yet it illustrates the way a universal psychic logic can be correlated with a particular affect. This preliminary example also indicates that anxiety is not given in the image, nor is it a product of the image's signification structure. Anxiety is correlated, just as pleasure and displeasure are for Kant, with the subject's particular position before the artistic object/image.

But even prior to the singular experiences of art that are associated with anxiety (e.g., uncertainty, sublimation, perverse position), it should be noted at the present stage that anxiety, just as Kantian pleasure, has to do with the fundamental human condition that enables enjoyment under strict constraints. These constraints are called in psychoanalysis "castration" and "repression" and "disinterestedness," "purposiveness without purpose" by Kant, thus referring to enjoyment as being immanently structured around a fundamental lack. Anxiety thus provides a new way of approaching the question of aesthetic pleasure that goes beyond the distinction between positive and negative sentiments, by tying our experience with art to the psychic logic of human enjoyment.

THE OBJECT OF ANXIETY, THE OBJECT OF AESTHETIC JUDGMENT

On a preliminary reading of the third critique, it may appear that Kantian aesthetics suggests an experience in relation to which the object is indifferent; aesthetic judgment neither produces cognition of the object nor the possibility of pointing to its aesthetic qualities in an objective manner. It takes a radical reconsideration of Kantian aesthetics on its own terms (and not by ignoring Kant's strict constraints on the act of judgment) to demonstrate the way in which the object of judgment is consequential to the subject of cognition. The relevance of the object of judgment can be shown through its function in eliciting an idea of reason, or by suggesting that the relevant object, rather than being flatly annihilated, is affirmed by negation.[15] The psychoanalytic notion of anxiety can indeed allow aesthetics to reconsider the place of the object in relation to aesthetic judgment. In his seminar on anxiety, Jacques Lacan claims that "anxiety is not without an object," implying that anxiety can be the cause of psychic events (such as repression) because it signals the presence of a real object. The real object, which is in itself indeterminate, can be substituted by an imaginary replacement.[16] Lacan claims that anxiety, although a universal state for the subject, is raised precisely because it signals a real encounter with an object, the nature of which has to be articulated within the particular domain of the subject. It is due to this real encounter signaled by anxiety that anxiety can never deceive; the affect of anxiety is not the product of interpretation or signification but rather is imposed on the subject as a subject of certainty. Anxiety for the subject has the status of a knowledge of an intimate experience that she or he possesses, even if exempt from it (as not all subjects are affected by anxiety). It is a universal certitude of a nongeneral experience.[17] Beyond the pleasure principle, both anxiety, in its Freudian-Lacanian sense, and aesthetic pleasure, in its Kantian sense, are not given to subjective interpretation and do not require actual personal experience to gain their certitude for the subject.

How should we understand the certitude that accompanies anxiety? Lacan's interpretation of anxiety follows (and modifies) the steps taken by Freud in his "Inhibitions, Symptoms, and Anxiety," in which Freud shows that anxiety emerges in the face of a danger whose object cannot be identified with an object from reality, nor with an object signifying the psychic loss of a primary pleasure.[18] Anxiety, according to Freud, is a signal of loss, not of the actual loss but of the danger of losing the real object. This danger can be described as that of not having the real object represented in the Other; the danger of not seeing the lost object represented in whatever image we face, of losing sight of the loss.

Anxiety does not only signal danger but also appears as a cause, a cause identified with the menacing moment of encountering the real. Hence, anxiety is both a signal of the possibility of the loss of the object and also the cause for fleeing from that object. This, to follow Lacan's reading of Freud's concept of anxiety, indicates that anxiety is not to be identified with the finding or losing of an object that actually could cause pleasure or displeasure. Anxiety, beyond the pleasure principle, is raised in relation to desire itself, which at its limit brings the subject into the domain of the unknown; it both marks an object signaling the possibility of reexperiencing loss and the possibility of encountering the real object of enjoyment that causes the subject to flee. We see, then, that an object, even if not the object of reality, is at the core of the very notion of anxiety.

If we import this paradoxical idea regarding the reasons for anxiety into the domain of beauty, then it can illuminate why beauty can cause anxiety in the observer. Beauty is opaque, immune to symbolization, as Kant has shown us. We cannot say why or in what this object before us is beautiful—we find ourselves as if estranged by the beauty of the object. As such, the object in reality judged as beautiful disables the subject from relating to it as an object of desire, that is, as an object that replaces the original loss of the object of desire. In beauty, losing sight of desire elicits anxiety in the observer. One answer to this predicament of loss is the perverse choice of identifying with the object of real loss, a choice that will relieve the anxiety of the subject but will intensify that of the observer, the Other of the scene. The encounter with beauty can thus be articulated in terms of the paradoxical object of anxiety: the subject fears losing in the beautiful object the signs of her or his own desire, and yet the beautiful object stands for the ultimate object of desire.

This introduction presents the core ideas that will be further developed in this book as part of a larger attempt to reconsider the place of anxiety at the heart of the aesthetic experience of art. The chapters here explore anxiety by reconsidering the four fundamental concepts of aesthetics: pleasure, beauty, the sublime, and the genius, and in this sense the chapters outline the fundamentals of Kantian aesthetics while reconsidering them in view of psychoanalytic anxiety.

Chapter 1, "On the Anxiety Prior to Any Judgment of Taste," explores the status of displeasure and of negative judgments of taste in Kant to show that both in Kant and in his later commentators displeasure has a necessary place. Further on in this chapter, psychoanalytic anxiety is brought into play as a moment that can be isolated in every judgment of taste. Anxiety is called for as a moment of hesitation prior to any judgment of something being beautiful or sublime.

Chapter 2, "The Beautiful Thing," examines aesthetic beauty in Kant to associate it with Freud's notion of the uncanny and explores the claim that beauty in the modernist experience of art is intensely present, and its affect can be associated with the affect of beauty as perceived by Kant. The discussion concentrates on doll images, extensively used by modernist artists, from the surrealists to Cindy Sherman's photographs, images that use the idea of dolls' beauty to elicit anxiety in the observer. Different possibilities of tying beauty in art to anxious affects are developed and explored.

Chapter 3, "Catharsis, Displeasure, and Anxiety," examines the notion of catharsis as an aesthetic affect that relates pleasure to displeasureable causes. Catharsis is enacted on the negative emotions of pity and fear to ultimately produce aesthetic pleasure. Freudian and Lacanian views on tragedy and catharsis are analyzed alongside philosophical attempts to settle what seems like an ethical incompatibility between aesthetic pleasure and the conditions that bring it about. This chapter distinguishes catharsis from anxiety in terms of the relation of these affects to the pleasure principle.

Departing from catharsis, chapter 4, "Toward Two Principles of Aesthetic Functioning," concentrates on the structure of anxiety in the subject, on the coordinates that structurally define anxiety, and on the aesthetic and ethical consequences of this structure.

Chapter 5, "Beyond the Sublime," addresses the problematic aesthetic notion of the sublime that in Kant is both associated with an object and, at the same time, is disconnected from any object of nature or art. This chapter reveals productive links between the aesthetic sublime and psychoanalytic sublimation in terms of their ethical implications. While for Kant the sublime has ethical implications because of its dependence on reason, for Freud and Lacan the ethical implications of sublimation have to do with the object of sublimation. The objects of sublimation and of the sublime, not being objects of reality, can account for the displeasurable affect, or the anxiety, that accompanies them.

Chapter 6, "The Subversion of Genius and the Dialectic of Creation," relates to Kant's idea of genius and to the fundamental paradox of "original exemplarity" defining the function of genius as the instigator of beautiful works of art. In an attempt to solve this paradox, the case of genius will be tested against Lacan's study of James Joyce's writing. Joyce will be considered as a writer of genius who has left generations of readers and critics anxious and perplexed. The anxiety that Joycean writing effectuates in its readers has to do with the way Joyce, the genius, makes use of language, of given forms that at the same time are symptomatic of Joyce's particular enjoyment.

CHAPTER ONE

On the Anxiety Prior to Any Possible Judgment of Taste

Can displeasure be aesthetic? What kind of relevance does pleasure maintain for aesthetic experience? What makes a judgment of an object as ugly an aesthetic judgment? Is aesthetic pleasure such that it sets the limit of the aesthetic (thus foreclosing displeasure)? These questions have obviously come to occupy aestheticians in recent decades not only as part of the ongoing commentary on Kant's aesthetics but as part of the attempt to find a way of reconciling the interests of an aesthetic investigation with the changing, apparently antiaesthetic, face of contemporary art. Modernism, so it seems, has made it difficult to distinguish beauty from ugliness, form from formlessness, pleasure from displeasure, and satisfaction from repulsion, thus undermining the usefulness of these concepts for delineating the nature of aesthetic experience. Displeasure and the displeasing effects of the encounter with the disgusting, repulsive, and ugly, especially associated with modernism in art, have convinced some aestheticians of the irrelevance of pleasure to the basic aesthetic experience or the irrelevance of any notion of the aesthetic to one's experience of art.[1] At the same time it is difficult to think of an aesthetics within which these primarily aesthetic concepts do not play a central role.

The aim of this chapter is threefold: (1) to show that the *aesthetic* domain, as it emerges from Kant and from many post-Kantian aestheticians, is constituted by *both pleasure and displeasure*, and that displeasure, rather than calling for a different aesthetics, is equally fundamental as pleasure to one's experience with art; (2) to suggest viewing pleasure and displeasure not only as distinct facts about possible aesthetic experiences (the former attesting to the presence of a beautiful object, the latter to the presence of a nonbeautiful one) but rather that *displeasure fulfills a necessary intervening role in every aesthetic experience*; (3) to expose the constitutive role of *displeasure at the heart of Kant's aesthetics* and to support the present endeavor of developing the notion of displeasure as aesthetic by contemporary studies that revive interest in the forms of displeasure and in ugliness.[2]

Establishing the place of displeasure within the aesthetic domain appears to demand considerable argumentative effort, especially since it relies on a retroactive interpretation of Kant "under modernist eyes." Psychoanalysis, on its part, regards pleasure and displeasure as fundamentally mingled, as they share the management of the "pleasure principle," to use Freud's term. The "pleasure principle" regulates mental processes so that displeasurable tension is avoided or discharged and pleasure is increased, but displeasure always remains part and parcel of the working of the pleasure mechanism, having its upper hand once tension increases anew. The pleasure principle is hence the fundamental navigator of psychic life, producing the dynamics of pleasure and displeasure. For psychoanalysis there is no simple lack or absence of pleasure: *everything is subjected to the pleasure principle* (a supposition that later in this chapter will be correlated with Kant's mutually bound pair of pleasure and displeasure).[3]

Freud gradually develops in his work the notion of anxiety that rather than standing as a synonym for displeasure subsumes both displeasure and pleasure. Already in 1917, in a lecture on "anxiety," Freud establishes the relation of anxiety to libido and describes the emergence of anxiety in hysteria, "where its unconscious correlate can equally be an impulse of similar character—anxiety, shame, embarrassment or, just as easily, a positive libidinal excitation."[4] In later years, Freud stresses the relation of anxiety to repression and refers to anxiety as a signal prior to the ego's ability to withdraw from or otherwise avoid displeasurable excitations.[5] Birth, for instance, which serves as a model for an anxiety state, is "of highly tense excitation, which is felt as unpleasure and which one is not able to master by discharging it."[6] Pleasure and displeasure both play an important part in the emergence of anxiety; anxiety is felt as unpleasure but in fact signals a moment of libidinal excitation.

Further on in this chapter, after describing the intriguing role of displeasure in aesthetics and reviewing its implications, I will suggest tying the aesthetic pair of pleasure-displeasure to the psychoanalytic concept of anxiety in its relation to the fundamental divide of the pleasure principle. This will lead to the claim that displeasure, for Kant, just as anxiety, for Freud, and later for Lacan, may appear as *prior, yet constitutive, of the very act of judgment* (of taste). In other words, it will be proposed in this chapter that the place of Kantian displeasure be reconsidered in terms of psychoanalytic anxiety, and that displeasure is regarded as fundamental rather than alien to aesthetic experience.

To establish the logic of the distinction of pleasure-displeasure, a relation left perplexingly open to interpretation by Kant, anxiety, as used by Freud and Lacan, will further present the possibility of *mingling pleasure and displeasure.* Anxiety signals something unpleasant that is also attractive and imbued with potential pleasure for the subject. Anxiety, therefore, has intricate relations with pleasure-displeasure; it both complies with the demands of pleasure and goes beyond the pleasure principle.[7]

Anxiety, in its psychoanalytic sense, is not tantamount to negative displeasure and resists the pleasure-displeasure divide. Yet for anxiety to hold more than heuristic value in articulating the nature of aesthetic experience, one obstacle has to be surmounted. If anxiety *transcends the distinction between pleasure and displeasure*, and hence *resists being correlated with definitely valued objects*, then how can it serve us in telling the ugly from the beautiful, that is, in actually making a judgment of taste? While the answer to this question permeates various parts of this book, it can be pointed out at the present stage that over and above some fundamental differences between the philosophical and the psychoanalytic ways of thinking about aesthetic experience anxiety cannot tell the difference between the ugly and the beautiful because it is prior to actual judgment. Anxiety is not a response that alternates with positive affects but rather is something that precedes the distinction of displeasure from pleasure. Anxiety will thus be established as prior to judgments that follow the dictates of the pleasure principle. Furthermore, the notion of anxiety does not contradict the possibility of aesthetic judgment, because for Kant too the judgment of taste does not reside in the positive characterization or knowledge of an object. Anxiety, just like aesthetic pleasure and displeasure in aesthetics, contributes nothing to the cognition of the object in reality, nor is it a sign that carries meaningful insights about that object, nor an effect with specific emotional content. Anxiety, just like pleasure and displeasure, is a signal marking the presence of a specific structure (a cognitive structure for Kant, a psychic structure for Freud and Lacan) that can be shown to constitute one's encounter with art. It is indeed the main purpose of this chapter to point to anxiety, precisely because it subsumes the divide between pleasure and displeasure yet acknowledges their distinct psychic value as related to aesthetic experience and as constitutive of the very foundations of one's encounter with art.

To further the argument regarding the place of displeasure in aesthetics, this chapter proceeds by first examining one problematic aspect of the *location of aesthetic pleasure* in Kant, which has to do with Kant's dilemma around the precedence or antecedence of pleasure to the mental state that leads to the judgment of something as beautiful. After that, further support will be found through examining the possibility of including negative judgments of taste (judgments that result in displeasure) within the aesthetic domain. The implications drawn from these interpretive difficulties will be later associated with the psychoanalytic concept of anxiety.

KANT AND AESTHETIC PLEASURE

Kant's aesthetics is guided by two fundamental tenets: aesthetic judgment does not provide cognition of the object concerned, and judgments of taste, although subjective, have universal applicability. The first supposition points to the fact that judgments of beauty, although formulated as if referring to a property of the object itself, in fact characterize the cognitive state of the appreciator: "an aesthetic judgment is unique in kind and provides absolutely no cognition (not even a confused one) of the object; only a logical judgment does that. An aesthetic judgment instead refers the presentation, by which an object is given, solely to the subject; it brings to our notice no characteristic of the object, but only the purposive form in the way the presentational powers are determined in their engagement with the object."[8] For Kant, attributing beauty to an object is a way of validating the universality of the judgment, because when one says "this is beautiful" it is assumed that everybody ought to agree on this judgment (even if in actual fact such an agreement may not be actualized). In other words, the subjectivity of aesthetic judgments is achieved through the subject's certainty that beauty is attributable to an object, while this attribution tells us something about the cognitive state of the subject (that of harmony between the faculties of cognition) rather than about the properties or essence of the object thus predicated. Since the purpose of aesthetic judgment does not lie in cognizing the object but in attaining a certain cognitive state that produces pleasure of an aesthetic kind, questions about the characteristics of the object that make it beautiful lie outside of aesthetic concerns. Thus in the third critique transcendentalism, which in the Kantian sense relates to what conditions our knowledge of objects, is here giving rise to no determined knowledge whatsoever. The free play of the cognitive faculties is undoubtedly transcendental, relating the enabling conditions for knowing aesthetic objects, "and yet in judgments of taste it hovers on its own,"[9] unsupported by empirical rules or by determined concepts.

Judging something as beautiful transcends the private domain of personal opinion. The universal validity of judgments of taste means that when we say "this is beautiful" we demand consent to this judgment from other subjects. Being however devoid of objective cognitive value, this judgment cannot be proven or explained. No law can explain where beauty lies or can justify one's way of looking at the object as beautiful. Hence, universal agreement regarding beauty does not rely on logical explanation or on empirical agreement among members of a given community.[10] A judgment of taste is agreed upon not on the basis of a majority vote, nor is it just metaphorically universal (that is, an agreement referring to no more than an intensity of emotions regarding a certain object); agreement is a logical demand from judgments of taste. It is for this reason that aesthetic judgments predicate objects as beautiful in a way that exceeds matters of personal liking. Agreement has to do with the kind of satisfaction experienced by a subject who assumes, as part of the very logic of her or his statement of taste ("this is beautiful"), that whoever is exposed to the object given to a judgment of taste will experience the very same pleasurable state.

This cursory presentation of Kant's main contribution to the history of aesthetics, that is, the idea that a judgment of taste is not a way to convey knowledge about an object, and that this judgment yet refers to a pleasurable cognitive state of universal validity, transfers the full weight of aesthetic experience to the judging subject. The subject, to present an aesthetic judgment, has to tie his or her judging act and the cognitive state that led to it, to the pleasure felt as a result. Pleasure has to fulfill some conditions to be considered a pleasure in the beautiful. Establishing the link of pleasure to the judgment of the beautiful by showing that aesthetic pleasure must be the outcome of the judging act and cannot precede this act is a heavy burden on aesthetic theory. An additional difficulty is posed by the fact that this pleasure resulting from an aesthetic judgment also has to be somehow associated with the pleasure discussed elsewhere in Kant's *Critique,* as what posits the necessary condition that triggers a judgment of taste in the first place.

This, indeed, is one of many places where commentators on Kant's *Critique* are confronted with an immense interpretive difficulty, the kernel of which can be found in §9 of the text. "Now this merely subjective (aesthetic) judging of the object, or of the presentation by which it is given, precedes the pleasure in the object and is the basis of this pleasure, a pleasure in the harmony of the cognitive powers."[11] Beyond the various proposals made by commentators for unpacking this passage, it clearly refers to two separate moments of pleasure, one associated with the presentation given to the free play of the faculties, and the other to the result of the harmonizing of these faculties. Attending to this question of precedence may shed some light on the nature of the pleasure assumed by Kant. As passage §9 indicates, pleasure is what accompanies a given presentation restricted by no determinate concept, that is, given to the free play of the faculties. Following the reading of Rodolphe Gasché of the passage concerned, what is involved in a judgment of taste is a free play of presentational powers; that is, it is this cognitive state itself and not the resulting adjustment of the faculties in the cognition of the object that is accompanied by a feeling of pleasure. Yet cognition requires also a mutual harmony of the cognitive powers of imagination and understanding with one another. Thus there is the pleasure predicated (immediately) of a state of mind (i.e., the pleasure in what reveals itself in the presentation) and the pleasure in the very activation of cognitive powers where these faculties are in harmony. "The pleasure to be predicated follows the pleasure felt," concludes Gasché.[12]

"The pleasure predicated of the pleasurable state of mind must be distinct from it. Whereas the pleasure felt . . . is a subjective and empirical pleasure, the pleasure that follows the judgment properly speaking is that of the universal communicability of the state of mind in question." Gasché claims that the distinction between the pleasure that precedes judging and serves as its condition and the pleasure that follows the state of harmony is a distinction crucial to one's understanding the nature of judgments of taste, their being concerned with the a priori rather than the empirical.[13]

Aesthetic pleasure is thus distinguished by Gasché from the feeling of pleasure. His interpretation suggests that in order to have aesthetic pleasure, pleasure should be tied to the state of mind we describe as the aesthetic experience of the beautiful, as the retrospective cause of its communicable nature. Other philosophical commentaries suggest various modes of relating these two aspects of the aesthetic experience. While Gasché proposes a distinction between pleasure and aesthetic pleasure, Paul Guyer approaches this suggested division of pleasure into feeling and mode of cognition by identifying two logically distinct acts of reflection. This move is necessitated by what Guyer perceives as Kant's description of the feeling of pleasure as both the product of judgment and the ground for the determination of judgment. The awareness of pleasure must logically precede the conscious conclusion that an object is beautiful, and yet the judgment of taste requires that everyone agree on a given pleasure, that the delight in the beautiful be explained by the harmony of the faculties produced by reflection on its object. Guyer, as a natural conclusion from this duality of pleasure, suggests the possibility of distinguishing between two sensations of pleasure: "the sensation of pleasure brought forth by empirical intuition and that produced by the harmony of imagination and understanding."[14] Guyer's view, however, is that judgments of the agreeable or the beautiful do not differ in the kind of pleasure they elicit but in the context and cause of the feeling in its particular relation to representation. Feelings of pleasure are qualitatively identical, even though they are sometimes occasioned by the higher cognitive faculties and thus possess universal subjective validity. Pleasure cannot be of a different order when succeeding the act of judgment; it simply refers to another phase of the reflective act.

Henry Allison interprets Kant's intention by splitting the subjective conditions of cognition that Kant formulates into the free play of the faculties and their harmony. When judgments of taste are successful, this means that in the free play between imagination and understanding in the act of "mere reflection," a harmonious relation between the faculties was produced, thereby bringing about a pleasurable mental state. When, however, "the outcome of the free play is a state of *dis*harmony, whereby the faculties hinder rather than help one another," a mental state of disinterested displeasure will be produced, hence a negative judgment of taste.[15]

The three commentators agree that *aesthetic pleasure is a consequent moment in the act of judgment*, even though a necessary moment, if the object is taken to have beauty. Pleasure, being always of the same nature, has yet to allow a distinction between the pleasure in the beautiful (or the sublime), pleasure in the agreeable or other kinds of pleasure that result from the play of the faculties (a play that takes place also in cognitive judgments). Hence the kind of pleasure involved cannot be discerned on the basis of the subject's sensual experience. Moreover, the need to locate pleasure as retroactively attributable to the harmony of the faculties does not rely on the actual performance of the subject experiencing pleasure. A judgment of taste, as Gasché emphasizes, is a matter of transcendentalism rather than of empirical facts. The location of pleasure is hence the fundamental *condition* for sustaining a notion of *aesthetic* experience in the first place. Pleasures being always the same and the experiencing subject not being the last authority on the nature of the pleasure involved both suggest the need to establish the logical grounds for determining the nature of pleasure. Since for Kant aesthetic experience cannot be defined on the basis of experience itself, locating pleasure as a result of the cognitive state of harmony establishes the grounds for understanding the universal nature of the experience of aesthetic pleasure.

The dispute over the necessary causality between pleasure and a communicable mental state further indicates that the pleasure felt while facing the object judged as beautiful is a pleasure whose logical place within the structure of aesthetic experience has to be constituted or/and invented rather than found. Found pleasure is a pleasure identified as the one given to the senses and hence is a pleasure that carries little interest for the aesthetic concerns of philosophy. Yet if the pleasure felt is not the decisive test for aesthetic experience, and pleasure in the beautiful is the pleasure that *results* from the communicability of a mental state, then there is indeed no reason to exclude the possibility of a route leading from the free play among the faculties predicated of a presentation to either pleasure *or displeasure*. While the relations between pleasure, free play, and harmony are open to interpretation, it is clear that displeasure cannot be excluded from this play at the outset. Allison, for instance, accounts for this possibility of displeasure by indicating that not every object is beautiful, because when "the normal concerns of cognition are suspended," the degree of attunement of the faculties involved may vary." "(T)here is certainly room for differences in the degree of attunement, as well as for the experience of something that is positively unappealing or disinviting to the mind in the mere reflection."[16] An object given to an act of aesthetic appraisal does not only suspend one's ordinary cognitive concerns with classification and explanation, but it also requires a high degree of attunement of the faculties. Lesser attunement will simply lead at the end of the free play to a sense of displeasure.[17]

Whether one agrees or disagrees with Allison's idea of "degrees of attunement," the point to be made here is that Allison's move is a typical one on the part of philosophers of art in their striving to restitute a place for displeasure within a Kantian model of aesthetic experience.

This lingering on the moot points among commentators of Kant aims to stress that displeasure cannot be excluded from aesthetic considerations,[18] and that both pleasure and displeasure are taken to be possible consequences of the cognitive route that has to be completed so an aesthetic experience can occur. While commentators differ as to how they understand the phases of this cognitive route, it is obvious that it is this structure, along with the resulting pleasure or displeasure, that constitutes an *aesthetic domain*. The free play of cognitive faculties follows the same cognitive path, whether the faculties eventually harmonize or disharmonize.

While the idea of *pleasure as consequence* accounts for its universality, the idea of degrees of attunement accounts for the degree of determinateness of the object that the aesthetic judgment predicates. Neither pleasure nor displeasure results from attaining objective knowledge of the object of judgment. A judgment of taste does not yoke concepts of reason, for instance, to create a "fit" between the faculties of imagination and understanding and an object. Only in the normal experience of objects the mind does not linger beyond what is needed to fit the intuition of an object to a concept of understanding. In the context of aesthetic experience, "the powers of imagination and understanding that become attuned in a judgment of taste are still free."[19] While judgments of taste manifest the a priori transcendental condition of every cognition, "what keeps a judgment of taste from becoming a logical judgment is . . . the 'without' of 'without interest,' 'without concept,' 'without purpose' . . . etc."[20] A judgment that concerns the beautiful "is not without an object," to refer to an expression often used by Lacan;[21] its object is judged as beautiful or not according to a certain degree of mutual animation of the cognitive faculties of imagination and understanding. A judgment of taste is not without an object, because while the pleasure associated with this judgment is elicited by an object, the judgment does not end with a pleasure associated with a knowledgeable fit with the object. The pleasure in a judgment of taste is associated with the free play itself.[22] Hence, no final correlation with an object can determine the difference between pleasure and displeasure.

This section has demonstrated that, first, either aesthetic pleasure or displeasure can result from the causal relation that each one holds with the cognitive route undergone by the judging subject; second, that displeasure need not be excluded from the aesthetic domain, and that the difference between a positive consequence (pleasure) and negative one (displeasure) can be a matter of the degree of accordance between the cognitive faculties that ultimately determine aesthetic experience; and, third, that the difference of pleasure/displeasure is not a matter of the fit of the cognitive faculties with an object. Both aesthetic pleasure and displeasure are in this sense "without an object."

These points are both attributed and not attributed to Kant. On the one hand, I wish to point to the compatibility between a notion of aesthetic displeasure, as suggested earlier (as a possible *outcome* of the cognitive route taken by the judging subject, in which the free play of the faculties *results* in displeasure), and the very foundations of Kantian thinking about judgments of taste. On the other hand, this reading of Kant, supported by the Freudian "beyond the pleasure principle" and necessitated by modernist changes in artistic practice and theory, cannot be associated with Kant and with the settling of moot points in his aesthetics, or with disagreements among Kantian scholars, unless an obvious caution is taken.

ARE NEGATIVE JUDGMENTS OF TASTE AESTHETIC?

Kant's attitude toward the notion of ugliness (or even of aesthetic indifference) is perplexingly enigmatic. The possibility of negative judgments of taste is, however, mentioned by Kant in contexts sufficiently crucial to require and justify an investigation of its place within Kantian aesthetics. Furthermore, claims Henry Allison, negative judgments can make a determinant factor for the exegeses of Kant's notorious §9, and it is on such grounds that Allison criticizes Hannah Ginsborg's interpretation of the pleasure of taste as self-referential, that is, as literally lying in the "universal communicability of one's pleasure."[23] When universal communicability is taken to be in itself the source of pleasure, when no distance is allowed between these two transcendental conditions, there can be no place for an analogous universal communicability of one's displeasure, and negative judgments of taste become irrelevant to aesthetics. Allison believes that such an exclusion is wrong.

Commentators' approach to the problem of negative judgments of taste varies. I refer only to three examples that represent the range of arguments in favor of or against considering such judgments aesthetic. On the one hand, critics such as David Shier[24] construct a case according to which Kant finds nothing ugly in his critique, despite one of the first sentences in the *Critique* that gives equal weight to pleasure and displeasure. Kant finds nothing ugly because within Kant's aesthetics every judgment of taste must be accompanied in the subject by a state of harmonious free play, a state that is always pleasurable. In this manner, the possibility of negative judgments does not constitute an option and is excluded.

An argument in the opposite direction is proposed both by Ruth Lorand and by Matthew Kieran. Lorand's main argument is that the negation of beauty can take place within the aesthetic domain.[25]

"(T)he very opposites of beauty do indeed give us a better grasp of the nature of beauty. The ugly, the meaningless, the kitsch, the boring, the insignificant, and the irrelevant, all are opposites of beauty which illumine it from several negative poles."[26]

Each one of these opposites, according to Lorand, causes displeasure by negating another aesthetic property. Lorand shows that not only do the various opposites of the beautiful involve aesthetic judgments but they define the constitutive limit without which the judgment of the beautiful would lose its significance.

Along a different path of argumentation Kieran claims that "subject matter we would ordinarily find disgusting might afford pleasure if it is artistically manipulated."[27] Kieran can recommend an aesthetic pleasure in the nonbeautiful, because this is grounded for him in a necessary distinction between aesthetic and artistic value. Divorcing aesthetic from artistic value explains why we value a work by Francis Bacon, and how artistic value can be attributed to what is aesthetically unpleasant and repulsive.

What can be surmised from this aesthetic dilemma regarding negative judgments of taste is that, philosophically speaking, judgments that account for displeasing experiences are felt to have a problematic yet necessary relation to positive judgments. Kant himself can allow us to reconsider the status of negative judgments in view of the distinction he makes in his essay "Negative Quantities" between logical and real oppositions. Kant distinguishes the logical values of propositions from their real values in qualities of objects. "Precisely because reality and negation *in objects* . . . are not themselves logical contradictions but rather real states which may be in physical opposition, the differences between them may admit of degrees."[28]

Negation can reflect in the reality of objects degrees of sensation and not mutually exclusive logical possibilities. This idea first allows us to settle the dilemma around displeasure and pleasure as involving real possibilities. A negative judgment is a real possibility and not a way to exclude what is negated, nor a way to mark the absence of pleasure in the judgment's result. The idea of "real opposition" can be enlightening also because it indicates that we need the definition of the cognitive law of harmony or conflict to settle the relations between pleasure and displeasure, since while they make real possibilities in every aesthetic experience, they cannot hold at the same time. This is particularly clear in the case of the sublime, where a state of felt pain *leads* to a state of aesthetic pleasure. These states do not exclude each other but rather are experienced as equally real; both are explained in terms of a cognitive structure/dynamic of relations among the faculties. In experiencing objects of magnitude, displeasure and pleasure both play a role, constituting together what Kant refers to as the experience of the sublime; displeasure constitutes a real phase in the appreciation of the sublime. The notion of real opposition can indicate that displeasure cannot be taken as an abstract logical possibility, or as a way to point to the lack or absence of pleasure, but is, in itself, a *positive fact*. Note that the "official" role played by displeasure in experiences of the sublime is only a side issue here. To prove the necessary role that displeasure plays in Kantian aesthetics, the territory in which the question of displeasure should be approached is the territory of the beautiful, where displeasure appears to pertain only to negative judgments of taste. It is my aim to show that displeasure in Kantian aesthetics pertains not only to judgments of the ugly or to experiences of the sublime but to the entire aesthetic project.[29]

Allison's way of making room for displeasure, and for the experience of the unappealing object within the realm of taste, draws on the structural affinity between positive and negative judgments. Pleasure and displeasure are two positive facts within the aesthetic experience, depending on the law of cognition to distinguish them.

While Allison incorporates displeasure by showing that it too is the outcome of a mental state of free play (an outcome of a conflict among the faculties of cognition), another mode of incorporating displeasure into the domain of the aesthetic is proposed by Gasché. The latter, in reference to the sublime, claims that "the pain that it [the imagination] suffers in not being up to that task [of providing a fundamental aesthetic measure for the logical estimation of magnitude] when it is confronted with certain magnitude of nature is a pain that it can feel only because it obeys the laws of reason from the very start. In its failed quest for the fundamental aesthetic measure, the imagination already seeks to realize the law of reason."[30] Gasché implies here an important point that can serve us in advancing the claim that acts of judgment involve displeasure due to indeterminable ideas of reason that yet determine the purpose of the judgment beyond the object being judged. According to Gasché, the indispensable role of reason in any attempt of the imagination to come to terms with an object of an unexpected measure makes pain unavoidable. Gasché's ingenious reading of Kant demonstrates here something that, at face value, goes against the grain of Kant's argument, in suggesting why the law of reason in fact provides the general basis of all one's aesthetic judgments. The pain felt in the case of the sublime does not stem from the realization that imagination is inadequate to its task but from the realization of "the imagination's supersensible destination."[31] Gasché aims in his book to show that the moral and the cognitive are intertwined in the pure judgments of the sublime and the beautiful alike owing to the role played by reason. In the previous quote he indicates *that pain is the displeasurable affect of the very oscillation between the aesthetic and the cognitive, that pain arises because,* given to the indeterminate purposiveness set by reason, the cognitive faculties sacrifice aesthetic comprehension of the sensible object. Gasché's analysis hence suggests that the aesthetic act is painful because it is intimately tied to its own limitation, and that the pain transcends the mere dimension of failure and is related to the presence of indeterminate ideas of reason in every such act. Although Gasché himself distinguishes the "restful state of the feeling of the beautiful" from the agitation of the mind caused by the effort imposed on the imagination when experiencing the sublime, the implied affinity between the two is evident. I further add to his analysis that in the case of the beautiful, just as in the case of the sublime, the apprehension of the manifold in one intuition is either not instantaneous (in the case of the beautiful) or impossible to attain (in the case of the sublime). Thus pain resulting from the oscillation between the aesthetic and the cognitive appears to be unavoidable in both cases, and in both cases the pain incurred points at reason as the constitutive law directing the aesthetic act.

To clarify the point that Gasché demonstrates through the feeling of pain, we can refer to the way Kant solves the antinomy of taste where the logic of judgment also can be described as an oscillation between the aesthetic and the cognitive, similar to the situation producing pain. A judgment of taste, claims Kant, does deal with objects of sense, and yet "there can be no doubt that in a judgment of taste the presentation of the object . . . is referred more broadly, and this broader reference is our basis for extending such judgments as necessary for everyone. Hence this extension must be based on some concept or other; but this concept must be one that no intuition can determine . . . such a mere concept is reason's pure concept of the supersensible underlying the object as an object of sense" (§57, p. 212). For Kant the conflicting demands posed by a judgment of taste are reconciled when we understand that the judgment applies to an object of presentation, while the universality of the judgment refers to an extended field where the law of reason, rather than of sensible forms, applies. The situation described by Kant is hence similar in its logic to the one described by Gasché as a situation producing pain.

The following points emerge from the preceding discussion:

1. The law of reason is present in judgments upon the beautiful and the sublime.
2. The involvement of reason in the aesthetic experience elicits pain.
3. It is not the nature of the object experienced that motivates the pain felt; while judgments of the beautiful achieve minimal objectification, judgments of the sublime "come into play only where the formlessness of the object thwarts even aesthetic objectification."[32] The cause of pain is not in the actual object of judgment.
4. The displeasurable pain involved in the sublime does not make this experience resistant to aesthetic considerations: the sublime is a strictly aesthetic experience.

One may conclude the following:

5. The pain inflicted in judgments of taste may be claimed to serve as a constitutive factor of every aesthetic experience. Pain refers to the absence of adjustment experienced, even if temporarily, in the aesthetic domain, yet it is not simply the inadequacy of the imagination that results in pain but the inadequacy of any faculty of the mind giving rise to an intellectual standard; pain is hence bound to pertain both to the experience of the sublime and to that of the beautiful.

Negative judgments result from the judging subject moving along a cognitive route similar to the one that leads to positive judgments. The fact that Kant is taciturn regarding this cognitive route along which negative judgments are produced may lead one to attribute to him the view that displeasure is necessarily mentioned within the third critique only because of the case of the sublime (itself appended in many ways to the case of the beautiful).[33] Yet if the primacy effect of mentioning displeasure in the opening remarks of the critique is taken literally, and if the place of reason in the judgment of the beautiful and the sublime alike is taken into consideration,[34] and given the fact that pleasure as the outcome of a universally communicable cognitive harmony is only retroactively associated with the judgment of taste, then it becomes clear that negative judgments must be structurally integrated into one's understanding of what aesthetic experience involves.

One can summarize this part by stressing that the function given to displeasure within the aesthetic domain attests to the fact that this domain is not characterized by the exclusion of displeasure but by the necessary presence of pleasure and displeasure alike as two positive outcomes of judgments of taste. Otherwise, the free play in which the cognitive powers are engaged to the point of harmony or disharmony could have taken but one direction (of pleasure), which is incompatible with the overall intent of the *Critique*. Displeasure must present a real possibility in aesthetic experiences of the beautiful and the sublime alike. Furthermore, when cognition judges freely, which is the law of aesthetic judgment, moments prior to consolidating a distinct (positive or negative) judgment are bound to be accompanied by pain.

Hence, aesthetic pleasure and displeasure result from the specific cognitive routes that serve as their causes, and these routes, before harmonizing or disharmonizing, involve moments of painful oscillations between the demand for a totality of the manifold, which is a demand of understanding and reason, and the demand for sensible exhibition, which is a demand of the imagination. So as a consequence of the reading proposed in these two sections, displeasure can be said to occupy two distinct functions in the judgment of taste. First, displeasure *accompanies the cognitive free play*, a phase in which it is associated with the failure that lies in wait before the cognitive faculties enacted in the aesthetic judgment; the immanence of failure is due to the totalizing, yet indeterminable, horizon of reason in the aesthetic judgment. Second, displeasure also is *one optional outcome of a judgment of taste*: once the conflict between the cognitive powers (that are bound to be in tension) remains unresolved, the subject feels displeasure.

ANXIETY IS PRIOR TO ANY ACT OF JUDGMENT

Since psychoanalytic anxiety goes beyond the pleasure-displeasure divide, it cannot be flatly identified with the displeasure referred to by Kant or described by his commentators. Anxiety can yet suggest ways of further locating aesthetic conceptions of displeasure and of motivating the necessary presence attributed to it. The following discussion of psychoanalytic anxiety aims to clarify the place of the anxious subject prior to the resolution of this state in either of the aesthetic attitudes of pleasure *or* displeasure. Yet given the use made here of psychoanalytic anxiety, it should be made clear that while I argue that anxiety can shed light on the nature of aesthetic displeasure, the true relevance of anxiety to aesthetic experience can be revealed only from within aesthetics itself, that is, through a reading of Kant's aesthetics (as the cardinal text of modern aesthetics exposing the deep dilemmas of this discipline). It is in view of psychoanalytic anxiety that a crucial point at the heart of Kant's aesthetics can be exposed. Lacan himself, in his seminar on anxiety, although bringing a few examples from works of art, does not use anxiety to formulate the case of art necessarily. Yet in the following I will refer to his work as a way to illuminate the affects that art produces in the subject. Lacan's aesthetics is in this sense derivative and cannot be straightforwardly applied to the aesthetic dilemma. The fact that Lacan's thought on art does not constitute an aesthetic theory yet somewhat paradoxically points at its affinity rather than distance from Kant.[35] For Kant the aesthetic experience of the subject in his encounter with art is only derivative of the experience in the face of beautiful nature, and the aesthetic domain itself is but a derivative of the ways the transcendental subject comes to know nature and its laws.

As a preliminary manner of formulating the function of anxiety in aesthetic experience, I can note that aesthetic pleasure is a pleasure conditioned by its particular location within the entire aesthetic experience. Aesthetic pleasure is located as the affect of a universally communicable mental state. Until aesthetic experience is affirmed and elicits pleasure, the subject, in her or his encounter with a presentation (an image, for instance) prior to that consolidation, has to undergo a phase of anxiety. The anxiety located prior to judgment hence represents a preliminary moment in which the subject's relation to the object of judgment has not yet been settled. The act of aesthetic judgment, rather than excluding the subject's desire, is understood to be an act of desire to encounter an object of satisfaction. Psychoanalysis will explain the anxiety evoked in the preliminary phase of this encounter in terms of the doubt elicited in the subject as to whether the object of desire will indeed be exhibited in the presentation. A positive answer settles the encounter in a beautiful object; a negative answer would maintain the fundamental inadjustment between the presentation and the subject's faculties attempting, unsuccessfully, to attune to the object. It is for this reason that the desire for the object is "felt as unpleasure," to use Freud's words. The pain that accompanies the encounter with the magnitude of the sublime similarly emerges from the fact that the imagination fails in totalizing the object desired in a manageable form. With the sublime, the failure is immanent, while with the beautiful, something of the subject's desire will ultimately be exhibited in the presentation, which is why displeasure is only temporarily experienced.

Thus through the reading of aesthetic pleasure-displeasure from a psychoanalytic perspective, the idea that displeasure is a necessary constituent of every encounter with a presentation judged freely can be pointed out. Kant's free play of cognitive faculties verges on displeasure, until that moment when the subject locates the possibility of pleasure as related to a mental state of harmonizing faculties (or when reason takes the place of imagination in locating an object, as in the case of the sublime), and to a presentation that he or she perceives as satisfactory. Displeasure is the signal of the free cognitive play that precedes its location in a definite structure (of harmony or conflict). It is only when pleasure becomes locatable, a condition that demands displeasure as its constitutive limit, that it can be defined as aesthetic. Note, however, that displeasure in this case is tantamount to psychoanalytic anxiety, since what is felt as displeasure in fact signals the state of the subject's desire, a desire to know how the object encountered is to be judged. The displeasure felt prior to judgment is a state of high excitation; the subject in search of an object of desire is gripped in an anxious moment subsuming pleasure and displeasure.

What are the parameters that define the moment of anxiety raised in the subject in front of an object (of beauty or sublimity)? I have mentioned that anxiety has a necessary link to desire, a relation realized in anxiety's necessary link to the specular image, the mirror reflection in front of which the subject authenticates her or his own ego through an Other. It is a fundamental psychoanalytic insight that to sustain the subject's desire, this desire has to be constituted by an Other. It is in the Other, the mother looking at her child, Nature looking at the scientist work, or the totem looking at the celebrating tribe, that the consistency of the subject, the subject's desire, is sustained. How are these relations between subject and Other established to constitute the subject's desire? The infant reflected in the mirror sees itself as self-possessed and in control of its own being, while its self-sensation is that of a fragmented body (the human child being born in a state that is radically premature and dependent on its surrounding).[36] Confronted with this discrepancy, the child constitutes the function of the Other (at this stage identified with the person of a parent) as what is responsible for the unitary image. It is the Other that sees something in the child that enables this unification into a coherent self-image. The child thus attributes to the Other the ability to see in it a One; the child locates in the Other that something missing in the child itself, as it is to itself, yet complemented by the look of the Other. It is the thing lacking in the infant and attributed to the Other that constitutes the desire of the subject, and it is that thing that when at stake anxiety arises. The Other is the symbolic function holding the secret of the subject's unified being, a secret felt to be absent from the child itself.

Yet that something lacking in the subject and granted by the Other through the gaze (the mother in a way affirms with her look the gleeful satisfaction of the child with his or her own image) cannot be concretely assigned to the Other, since the subject knows not what she or he is for the Other, what the Other wants of her or him. The absent object of lack remains evanescent, impossible to grasp. The position of the Other remains hypothetical and .can never be occupied by the subject. The child or the subject imagines the Other has in his or her possession something that the Other would rather keep to itself.

What is the status of this lacking object? Lacan says that the paradigmatic object of lack is the phallus. It is a lack that marks the castration of both male and female in regard to the possibility of absolute satisfaction. It is only the Other (the primordial father, the unknown couple copulating behind the wall) who has access to the enjoyment of which the subject himself or herself is deprived. This is the imaginary aspect of absence; the subject interprets the missing thing as being in the possession of an enjoying Other. What is lost to the subject is taken to be attributable to the enjoyment of the Other, that Other in whom nothing lacks, since it is at the expense of the subject who has been cut off from the possibility of total self-enjoyment that the Other can be satisfied.

To return to the subject's specular image in the mirror, the correlation between the subject and the image leaves out a remainder, a remainder that also could be described in terms of the discrepancy between the two; between the decomposed *selbst-Gefühl* of the subject and the consistency of the unified image. It is this remainder that marks the constitution of the subject's desire, in that it marks a moment of radical lack located in the Other and yet necessary for the self-consistency of the subject's image

I (Unified Image) – S (Decomposed Self) = OD (Object of Desire)

The element of lack is located or demanded from the Other, and as such it is fundamentally paradoxical. While this element is eternally missing from the subject's domain and signals the Other's privileged possibilities of grasp, this missing element in fact remains unrecorded, missing also from the domain of the Other. The object of lack remains outside of the subject (whose fundamental sensation is incompatible with the complete image) and outside of the domain of symbolization attributed to the Other (as it is the element excluded from the image), and yet it is constituted by both. It is an object that is imaginarily ungraspable; it has no representation in the mirror image, yet it can be substituted by perfectly graspable objects for the partial satisfaction of desire, substitutes that exhibit this object yet at the same time leave it beyond their grasp. The object concerned is incarnated in substitute images yet it itself is only reproduced as a remainder from the specular image, an object "whose status escapes from the status of the object derived from the specular image, escapes from the laws of the transcendental aesthetic, this object whose status is so difficult for us to articulate that it is through it that there have entered all the confusions of analytic theory, this object *a* whose constituting characteristics we have only begun to outline and which we bring here onto the agenda, this object *a* is the one which is at stake everywhere Freud speaks about object when anxiety is involved."[37]

This object *a* is an object of demand, a demand directed at the Other as a demand for love: "What is in me that is more than my image?" This demand, which cannot but remain unsatisfied, is required so that desire is kept alive. In Seminar V Lacan formulates the relations between the demand of the subject and the desire of the Other in terms of the signifier *phallus*. The phallus marks the desire of the Other insofar as the Other is a real other, another human being. In relation to this signifier, the subject cannot fail to recognize, through the intermediary of this other, the fact that he or she also is marked by the signifier, namely, "that there is always something which remains beyond what can be satisfied through the intermediary of . . . the demand."[38] It is through the signifier of the demand, in other words, that the subject must encounter her or his desire. Object *a* is the unexhibited object of the demand for love that enables this encounter; as such, it is an object that cannot be captured in the image. It is an object that cannot be represented; an object of desire whose image remains invisible, yet its presence stimulates the subject's desire and attraction to the image before her or him. The meaning of this invisibility is that the object that causes the subject to desire must always loom in the visual field of the Other for the subject's desire to be sustained. Moreover, "The more man approaches, circumscribes, caresses what he believes to be the object of his desire, the more in fact he is deviated, turned aside from it, precisely because of the fact that everything that he does on this path in order to get closer to it, always gives more body to what in the object of this desire represents the specular image."[39]

Anxiety is connected both to the inability to locate the object of lack in the specular image and at the same time to the possibility of encountering the object of desire in the Other. This ambivalence of anxiety has its roots in Freud, who aims to disconnect anxiety from the economic factor. Freud claims that anxiety affects the pleasure-unpleasure agency, but it is not caused by repression. Thus as anxiety arises before *a possibility* of the dreaded situation setting in, a shift is marked in anxiety's connection to the dreaded object: "Anxiety has an unmistakable relation to *expectation*: it is anxiety about something. It has a quality of *indefiniteness and lack of object.*"[40] Anxiety is hence the signal of the subject's dialectic relation to the object of lack, the object as visibly unlocatable in the image produced in the domain of the Other (the danger has not set in but is yet present as a possibility), and the object as imposing itself as real on the subject (as an object of lack that yet exhibits a surplus remainder in the domain of the Other). This dialectic points to the fact that the object of lack is real (it belongs to the realm of enjoyment), is imaginarily occluded by a concrete object or image (for instance, the phallus the mother lacks that constitutes her desire), and is symbolically invisible (not given to representation).

I have singled out three parameters by which anxiety should be approached: *desire* (for an object of lack), *Other* (as constituting desire), and *image* (as the domain that produces the object of desire as its effect). It is within the structure created by these three terms that the place of anxiety can be articulated. Lacan offers the example of Hamlet to explain why the oscillation between the lack as the effect or remainder of the specular image and the lack occluded by an imaginary object brings on anxiety. While obviously idiosyncratic, Lacan's interpretation helps clarify the point at issue: the place of anxiety in the overall structure of desire.

In the play, Hamlet chooses to trap the conscience of the king by staging a play within a play that aims to mime the king's crimes. Surprisingly enough, says Lacan, once the play is staged, it is Hamlet who is seized by a crisis of agitation rather than the king, who stays absolutely calm. Moreover, Lacan reminds us, critics have noticed that the attire of the sham king closely resembles that of Hamlet himself rather than that of the king in the play within a play whom the staging of the play aims to trap. This and other similarities between the murderous character in Hamlet's staged play and Hamlet's own person point to the fact that Hamlet causes *himself* to be represented on stage rather than the king he aims to trap: "It is himself, carrying out the crime in question, this character whose desire cannot be roused to accomplish the will of the ghost, of the *fantôme* of his father, this character attempts to embody something; and what it is a matter of embodying passes by way of his image which is really specular here, his image not in the situation, the mode of carrying out his vengeance, but of assuming first of all the crime that must be avenged."[41]

Lacan's point in this analysis is that Hamlet produces through the play his own specular image in the hope that once the object of his desire will be located there, on stage, his desire will be constituted and he himself will be driven to action. In this play within a play, so it turns out, Hamlet indeed stages himself as passionate enough to pursue his desire, unlike the situation in the reality of the play itself, where he practically declines the decree of this ghost-father. But the specular image, constituted by the play within a play, fails to attain its purpose, Hamlet's desire remains blanked, and at the moment he has the option of killing the criminal, he holds back from striking him because the king is praying, and a death blow at that moment will send the king directly to heaven. Hamlet recoils, and the desire that should have been constituted by the object of lack in the play within a play has failed to appear.

The reversal of the specular image, made to mirror Hamlet rather than the king, is enacted again through Hamlet's melancholy over Ophelia's death. Hamlet identifies with Ophelia as part of his melancholic identification. It is not with her sorrow that he identifies (as the reader remembers Hamlet was alienated from this sorrow when she was still alive), nor is it her loss that he mourns. Rather, a melancholic Hamlet identifies with the sorrow he has left behind with her death. Following Freud, we know that melancholy is the state of mourning the other who stood, until her disappearance, as the object of lack for the subject.[42] We become melancholic when we lose the object loved for occupying the place of the loss, for sustaining our own consistency around what we lack. Hamlet can relate to Ophelia as an object of his desire only when this object has just disappeared. He identifies with Ophelia as an object of melancholia; he does not mourn her departure as an object of desire. Desire goes beyond the image, although the object of desire, says Lacan, can be reintegrated on the stage by identification, "precisely in the measure that as object it has just disappeared. . . . This object of desire, this retroactive recognition, this object which was there, it is along this path that there is placed the return of Hamlet, that which is the high point of his destiny, of his function as Hamlet."[43]

Hamlet takes a threefold position toward his desire; through the attempt to study the object of desire in the specular image of the play within a play, through the melancholic identification with the object just disappearing, and through the anxiety of the spectator. Hamlet, in other words, is the character whose function is *to refuse the encounter with the object of desire, a refusal that causes anxiety in the spectator.* By producing specular images of himself, in which he refuses to see the missing object that would have placed for him the object of his desire, he leaves the object of lack occluded. In identifying with the object of melancholia, he again occludes the place of lack in the Other. Hamlet, throughout the play, does not solve the place of desire and leaves no place in which the object of desire (as an object of lack) can be located. In his crime, in his mourning and insanity, the Other remains complete, divulging no trace of the object causing the subject (Hamlet) to desire. Hamlet refuses to touch the place where the desire of the Other constitutes his own.

Thus while Hamlet is melancholic, the spectator watching the play is stricken by anxiety, because through the play within a play, the spectator comes across Hamlet's dilemma in front of the object of desire to which Hamlet keeps refusing. Hamlet, through his engagement in play-staging, through his playful speech, is engaged in a free play with what he refuses to locate, even as indeterminate and invisible: the object of his desire.

It is through this particular case of Hamlet that we can learn something about the universal, constitutive nature of anxiety. Anxiety is universal, precisely in the Kantian sense of the term; just like pleasure, it is not bound to be elicited by any performance, in every encounter with a given object. Anxiety is wholly dependent on the subject experiencing it, which makes its universality a product of a particular experience. Although anxiety is located in a structure that generally defines the subject's position vis-à-vis an object of desire, anxiety has an immanent place in aesthetic experience. The constitutive moment of anxiety, as necessitated by the aesthetic experience, is exemplified by *Hamlet* as it can be exemplified in a painting by Rembrandt or in a novel by Virginia Woolf. The experience of the beautiful, the sublime, or the tragic can be elicited only when an aesthetic anxiety is at play prior to judgment. Hamlet's case yet exemplifies a particular mode of eliciting anxiety, as here anxiety is prolonged, and the location of the object of desire is infinitely evaded. The curtain lifted provides no relief for anxiety, whereas in other works of art, anxiety is facilitated at some point. Granted that *anxiety is the signal of the possible loss of the object of desire*, as claimed in this chapter, anxiety makes a signal without which a judgment of taste cannot take place. Pleasure can be brought about only when the doubt accompanying the lifting of the curtain, the doubt whether the cognitive faculties will indeed harmonize, precedes it. Just like Descartes's *cogito,* that at a moment of utmost doubt gains a certainty of its being a subject of thought, so Kant's subject of aesthetic judgment, at a moment of utmost anxiety, earns the certainty of encountering an object of satisfaction (or dissatisfaction) in the artistic image. The question of art, the question of whether art will relate to the subject's desire, cannot be settled unless anxiety enables its location vis-à-vis the subject's desire. Doubt is driven away only when the place of the lack is marked in the presentation, by bringing forth, for instance, an object playing the part of the object of lack, the subject's object of desire. When the curtain is lifted and the spectator sees something rather than a void, anxiety is facilitated. Anxiety, just like aesthetic pleasure in Kant, must be constituted, invented, and sought out rather than found. It takes the subject in search of the object of desire through his or her encounter with art, and this search is bound to bring on anxiety, which is why anxiety must fulfill a constitutive part in every aesthetic encounter with art. When the artwork engages the spectator in an aesthetic experience and brings back to her or him, from the place of the Other, a remnant of what she or he, the subject, lacks, it is then that the immanence of anxiety, as prior to that moment of invention, becomes evident. Hamlet's misgivings regarding the object of desire that has remained indeterminate are hence reproduced in a way, whenever the subject is engaged in an aesthetic judgment.

For psychoanalysis, anxiety is locatable. Psychoanalytic anxiety is not the Heideggerian one, tantamount to the human condition itself, an anxiety that is everywhere: "*That in the face of which one has anxiety is Being-in-the-world as such*."[44] The structural location of anxiety as a signal produced within the human psyche in a particular kind of encounter it has with the image can provide important insights into the place of aesthetic pleasure and displeasure. Anxiety arises vis-à-vis an object of lack and signals the subject's position toward the possibility of coming across what the subject desires—the object the subject lacks and serves as the cause of desire, an object that repels and attracts at the same time. The moment of anxiety is the moment before the curtain is lifted to reveal the stage, when the observer senses an anxiety not knowing whether the object that causes desire will reveal itself in the theater images about to be exposed. Similarly, anxiety can be located within the structure of the mirror image, where the subject/baby, looking at its image, then looks around to search the gaze of the mother, the mother here functioning as the instance that can endorse this ideal image. What the subject searches for in the image is a confirmation of desire, that is, a confirmation that the object that is lacking (exemplified in the case of the baby in the mirror by what it lacks in terms of self-control over its body, control that is still missing but is represented as an illusion in the image) will be fulfilled/located in the domain of the Other. It is the possibility of failing to secure this confirmation that raises anxiety.

The idea that anxiety is first to be approached by locating it is not a theoretical matter but, rather, from a psychoanalytic point of view, affects the clinical treatment of anxiety. When Jacques-Alain Miller describes Lacan's seminar on anxiety, he claims that this work with the title "*l'angoisse* is a work where anxiety, strictly speaking, is not a problem, where it is not a matter of treating it, but of giving it a conceptual place, with reference to the concept of anxiety in Kierkegaard."[45] This idea of conceptually locating anxiety rather than solving it clearly bears on the place of affects in aesthetic experience. Kant's aesthetics locates pleasure and displeasure within the practice of reflective judgments, not as something to get over, to be solved, but as forming a structure within which both pleasure and displeasure can be located.

Apart from the fact that Kant has taught us that displeasure is not a "problem" to be excluded from aesthetic considerations, he also has indicated that the object of aesthetic judgment, the one the third critique is busy locating, is not the object in reality, and that prior to aesthetic judgment, the subject is oscillating between various possible sensations. How does the intricate position of displeasure in Kantian aesthetics relate to the Lacanian idea of anxiety as emerging in front of the real object (rather than the object in reality) whose representation in the image one is facing, is missing, yet feared?

Gasché has pointed out that Kant's *Critique* itself attests to the place of reason both in judgments of the sublime *and of the beautiful.*[46] That is, the "not without an object" and the hesitation before a suggestiveness of sensation (pleasure or unpleasure) can be applied to all judgments of taste, putting the subject in an anxious position until the safe shores of reason have been reached and a judgment of taste can be performed. I suggest that the fact that displeasure cannot be dispelled from the domain of aesthetic experience, the fact that sensation and the perceptual experience of pleasure cannot attest to the presence of a pleasurable affect according to transcendental logic of aesthetic judgment, and the fact that between the pleasure in sensation and the aesthetic pleasure there is a gap that has to be surmounted—all of these indicate that aesthetic experience is an attempt to circulate or fix an object, that object occupying the subject's field of vision, which the subject strives to aesthetically determine. The object of aesthetic experience can only be approached through negation, through the anxiety that may be taken to signal the presence of this object, the impossible object, the cause of desire, with which judgments of taste and experiences of art are engaged.

This chapter has concentrated on the attempt to *locate anxiety* as well as displeasure within the aesthetic act of judgment, that is, to locate anxiety in a structure in which the subject is engaged with an object of desire or of aesthetic contemplation. The following chapters will each address another aspect of anxiety through the inquiry of an aesthetic concept.

CHAPTER 2

The Beautiful Thing

"There is a certain relationship between beauty and desire" writes Lacan in his seminar on ethics,[1] and it is this relationship that will serve us, in this chapter, to clarify how the experience of the beautiful can be related to anxiety. Kant apparently excluded desire from the realm of aesthetic judgment by the notion of *disinterest*, and yet, in view of Lacan's words above, the place of desire has to be reconstituted in Kant in order to relate beauty to anxiety. Kant claimed that while the agreeable is a liking "conditioned pathologically by stimuli," and the good is "a pure practical liking," a judgment of taste "is merely *contemplative*, i.e., it is a judgment that is indifferent to the existence of the object."[2] For Kant, the absence of desire appears to condition the existence of a judgment of taste, whereas Lacan's view of beauty associates the beautiful object essentially with agony and desire. While at face value these perceptions of beauty may seem incompatible, the patent difference between them can reveal a more intricate picture of interesting affinities. Kantian disinterest or indifference toward the existence of the beautiful object does not necessarily reflect an absence of desire. The function of desire in judgments of taste is marked not only in those places where Kant assigns an *interest* to judgments of taste or recognizes the (moral) feeling elicited by beauty but also in the very tension immanent to the judgment of beauty between the sensible and the supersensible. These are the hidden affinities that I will utilize in order to preserve the notion of beauty as central to the aesthetics of anxiety. It also will enable me to retrospectively explain how Kant's notion of beauty, which in so many ways could have been considered irrelevant to an aesthetics of anxiety, and to the appreciation of art in general ever since the first forerunners of modernism appeared (in the nineteenth century and even earlier), continues to occupy the central stage in aesthetic theory with an unremitting intensity.

In this chapter, a psychoanalytic "reading" of Kantian beauty is presented, according to which the beautiful object is *split between its actual instantiation as an object in reality and its transcendental reference to the judging subject's desire*. According to Kant, while a judgment of taste treats the object in reality as its relevant domain, the judgment also requires that the limits of the sensible are transcended (as indicated, for instance, in the solution to the antinomy of taste, where it is acknowledged that a judgment of taste *cannot* be proven by reference to a concept of understanding, a concept that seeks correspondence with a sensible intuition).[3] Following the psychoanalytic "reading" of Kantian beauty, the experience of beauty will be shown to be imbued with anxiety, because this experience refers to an indeterminable concept of reason, or, in Lacanian terms, to the real object that causes desire.

The main context in which Lacan explores the question of beauty is that of tragedy. Lacan claims that beauty is the limit of the tragic, "the point at which the ungraspable thing pours its euthanasia [mercy killing] over us."[4] Thus he associates beauty with an indefinite thing, which is agonizing, menacing, and even lethal. It is "the function of this barrier of beauty under the form of the agony which the thing requires of us for us to join it."[5] For Lacan this power of beauty has to do with its essential relation to the Thing, the Thing that also can be referred to as the object-cause-of-desire. The object-cause-of-desire is not the substitute object actually desired but an object that marks "the subject's access to his relationship to death" in a blinding flash. The beautiful, in other words, is the object most related to the death drive, as beauty refers to what cannot be articulated in symbolic terms. The beautiful is predicated in tragedy in a way that marks it both as a form of protection from death and as a limit impeding the access to death. The beautiful image stands for the desire to what lies beyond, the death drive being, let us remember, a drive toward ultimate inertia, that is, enjoyment beyond excitation and satisfaction.

In this sense the tragic figure, Antigone, for instance, in her desire to go beyond human life, embodies in her beautiful image that which both attracts and repels. There where the human subject defies signification and universal meaning is where the subject's encounter with her own death is assumed. Antigone embodies ultimate beauty because she defies death, not only the death of the organism (by risking her life in declining to obey the ruler) but the symbolic death of common belief and meaning (by rejecting human law and the limits of signification). Beauty for Lacan marks the limit of "the second death," that is, the limit that human life can only briefly cross, and it is by the power of this limit that beauty gains its effect on the observing subject.

Psychoanalytic thought identifies the "beyond" of the pleasure principle with the loss of signification. After all, what sense can be given to a compulsive repetition? How can animation of the inanimated be made to signify if our historical memory fails to bring on any relevant reminiscence of such indeterminate existence? What brings "in a flash" this beyond, and is the cause of our anxiety, is what also fails signification. Lacan indeed describes the tragic as the limit of the symbolic; beyond the pleasure principle is where human actions cannot be made to signify, in terms of a social rule, a religious belief, an ideology, or any other unification by meaning. Antigone in this context is presented as a tragic figure precisely because her desire aims beyond the limit of the law, and of social significance.[6] This desire of Antigone is intolerable, as the chorus itself attests in the play. Antigone is intolerable in her beauty and splendor, which is something, Lacan implies, that pertains to all tragic characters: "Tragic heroes are always isolated, they are always beyond established limits, always in an exposed position and, as a result, separated in one way or another from the structure."[7]

So beauty, in its unbearable splendor, is considered in the context of psychoanalysis to signify the limit of symbolic human structures. The beautiful image cannot be transformed into goods (which is why Lacan assigns the concept of the good to a different register than that of the beautiful) nor into a meaningful object. In its opaque splendor the beautiful stands as an object of desire occupying the place of *das Ding*, the Thing. For psychoanalysis, the power of beauty is embodied in the necessary role that beauty fulfills in the structure of desire by standing for the limit of desire to which the subject is drawn but at the same time from which the subject is averted. This power, Lacan reminds us, is exemplified in many cultures by the fact that one is forbidden to touch the beautiful object.

But beauty within psychoanalytic thought has an ambivalent position; it does not only take part in constituting the cause of desire, but it sometimes can be said to suspend or disarm desire. This, claims Lacan, can be observed "with the precision of a Geiger counter" in clinical experience. "It is at the very moment when a thought is clearly about to appear in a subject . . . a thought that one recognizes as aggressive relative to one of the fundamental terms of his subjective constellation, that, depending on his nationality, he will make some reference to a passage from the Bible, to an author, whether a classic or not, or to some piece of music."[8] Thus the beautiful thing also can mark the limit of desire by signaling that we have reached the borders of a phantasm, therefore averting the subject from the menacing place by means of the beautiful appearance that disarms and blanks out desire.

Hence, the beautiful object maintains paradoxical relations with the desiring subject, as it causes agony or suffering with its very power of attraction. But can the beauty referred to by psychoanalysis be somehow related to the beauty addressed by aesthetics and art history? Before turning to the case of beauty in modernism in the next section, it should be noted that, for Kant, the nonconceptual nature of beauty, the fact that beauty does not lend itself to signification or cognition, is what prepares the subject for the free play of its faculties. This play conditions aesthetic pleasure, as demonstrated in the previous chapter. However, it also may be possible that the nonconceptual, unsignifiable nature of beauty in Kant points at the opaque front of the beautiful image, which human cognition cannot decipher by its routine cognitive modes.

AESTHETICS BEYOND BEAUTY?

Modernist art, from the mustached *Mona Lisa* of Marcel Duchamp, to *How to Explain Pictures to a Dead Hare,* by Joseph Beuys, has become identified as a practice that actively renounces beauty. Beauty is renounced by striving to maintain either a clear territory for an art that exists outside of the beautiful, and that does not recoil from ugly or revolting objects, or at least a territory indifferent to beauty. Paradoxically, it may seem that in order to delineate an aesthetic experience specific to modernist art, we depend on the distinction between the beautiful and the nonbeautiful, as much as classical art was dependent on a distinct territory of beauty (even if, as Kant indicates, beauty in the eyes of the observer can be the result of beautifying something given as ugly outside of art). Modernism, however, despite continuing in some senses the dialogue between art and beauty, can hardly be regarded as being an uninterrupted continuation of the classical aesthetic agenda.

Duchamp's *Fountain* marks a point of radical change in what had been considered, until this artistic event, the necessary association of art with beauty. This radicalness is described as a reshuffling of the whole aesthetic agenda to replace the question of beauty with the question of art,[9] or as a radical change in the position of the aesthetics of pleasure and beauty vis-à-vis art, a position that has now become totally irrelevant (as the situation of the early 1950's is gloomily described by Danto).[10] After Duchamp, art and art criticism appeared for a certain period of time to run a fierce battle against beauty, to the extent that saying an artwork was beautiful was taken as a way of downgrading it, of diagnosing the piece of art as anachronistic. Art became conceptual, political, an art of discontent with regard to the spectator's aesthetic sensitivities. The apparent demise of beauty went hand in hand with a questioning of the relevance of pleasure to aesthetic experience, as alongside the view that beauty is irrelevant to art the possibility of an aesthetic experience tied to sensations such as disgust, revolt, and displeasure emerged. In other words, modernism enters the scene of art in the name of ugliness, pleasing or displeasing, and in the name of disgust (elicited by the beautiful or the ugly), so that these are marked as the constitutive signs of the artistic revolution brought about by modernist art in general, and by Duchamp's art in particular. Obviously once pleasure and beauty no longer work as distinctive features of the aesthetic, art and non-art are automatically conflated.

While these demarcations of modernism are sustained, modernist art and postmodernist art continue to produce objects regarding which the question of beauty or ugliness is far from abated but is rather raised, in many senses, with special intensity. The uncompromising presence of beauty in art objects is something constantly taken into account in the contemporary production of art.[11] Thus a general ambivalence exists regarding the status of beauty in contemporary art, as either a totally anachronistic concept or as a notion that opens up new vistas for thinking about art.[12] This ambivalence is particularly emphasized here to point first to a historical moment in which the question of beauty can still be considered central to art, although beauty is no longer officially tied to an aesthetic experience constituted by positive feelings. The question of beauty persists, although it does not seem to serve any official purpose of artistic expression. Second, the ongoing occupation with beauty, despite the fact that beauty is no longer taken to form an integral part of aesthetic conceptions of art, suggests that *beauty fulfills another constitutive function in aesthetic experience, a function that transcends artistic revolutions and radical changes of taste.*

When examining this ambivalence and the paradoxical status of beauty in art theory and practice, the potential contribution of the psychoanalytic notion of beauty to the discussion becomes evident. The present calling for the notion of beauty in psychoanalytic thought is motivated by the fact that beauty cannot be simply restituted as being on the aesthetic agenda, without a radical rethinking of its meaning. Modernism presents itself as such a radical change that beauty, even if proven to play a significant role within the modernist artistic practices, cannot be simply reinstated within aesthetic considerations without further ado. A radical rethinking of the notion of beauty is suggested in this chapter based on Freud's and Lacan's references to the beautiful.

Thus this chapter advances a rather paradoxical claim—that beauty, which in aesthetic terms is not an objective property of the object, and in psychoanalytic terms refers to the desire of the subject and does not involve the object, *in the object is yet universally constitutive of aesthetic experience*. That is, while the object unto which aesthetic judgment is directed is, in a way, not the object of the aesthetic experience, a fact acknowledged by Kant, but also by Heidegger, Derrida, and Danto, the beauty ascribed to the object of aesthetic judgment nevertheless plays a necessary function in the constitution of an aesthetic experience. Thus while the difference between the beautiful and the ugly in objects is presented as being inconsequential to the aesthetic judgment, the beautiful thing is a condition, a cause for aesthetic experience. So how can beauty be both inconsequential and necessary? This is the question for which psychoanalysis, by binding beauty with desire, can provide an answer.

As suggested earlier, the fact that the difference between the beautiful and the ugly cannot be substantiated by aesthetic theory has already been noticed in traditional aesthetics and should not be attributed to a newly invented modernist move. This diffuseness of limits is already suggested by Kant, who claims that fine art is capable of describing things beautifully, even if in nature we would dislike or find these things ugly.[13] Within the context of art the ugly does not undermine the possibility of drawing aesthetic pleasure from it, nor does it contradict its being transformed into an object judged as being of pleasing beauty. It is only the ugly arousing disgust ("that cannot be presented in conformity with nature without obliterating all aesthetic liking and hence artistic beauty") that is incompatible with an aesthetic judgment of taste. Kant thus attests to the intimate relations between the beautiful and the ugly in the context of art, a relation also acknowledged by Lacan: "The forms that are at work in knowledge, Kant tells us, are interested in the phenomenon of beauty, though the object itself is not involved."[14] Yet although the object is not involved, it is needed to support something, that is, its beauty, and for Lacan what makes the beautiful object needed is the support it gives to a form of suffering. Thus what could have been surprising outside the context in which Lacan discusses the problem of the beautiful, the fact that beauty is agonizing, is not puzzling at all; nor are we surprised when Lacan claims that what is needed to grasp the role of beauty is an acquaintance with Sade. There, claims Lacan, in Sade's notes, the victims are always described as being adorned with beauty and grace, a necessity that can only be explained by "the prospect of the image that is silhouetted behind it and threatens it,"[15] a prospect, Lacan believes, that we find in every form of beauty. What the beautiful image keeps hidden yet supports is the object beyond the limit, an object therefore pleasing and agonizing at the same time: "Suffering is conceived of as a stasis which affirms that that which is cannot return to the void from which it emerged."[16] The meaning of this limit in which beauty is involved will be discussed later. At this point it is clear that beauty plays a role necessary for the operation of the aesthetic on us, readers and spectators, and that the beauty involved is there within the object, although the object itself is not involved in its beauty.

To return to the contemporary, postmodern change in the conception of beauty, the attempt to commensurate beauty with ugliness and pleasure with displeasure has created a difficulty in attempting to formulate an aesthetics appropriate to the spirit of contemporary art. Danto, for instance, recounts in his book the story behind the two shows exhibited in the Hirschhorn Museum in Washington: the first, "Distemper: Dissonant Themes in the art of the 1990s," was presented in 1996. The second, presented three years later, was antithetically called "Regarding Beauty."[17] Visitors to the earlier show (no less than visitors to the second show) reported, according to the curator, that they found many of the pieces presented beautiful, although the show exhibited works with no particular interest, or any concern, for that matter, for beauty. Facing these routine attributions of beauty to the "wrong" objects, how are we to grasp Kant's view that beauty is not in the object? How should we decide whether an object indifferent to beauty should be judged aesthetically? Danto himself suggests distinguishing a beauty that is integral to the meaning of a work from beauty that is only accidental to the work. Yet for that purpose, for establishing this distinction, Danto must break off from Kant; beauty is important to current aesthetics as much as ever, yet to have the notion of the beautiful work we must go beyond Kant's nonconceptual beauty and tie current beauty to the larger experience of the work, that is, "beauty belongs to meaning."[18] I mention this solution proposed by Danto to point to the difficulty of preserving the fundamental coordinates that define beauty in aesthetic judgment when things that ostensibly are not being made to please are taken to be beautiful.

Thus between attempts to show that beauty and ugliness are intimately tied, or are both useless predicates of art, and attempts to save the day for beauty, modernism seems to have irreversibly problematized the notion of beauty in ways previously unknown in the history of art and aesthetics. However, rather than claiming that modernist art transcends the distinction between beauty and ugliness, thus causing art to lose its aesthetic distinctness, the persistent presence of the question of beauty indicates that aesthetics cannot transcend these categories nor ignore their segregating effect. Indeed, aesthetic approaches that wish to go beyond traditional aesthetic categories (of beauty and pleasure, ugliness and displeasure) without obliterating the cardinality of these very categories to aesthetic experience and to the philosophy of art[19] are of the most radical and significant attempts to deal with the problem of art and to reconsider the status of aesthetics regarding contemporary art. In this context one should consider the works of Thierry de Duve, Hal Foster, and the work that emerges from psychoanalytic approaches to art as part of this project of radically rethinking aesthetic concepts as being essential to any notion of aesthetic experience.

The artistic case to be examined in this chapter is that of doll images, as perceived in the symbolic order of our culture; images that by their very definition are tied to beauty and infantile innocence, and as such are destined to elicit pleasure. Dolls represent themes that are officially rejected by modernism, and yet doll images are widely used in the art of the twentieth century, thus revealing how they touch ambiguously the limits of these themes (beauty and natural innocence) and indicating the paradoxical status of beauty in the context of contemporary art. Yet historically the doll is not only a prop in children's games but also a device in various rituals and ceremonies of a malignant nature. Within this ambivalence, dolls, in their innocent and menacing aspects, are paradigmatic for the relation of beauty to anxiety. As indicated previously, psychoanalysis points to the relation of beauty to the limit of desire, thus implying the necessary link of beauty to anxiety; the doll image appears to embody this ambivalence in its very function in cultural and artistic practices.

THE UNCANNY IN FREUD

"The liking for the beautiful carries with it directly a feeling of life's being furthered, and hence is compatible with charms and with an imagination at play."[20] If beauty, according to Kant, revives and furthers one's feelings of life, then Freud's uncanny seems ill suited to this Kantian conception, as it is triggered in the subject by an insoluble hesitation as to whether a given object can be cognized as animate or inanimate. How can this stupefying effect be correlated with a feeling of life?

It should first be noted that for Freud, just as much as for Kant, "a feeling is only aesthetic if it is universally applicable,"[21] and as I will show in this chapter, the universal demand is implemented in both aesthetics (the Kantian and the psychoanalytic), in terms of indeterminacy that is "furthering of life feelings." To embark on this investigation, I examine Freud's literary example, which involves a doll image,[22] the doll Olympia from A. T. Hoffman's *The Sandman.* This doll image elicits in the reader a sense of the uncanny, in that it keeps the reader hesitant as to whether the doll is animate or inanimate, a living beauty or an inanimate object. This idea that the doll represents the impossible encounter between innocent beauty and uncanny effects (the uncanny being, according to Freud, one type of anxiety that the encounter with art can elicit) may provide a preliminary explanation about the way the beauty in general, and the beauty of dolls in particular, should be approached. Doll images suggest an aesthetics that exceeds the distinction between beauty and its opposites, between the pleasing and the anxiety-provoking object. Surely if the doll raises a sense of the furthering of life feelings, then these feelings in view of the beautiful are definitely not of a pleasant kind. The doll agonizes both the character in the story and the reader attempting to decipher what is behind this bizarre creature. The doll serves Hoffman to stage the ultimate irresolvability of whether one faces a case of an organized conspiracy against the hero, Nathanel, or a case of delirium on the hero's part.[23] Between these two interpretive possibilities, the doll stands as a walled enigma. Freud, it must be stressed, is not interested in the literary aspect of this ambiguity. The events of the story *should* be ambiguous to cause an uncanny feeling; the intimidating figures of Copelius and his partner must be both convincing as incarnating externally encountered evil and as psychically imposed misrecognitions of the world around on the part of the hero. The doll embodies this ambiguity of the inside/outside, animate/inanimate, and planned/imposed nature of the events and of the figures involved.

Psychoanalysis, as is well known, runs against the common view of childhood as a time of innocence. Whether we address the early Freud, who saw neurosis as the result of a traumatic encounter in childhood with mature sexuality, or whether it is the later Freud, who treated psychic reality as a series of formations (such as fantasy, symptom, or the dream), fixated at a moment of early repression, in any case psychic reality cannot be characterized as innocent, even when its external products may appear to be so. The young infant sucking with angelic innocence his mother's breast implements an infinite demand that can never be satiated by satisfying the physical need. This state of insatiability continues to hold during the child's early life, even when no hunger is felt, and later, when demands made to the Other take infinitely diverse forms.

Examining the doll image from this point of view clarifies from the outset that the doll cannot be perceived as a reflection of infantile innocence, nor of asexual beauty, but is, by necessity, an impossible materialization of these features together with their opposites. From a psychoanalytic point of view, the doll, in its artistic imagining, can indeed be seen as the place where beauty and the shattering of innocence coalesce; where pleasure (associated with childhood games, for instance) is tied to an uncanny feeling (possibly associated with an air of sexuality or of secretiveness effectuated by the doll) that agonizes the subject.

When Freud published in 1919 "The Uncanny," he referred by this concept to occurrences where the subject comes across an object or event, habitually familiar to the point of utter automatism of perception, and feels this object or event to be strange and intimidating. One phenomenon responsible for turning the familiar and habitual into the strange and uncanny is that of a repetitive occurrence that imposes itself on the subject time and again. For example, the dreamer walks in a small town in Italy and finds himself, as if against his will, returning to a morbid narrow street, empty of people and with figures of women drawn on buildings' windowpanes. The dreamer is stricken by the anxiety Freud names "uncanny" when finding himself for the third time in the same street, which he has been striving desperately to detour. This involuntary return, says Freud, is imposed by what attracts and draws the dreamer beyond his conscious displeasure in this frightening and strange street.[24] It is this "other will" that turns the automatic mechanics of walking into something that is neither innocent nor really against the subject's will. It is therefore the type of occurrence that subjects tend to interpret as meaningful, as carrying secret significance for them. Repetition can thus be said to be of a paradoxical nature, as it transcends life itself, so to speak; that is, the uncanny feeling elicited by repetition signifies the presence of another drive, beyond the drive to pleasure or the drive to life—the death drive. Lacan will later claim that "every drive is virtually a death drive,"[25] because every drive involves the subject in repetition, and every drive is an attempt to go beyond the pleasure principle, where enjoyment is experienced as suffering.[26]

The automatism of repetition is linked to pleasure, claims Freud, the principle of pleasure being the fundamental navigator of psychic life through a stimulation that causes suffering until a point of discharge that brings about relief and pleasure. Yet the psychic dynamic involved goes beyond the stimulation and discharge of energy, since this dynamic draws the subject to something that is displeasing to him. The subject senses anxiety where the demands of pleasure have been transcended. Beyond the pleasure principle, the subject orients himself or herself toward an inorganic state of inertia, the fundamental mode to which all existing beings strive to return.

Repetition compulsion thus has a complicated relation to pleasure, which the Lacanian *jouissance* aims to grasp. Repetition, in its displeasing effect, marks the vivacious power of the drive toward which the subject moves in repetition. By associating repetition to the drive, Freud suggests that this mechanism, in its very automatism, touches the living substance, the vibrating factor in every subject (the effects of unfamiliarity and uncanniness signal this very factor). While the effect of the drive movement is displeasing for the self, the real object of the drive magnetizes the subject with its power of absolute enjoyment. The movement of the drive embodied in repetition (a signifying mechanism that marks the limits of its own functioning) signals the death drive inherent in every living substance, since it represents in the real what returns to the inert, immobile state of being, beyond pleasure or suffering. The repeated element therefore transcends the distinction between pleasure and displeasure; while finding himself time and again in the same morbid street stimulates the dreamer's displeasure (as he feels a repulsion that drives him away from this street), the recurrent encounter also signifies the unconscious desire to get close to what the dreamer consciously rejects and aims to push outside his field of vision. The uncanny thus signifes an affect elicited when the subject comes close to the thing he is driven to yet has been suppressed. The recurrent encounter must therefore also involve pleasure, although not a pleasure that can be clearly distinguished from displeasure.

In referring to Freud's *Unheimlich,* Lacan says that Freud has shown us that everything starts from imaginary castration, a lack of which we have no image (which refers to the mother's desire beyond the child, namely, to an imaginary phallus). "When something appears there," in the place of imaginary loss, an uncanny feeling is elicited, because "the lack is lacking."[27] What appears in this place of lack, the image that supports it, is an image raising anxiety, "revealing to us the nonautonomy of the subject." The object in the place of the imaginary lack, in other words, somehow dispossesses the subject of its place vis-à-vis the desire of the Other. To put it differently, since the Other should desire (i.e., lack something) in order for the subject's desire to be constituted, an image in the place of lack signals the lack as lacking, since it marks the complete Other as lacking nothing, thus raising anxiety. My desire as subject, says Lacan, is determined by my being the object of the desire of the Other "insofar as it exiles me from my subjectivity by resolving of itself all the signifiers to which this subjectvitiy is attached."[28] The encounter with the beautiful object is the encounter with the object occupying the place of lack that marks the kernel of the Other's desire. The effect of this encounter is dual. The beautiful object, like the doll in "the Sandman" (that on Freud's interpretation epitomizes the threat of stealing the hero's eyes from him), both locates the subject's desire (marking the threat of castration as the stealing of Nathanel's eyes) and dispossesses him from this place of desire (the doll appears as planted by the menacing Other, dispossessing the subject of his own desire).

This duplicity can further elucidate why for Freud the uncanny is beyond the pleasure principle. For Freud, anxiety refers to a primary phase when the ego has not yet been differentiated from the external world. It is in this manner that the anxiety that accompanies repetition is linked both to the source of life itself and to the place where movement has absolutely become absent, where death resides. Beyond the pleasure principle, Lacan would later claim, nothing is lacking, and the image of lack is unsignifiable.[29] It is for this reason that what brings us closer to the possibility of nonlacking pleasure elicits anxiety, since we, castrated as we are, recoil before such a possibility.

The experience of the uncanny brings back something familiar that has been repressed. Thus the uncanny emerges where primitive beliefs that have been superseded gain a sudden affirmation (for instance, when a wished-for death of a hated person is actualized soon afterward, taken as a proof that a wish of the heart can gain power in actual life as part of a primitive animistic view of the world surrounding the subject.) Likewise, where infantile complexes that have been repressed return with vivid and real force (as is the case with the sandman of Nathanel's childhood who returns in the later figure of Dr. Copelius to reactivate the torturing fear from blindness harassing the hero of the story), an uncanny effect is produced. These examples illustrate the impossible point of view that the uncanny materializes; it is a point of view that combines the primary perspective of the infant with that of the adult who has already repressed her primary desire.

At this stage in Freud's thought, when "The Uncanny" is published, it is still difficult to say whether the anxiety accompanying the uncanny is the cause or the result of repression. That is, is anxiety to be understood as displeasure caused by the encounter with an event or object that has been repressed, or is anxiety a cause that precedes repression? In "Beyond the Pleasure Principle" (1920),[30] Freud already points decisively at repetition compulsion, or the return of the repressed, as having its source in the inanimate, inert occurance that precedes the endless process of charge and discharge of psychic energy imposed by the principle of pleasure. There is thus a certainty in anxiety, a certainty that has to do with the encounter with something absolute and nondialectic, that therefore necessitates repression as its result. Whenever the subject will come across formations that signify what is infinitely unrepresentable, the registered yet unrepresentable memory of undifferentiated inertia preceding repression, anxiety will arise (this aspect of anxiety as cause is extensively discussed in chapter 4).

If anxiety is not the product of repression, then it must itself be an unconscious formation, a formation that imposes its presence through the blocking effect of repression. From "Beyond the Pleasure Principle" it is clear that anxiety is unique among unconscious formations, since its object is not the repressed but is beyond/before repression. In a later article, "Inhibitions, Symptoms, and Anxiety" (1926), Freud explains why anxiety is related to what transcends life itself, that is, to beyond the pleasure principle.[31] Here he points to the fact that had anxiety been the result of repression, had it been subject to the control of the pleasure principle, then we would have faced here a paradox: repression works in order to relieve the subject of tension; repression thus satisfies. Anxiety, on the other hand, within the economics of pleasure/displeasure, should be taken as dissatisfying, as having to do with energetic charge, and thus as distinct from repression. An overcharge of energy, but not a discharge of energy, can cause anxiety. Thus within the economics of psychic energies, anxiety is opposed to repression.

It is for this reason, says Freud, that anxiety should be understood as being there "from the beginning," so to speak, as involving what precedes the energetic cycle of charge and discharge, of pleasure and displeasure. Anxiety hence cannot be integrated into the movement of the energies of life but is rather to be grasped as a real state of being, registered in the subject's body from the moment of birth when the danger of being separated from the mother's body produced the first moment of anxiety. This psychic real state of anxiety recurs later at various moments (facing the threat of castration, the danger of an object loss, or the imposition of the superego imperatives), when a similar danger for the subject, that of losing her imaginary unity with the object, is marked by anxiety. The anxiety effectuated by repetition hence does not signify the return of the repressed as Freud claimed in "The Uncanny," but, rather, signifies the real thing prior to repression, which cannot be represented yet whose presence can be indicated through the very occurrence of anxiety itself.

It was shown previously, that Lacan further qualifies the structure of anxiety raised in front of an object that occupies the imaginary lack (of unity in the Other). Lacan also will instruct at a later stage that "the metaphor of return to the inanimate—which Freud ascribes to every living body—the margin beyond life that language assures the human being due to the fact that he speaks . . . is precisely the margin where this being places in signifying position . . . the body itself."[32] In other words, the Freudian idea of "beyond the pleasure principle" is simply a way to point to the dialectic in which the speaking being is seized. The repetition of signs/formations is not just a mechanism of language; it appears as that through which the subject "gets a glimpse," so to speak, of what lies beyond language/life. The return to the inanimate is the return to the retrospectively assumed prelanguage state of the real, to the limit where language stops. It is a place of nonbeing which language can suggest only from the point where the subject is already a speaking subject. Anxiety thus signifies the paradoxical existence of the intimidating and enjoyment in one and the same formation of language (visual or textual), thereby also indicating something about the possible function of art and its modes of expression and figuration. Beautiful images present obvious candidates for occupying the structural place of the nonhuman at the limit of signification, which at the same time signals the limit of life symbolized.

The intricate relations that Freud describes between anxiety and the limit of life, embodied in the uninterrupted movement of the drives beyond the living substance clarify the set of examples he employs to illustrate the causes of the uncanny, examples around which a hesitation appears as to whether the object concerned is inanimate or animate, a dead object or a living body, a moving substance or a mechanically moved thing, a human being or a fabricated reflection.[33] These intricate relations also are linked to the role Freud assigns to art in connection to anxiety: in art, as the product of imagination and creativity, one cannot distinguish between the uncanny produced by what has been repressed and the uncanny produced by an infantile belief that has been superseded. Art as an imaginative, creative act does not obey the reality test; it transcends it. The art of fiction can produce an intensified effect of the uncanny, even though, paradoxically, many things that may have been perceived as uncanny in reality are not seen as such in art. In other words, for Freud, art has the ability to create, by the power of the imagination, an intensified effect of the uncanny that is not subjected to the modes of its production in reality. The effect of the uncanny refers to a psychic event that precedes the distinction between reality and imaginative reality. It is this indistinguishability that exceeds the breaking test of reality, for which Lacan will coin the concept of "the Real."

Freud explicitly indicates that the uncanny is an effect produced where the distinction between inanimation and animation collapses. Indeed, the horror in face of what was perceived as a living being and turned out to be a machination and the anxiety felt when an object perceived as inanimate (a house, a wall, a cave) turns out to be animated are both produced when we face entities that are neither alive nor dead and as such transcend (or precede) the differentation of objects. The speaking cave, the inanimate animated, materializes the power of the life drive inside the dead body, signifying the presence of the material of life, what Freud refers to elsewhere as the "libido," as if distinct from the inanimate body. Alternatively, the machinated doll, the animated object turning inanimated, materializes the imposition of the death drive on the living body. That is, what activates the inanimate body that looks alive is not life but only an imposing, automatic movement, the movement characteristic of the body carrying itself on as if without vivid volition, but in fact just like the movement of language, it is a movement beyond life itself, in the striving to reach the state of ultimate inertia.

FROM KANT'S *AESTHETIC IDEA* TO THE SURREALIST DOLL

In §17, a paragraph dedicated to the ideal of beauty, Kant unfolds the intricate relations between the mental representation of a beautiful thing (an archetype of beauty) and the production of an intuitive form on the basis of such an ideal so that this form will elicit a judgment of taste. The ideal of beauty points to the fact that an idea of reason, representing the demand for a maximum (of beauty), looms in the aesthetic judgment as an indeterminate standard of taste. Kant sets the human figure as a standard of beauty, "the only form of beauty that expresses something absolutely and unconditionally valuable, namely, the moral autonomy of which humans alone are capable," and yet "there is no determinate way in which this unique value can be expressed in human form." The human figure as ideal cannot itself be conceived to be discovered by any mechanical process through average measures of humans actually encountered.[34] While stressing that the unique value attributed to the human figure has no determinate way of expressing itself, the ideal of beauty sets a crucial relation between aesthetics and ethics, between moral ideas and their visibility in beauty.[35] This passage in Kant, in other words, shows that the leaning on (indeterminate) ideas of reason in intuiting a beautiful form is indispensable. Even if the idea playing a role in the production of beauty is merely a general idea and not a determinate one, without this component of "spirit," without leaning on a nonmechanical standard of beauty, the beautiful would have been no more than an empty form. Gasché, in his reading of this paragraph in Kant, stresses even further how the ideal of beauty goes against the formalist reading of Kant, exposing the extent to which "the faculties involved in the creation of aesthetic ideas seem to be imagination and reason."[36] For Gasché, no judgment of taste makes sense outside the realm of ideas of reason and morality. The beautiful in Kant is, in the profoundest of ways, a symbol of morality.

In order to negotiate the nonconceptual reflective judgment with an ideal of beauty necessary as a standard and presupposing a determined concept of reason (such as the human figure), Gasché recruits what he calls a symbolic dimension to be added to the schematic side of forms. His claim is that reason, both in its theoretical and practical aspects, is intertwined with judgments of taste, an elementary intertwining "in advance of their ordinary, and mutually exclusive, employment."[37] That is, judgments of taste bridge the abyss between cognition and morality, understanding and reason by interconnecting a sensible intuition (in the shape of a form) and ideas of reason (even if merely indeterminate ones). Imagination collects the intuited manifold of an object into a presentation of a concept in general; imagination in that fashioning yet strives to produce the ideal of beauty, an ideal that for Kant "is a mere idea, an idea which everyone must generate within himself and by which he must judge any object of taste."[38]

So the ideal of beauty introduces a standard that is a mere idea that can only become palpable when implemented particularly in a presentation. This faculty of intuiting a form for an idea of reason is exhibited in the aesthetic idea and is the faculty Kant calls "spirit,"[39] a faculty that points to the crucial role of the imagination in presenting ideas spiritually. Aesthetic ideas are not solely presentations of ideas of reason, but rather they only strive toward something that transcend the bounds of experience, which is why the imagination should execute its nonconformist powers and wild attempts to go beyond the bounds of what can be experienced.[40]

This discussion of aesthetic ideas in Kant is raised here to clarify the relation between judgments of the beautiful and the image implementing the ideal of beauty. The beautiful cannot be semanticized nor embodied in an image; it can only be intuited through a form that strives to grasp the spirit of an idea. This Kantian approach to the interface between imagination and reason in the judgment of taste is referred to also in Lacan's approach to Antigone and in Freud's analysis of the uncanny, as in both cases the status of the image is ambivalent. The doll image is in this respect also a mode of exhibiting beauty in an image, yet as a mental representation of a standard of a maximum, the doll oscillates between the exhibition of an idea and the impossibility of finding a measure or way of determining a form for the ideal of beauty. The doll image thus refers to an ideal of beauty without being in itself an embodiment of this ideal or of any other idea of reason. In what follows, I will therefore demonstrate how the doll maintains an insoluble split between the schematic form and the idea of beauty or innocence embodied through this form.

In a catalogue published on the occasion of an exhibit in the "Tate Modern" in London in the winter of 2001–2002, under the heading "Surrealism: Desire Unlimited,"[41] Hal Foster refers to the image of the woman as fetish and as an object shattered by surrealist aesthetics.[42] Foster argues that the doll photographed by Man Ray, or the doll manufactured from different materials by Hans Bellmer, cannot be easily subsumed under the distinction feminine/masculine. True, the surrealists were mostly men who created images of women from a masculine point of view, but a perspective that subjects the woman image in surrealist art to the distinction feminine/masculine is too schematic to grasp the surrealist main dilemma. Foster in fact adopts a psychoanalytic viewpoint to argue that it is difficult, or even misleading, to interpret Bellmer's dolls simply as a way of turning the woman into an object of masculine violence; Bellmer's dolls undergo a series of mutilations, dislocations, and distortions of form and are subject to sadistic treatment under the hands of the artist, who assembles their parts into artistic objects. In a Kantian spirit, one may argue, Bellmer intuits a doll form as a way of imaginatively going beyond the sensible and symbolic divisions. The doll exhibits an indeterminate idea of sexuality that needs the full power of the imagination to be presented in mere form.

Foster further argues what can suggest the range of possible incarnations of the beautiful. What can the image of a doll grasp and structure with regard to the idea of beauty? Through the sadistic scenes that Bellmer creates for his dolls, a masochistic sexuality appears: "In his erotic manipultation of the dolls he explores a destructive impulse that is also self-destructive. In this way the dolls may go inside sadistic mastery to the point where the subject confronts its greatest fear: its own fragmentation and disintegration. And yet this may also be the greatest desire."[43] The doll is both mastered and threatens to disintegrate, and if we follow this argument of Foster further, it can be argued that the image of beauty is produced by collecting the manifold in a form imbued with spirit, and as such, the image of beauty can exhibit both a totality of form and the danger of a disintegration of this totality. The image of beauty, in Kant as in the art of Bellmer, is a conflictual image constituted by the incompatible use of imagination to transcend the limits of sensibility. This conflict both clarifies why the beautiful image cannot be reduced to a concept of beauty and why the beautiful image raises anxiety in the spectator, anxiety signaling the danger of disintegration that the image exhibits.

The conflictual use of doll images by Bellmer can be associated with two points Lacan made with regard to the image of beauty. First, the splendid figure of Antigone is one that "represents the radical limit that affirms the unique value of his being without reference to any content, to whatever good or evil Polynices may have done."[44] What is essential to the tragic image of Antigone, in her terrifying splendor, is the fact that her deeds cannot be identified as responding or corresponding to good or evil values. Antigone, just like Bellmer's dolls, is beyond the symbolic divisions between man and woman, good and evil, and so forth. The aesthetical idea, while clearly linked in Kant to practical reason and questions of morality, can hardly be said to be moral in its content. The idea of beauty and the idea of femininity or goodness transcend the sensible divisions one can enact on usual objects of cognition.

Second, Lacan refers in the context of beauty to the economy of masochism, as reducing desire to objecthood: "The position of the perverse masochist is the desire to reduce himself to this nothing that is the good, to this thing that is treated like an object, to this slave whom one trades back and forth and whom one shares."[45] Within this masochist economy, the subject is reduced to a commodity as a matter of unconscious choice. The masochist, to ward off the anxiety from disintegration, replaces the pain of crossing a certain line at the limit of which the beautiful object stands, with the pain involved in being a commodity, a good to be shared. This point explains why not all forms of pain, not all objects at the line of desire, elicit anxiety (a point that will be discussed at much later length in the next two chapters). In the case of masochism and other forms of perverse pain, the subject of perversion is not affected by anxiety; the spectator, however, is. The perverse subject identifies with the object that may imaginarily fill the place of loss. The pain that ensues for the masochist is therefore a pain and not anxiety, and it is a pain full of enjoyment.

The doll, in other words, sustains the duplicity of marking a symbolic lack, on the one hand, and of blocking the imaginary loss, on the other hand. So the doll image causes dismay because it marks the place of the missing object, but it also blocks this place, causing the loss to be lost. In that the doll image illustrates the working of the beautiful image as intuiting an idea that no object can determinately exhibit, an idea yet indeterminately presented in a particular form.

In Freudian terms, the doll is not an object for the torturing acts of dominance by the creating, masculine subject; the doll rather represents this subject himself or herself. The horror in face of the threat of disintegration that the doll embodies is also the most desired state, a source of immense attraction, since it marks the return of the subject to the state that eludes the safe outlines of the self, where subject and external objects are undifferentiated. Bellmer does not just desire his dolls as objects of his sadism but treats them also as objects of identification, and it is this very identification full of desire that constitutes the shocking, horrific effect of the encounter with his art. Bellmer's dolls, being on the verge of decomposing (Bellmer accentuates the tentative being of the doll as assembled of parts), thus refer to a state of inertia in the beginning of life (before the infant's separation from the maternal body, prior to the ego's separation from the object) or to a state of nonexistence that terminates life. The anxiety effectuated by the doll image touches on a state either prior to or beyond the economy of sexuality and of psychic representations of pleasure or displeasure, good or evil. From Brancusi to the phallic photographs of the human body executed by Man Ray, the distinction between the feminine and masculine is totally blurred. Foster, in his book,[46] has indeed characterized surrealism in general and "dolls" in particular as an artistic practice that surrounds the uncanny, signifying the indistinction between life and death, the confusion between repetition compulsion and the return to repressed desires, the collapse of the dualism of inside/outside.

The psychoanalytic interpretation of Bellmer's dolls developed here positions beyond the effects of misogyny so blatantly marked in these images, another dimension of anxiety that makes the opposition feminine/masculine irrelevant. The particular position of the subject vis-à-vis such an image is precisely *not* dictated by social considerations or ideologies; the observer given to the uncanny effects of the doll oversteps the social patterns of the feminine and masculine positions and observes the doll as an object that eludes the symbolic patterns of conventional mapping (according to patriarchal, political, or other social-ideological criteria). In this, the doll image reproduces the same resistance to symbolization with which Lacan has characterized tragic heroes.

For this very reason, the doll cannot be regarded as exhibiting a determinate idea (of reason) or concept (of understanding); the doll disavows sexual difference; it is "a faltering at the threshold of the genital order in which such difference is established."[47] It is because the doll is located at the limit of integration, and yet refers to a stage prior to the danger of separation (between mother and child, between subject and object, between man and woman), that it elicits anxiety in the observing subject. The doll refers to an absolute Thing that cannot be semanticized nor dialecticized.

FROM INTIMACY TO ABSOLUTE EXTIMACY: THE SUBJECT AS DOLL

"*Das Ding* is at the center only in the sense that it is excluded . . . in reality *das Ding* has to be posited as exterior, as the prehistoric Other that it is impossible to forget . . . something strange to me, although it is at the heart of me."[48] With these words Lacan refers to the Other as a core of absolute strangeness inside the subject, an irreducible core for which he coins the adjective "extimate" (an "ex" added to the suffix of "intimate"), indicating the problematic split between inside and outside that is yet constitutive of the relation between subject and Other.

From the staged photographs of Cindy Sherman as a Hollywood doll, photographs that stage her as the heroine of the scenes she herself directs, through the works of Mariko Mori and Tony Oursler, to those of Uri Katzenstein and Charles Ray's "Self-Portrait" of 1990, the doll image does not appear as an object given to the masculine, externally imposed gaze but as an image split by the gaze observing it. What does this split amount to?

Freud had shown us that the doll in Hoffman's tale is a "materialization of Nathaniel's feminine attitude towards his father in his infancy . . . Olympia is, as it were, a dissociated complex of Nathaniel's which confronts him as a person, and Nathaniel's enslavement to this complex is expressed in his senseless obsessive love for Olympia."[49] Contemporary art exhibits doll images that, like Hoffman's, refer to an aspect of the psychic position of the one (author, hero) who created them. Yet the anxiety that is effectuated by their presence points to the fact that the doll image is not just a way to represent an inner world. The doll is an image that irresolutely combines intimate familiarity with a strange object located at the very heart of familiarity. The doll, in its aspect of extimacy, presents the idea of strangeness in intimacy that constitutes the beautiful figure, the image of splendor. The doll image represents the refusal to *Aufhebung* and retains an absolute strangeness that cannot be reconciled with the familiar form.

Self-representations implemented by artists by doll images stress the mechanic, industrial, inanimate, and artificial side that characterizes the doll (whose body is made of industrial stuffing, attired in a wide range of absurd costumes, or is petrified in an artificial pose), thereby indicating that the doll is alien, strange to the artist who created it. The doll as a self-image confounds the distinction between animate and inanimate, between natural and artificial, between feminine and masculine ("the doll," among a series that impersonates artist Uri Katzenstein, can have the masculine face of the artist and a feminine or an androgynous body carrying the well-individuated head; see Figure 2.1). The doll presents an image of the self through an alien body. "The voice is Jacob's voice, but the hands are the hands of Esau" says the Old Testament of the father confused between the familiar, loved aspect of one son and the foreign, unfamiliar trait of the other son. That is, the only way to represent the creative artist is not by being faithful to the personal, intimate, familiar parts that make him or her a unique individual but through an object that carries some features of the artist, yet in a body that is petrified, foreign, imposed—that is, through the image of the doll.

This idea of materializing the artist's personality or uniqueness of the artist by placing his or her familiar face or another identity trait on top of a doll body is also typical of Mariko Mori's self-presentations (as in Figure 2.2). Here the doll-image of a pop star is accompanied by a pop song sung in the voice of the artist herself.[50] The irreducible presence of the Other in the machinated form of a doll becomes the constitutive idea of subjectivity. This Other is nothing but the function that possesses the solution to the enigma, "How am I being seen as an object of observation?," an enigma that remains eternally unsolved yet critical for the artist's self-image. In this

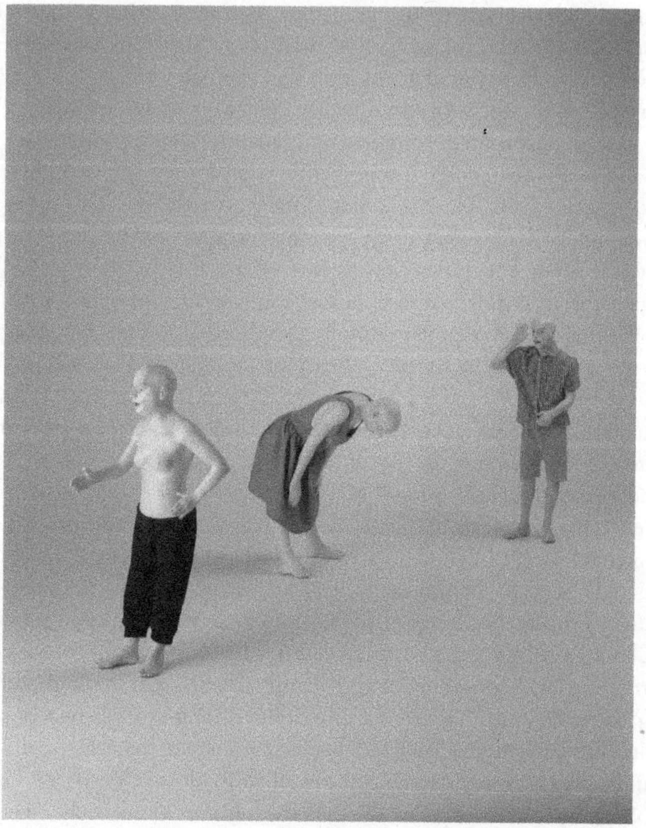

Figure 2.1. Uri Katzenstein (b. 1951). *Home* (detail). 2000–2001. Collection of The Israel Museum, Jerusalem Purchase, ARTVISION Acquisitions Committee, Israel.

respect the artist's self-presentation is controlled by a gaze positioned at a point from which the artist cannot perceive himself or herself. The artist "cannot see himself from the point from which he is seen," claims Lacan in Seminar XI,[51] thereby pointing to the fundamental paradox of creation. The artist can represent himself or herself from where this representation can never lead to self-knowledge or to self-awareness, since the route to self-knowledge passes through an uncanny image. Something that is absolutely unfamiliar and inhuman, "beyond the texture of life," marks the real existence of the artist as a body and as a living being. It is that which is beyond life, here materialized by the doll, which breathes life into the doll image, making it the paradoxical formation that represents the particularity of the artist as subject other to herself or himself.

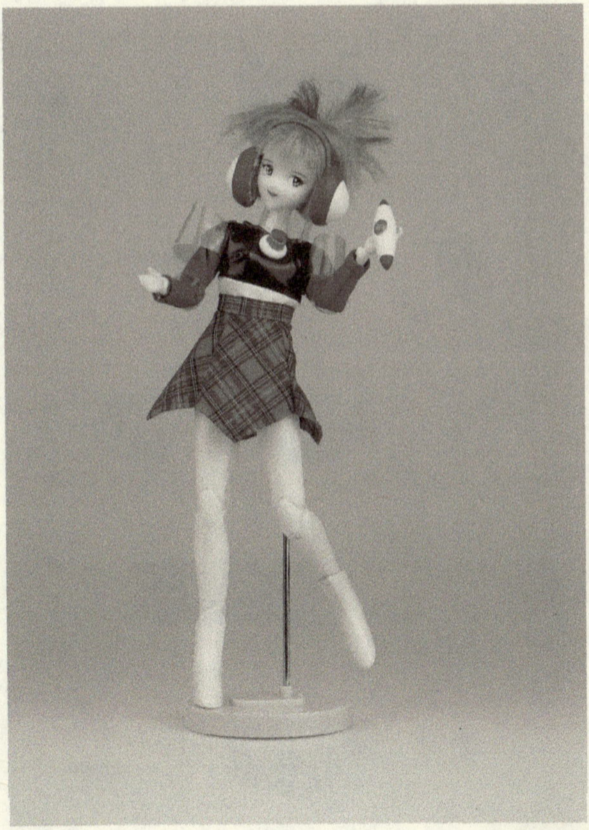

Figure 2.2. Mariko Mori (b. 1967). *Star Doll.* 1998. Doll with microphone, earphones, white boots, white stockings, red plaid skirt, top in blue, black, and white, transparent bracelets, yellow shoulder pads, brooch, and blue hair. 10¼" high. Ed. 99/XX, signed and numbered. © Parkett Publishers and Mariko Mori.

FROM THE UNIQUENESS OF BEAUTY TO THE EFFECT OF REPETITION

In 1994, American artist Lorna Simpson created a work called *Wigs* (Figure 2.3), which presents a series of wigs in various colors and shapes; a kind of catalogue cut off from any concrete human context. This work appears to be a late incarnation of Andy Warhol's works from the 1960s, which stressed the mechanistic aspect of repetition, as in the work reproducing numerous times the lips of Marylin Monroe, or Warhol's *Triple Elvis* of 1963, which presents a multiple reproduction of Elvis's figure, where the figures are finished as fading

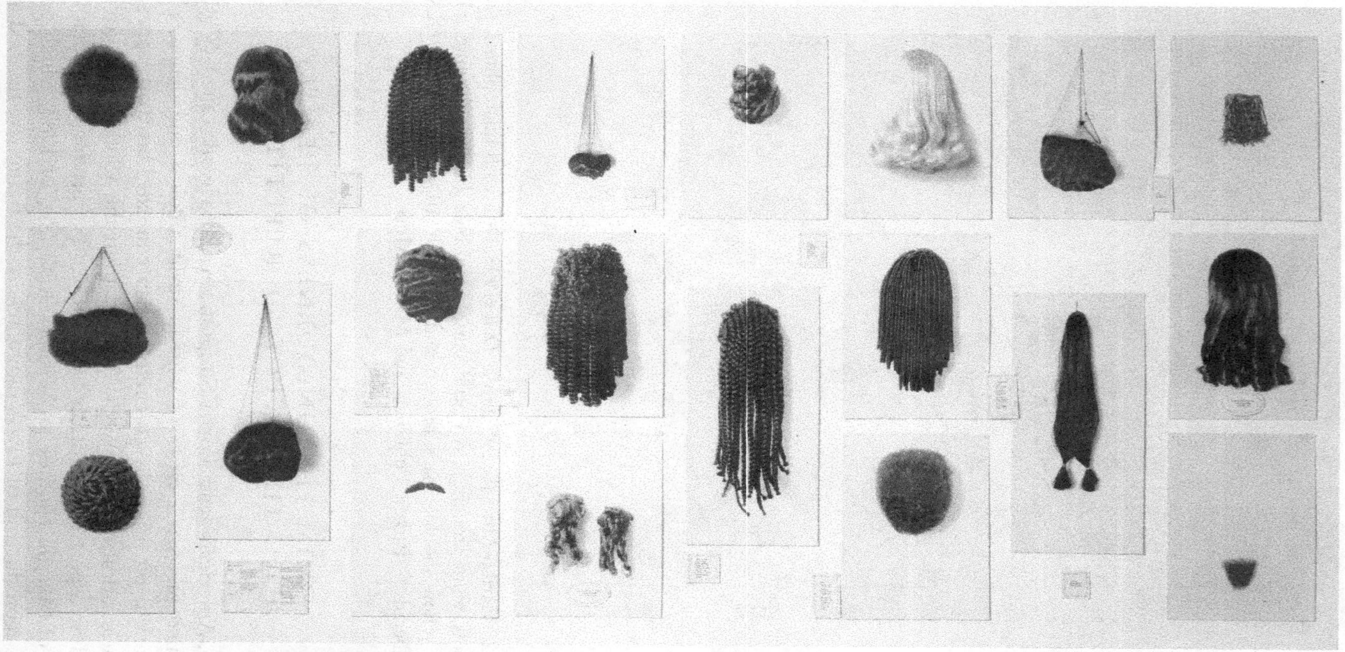

Figure 2.3. Lorna Simpson (b. 1960). *Wigs.* 1994. Collection © Walker Art Center, Minneapolis. T. B. Walker Acquisition Fund, 1995.

in color and contour. To this list also belong Charles Ray's dolls, engaged in an orgy, or posing for a family snapshot (Figure 2.4), where all marks of individuality have been erased from them; in the family scene presented by Ray, the observer faces four figures of almost identical height and body shape, with only the sexual organs marking the difference between father and mother and son and daughter. To this list one can add a work entitled *Mamelles*, by Louise Bourgeois (1991), which presents a series of breasts/udders inside a mold, body parts that are cut off the human body but repeated as products of a molding process (Figure 2.5).

In all of these examples, the doll, or parts thereof, is presented in a series that in itself also serves to constitute the doll image. The dolllike character of these images embodies a standardized conception of objects, since the mechanistic repetition indicates the artificial, representative nature of the doll (as evidenced, for instance, in the use of many wigs rather than one; one would have created a different effect without the present emphasis on the standardized nature of "personality" or "style"). Following this standardization, the very possibility of perceiving the doll as representing a particular object or

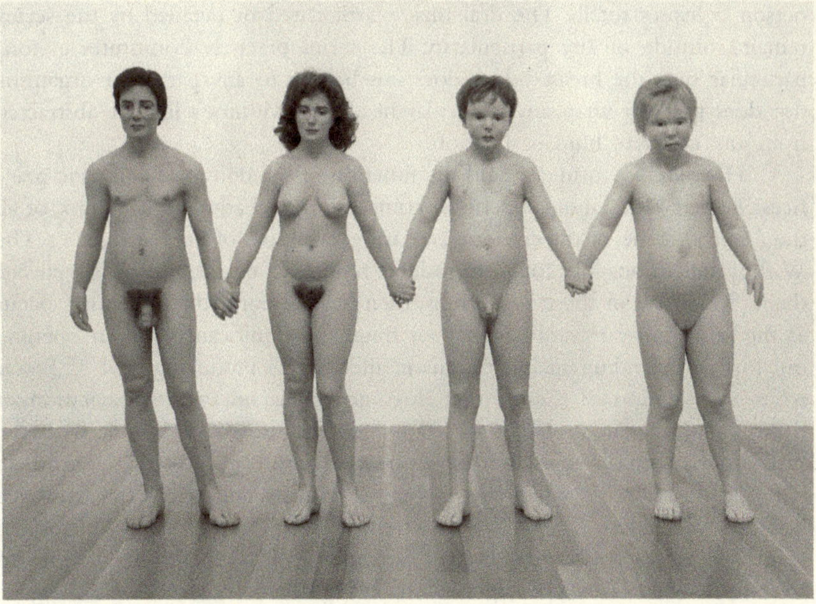

Figure 2.4. Ray Charles (b. 1953). *Family Romance.* 1993. New York, Museum of Modern Art. Mixed Media, 53" x 7'1" x 11" (134.6 x 215.9 x 27.9 cm). Gift of the Norton Family Foundation. Digital image © 2007 The Museum of Modern Art, New York/SCALA, Florence. Courtesy Donald Young Gallery, Chicago.

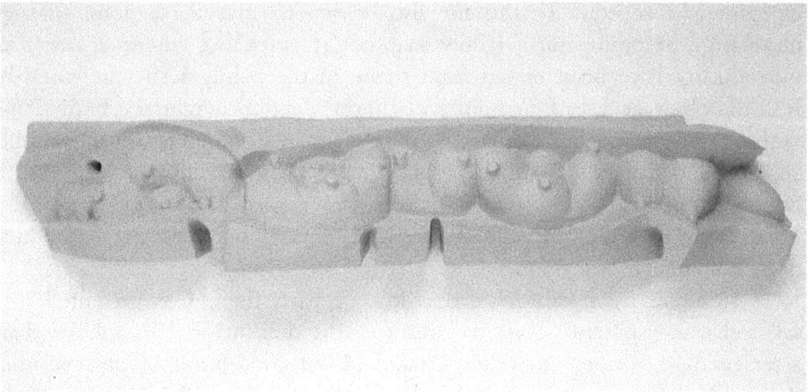

Figure 2.5. Louise Bourgeois (b. 1911). *Mamelles.* 1991. Rubber, fiberglass, and wood; wall relief. 19 x 120 x 19" (48.2 x 304.8 x 48.2 cm). Courtesy Cheim & Read, New York. Photo: Lee Stalsworth. Art © Louise Bourgeois / Licensed by VAGA, New York, NY.

person collapses totally. The doll image, articulated or detailed by the series, remains outside of any particularity. The series precisely constitutes a non-particular sign; the breast/udder does not belong to any particular organism, nor does the wig wrap any particular head, and Monroe's lips are abstracted from any concrete human situation.

How are we to understand the function of the doll in such artistic practices? Foster writes about repetition compulsion in Warhol's art: "Think of all the *Marilyns* alone, of the cropping, coloring, crimping of these images. . . . The Warhol repetitions not only *re*produce traumatic effects; they also *produce* them. Somehow in these repetitions, then, several contradictory things occur at the same time: a warding away of traumatic significance *and* an opening out to it, a defending against traumatic affect *and* a producing of it."[52] Foster refers to a notion of trauma that does not focus on the representation of the traumatic event itself but on trauma as the missed encounter with the real thing. Trauma itself cannot be represented, and the most that art can do is repeat the moment when the encounter with its unbearable real existence is missed. Repetition here does not reproduce an event that happened in reality—it is not a representation of anything at all. Repetition functions to screen out what cannot be represented, and by that very screening it suggests the presence of trauma.

Freud, in his 1932 article about anxiety, claims as he did in his 1926 work that anxiety signifies for the ego a possible danger facing it.[53] In reaction to the danger of separation from the mother, or the danger of separating from a loved object, and so forth, the ego, sensing anxiety, defends itself by repressing the danger. Yet the effect of repression will be a fixation that will channel every new stimulation similar to the one that has been repressed to repetition. That is, although the situation of danger is no longer relevant, the repetitive reaction continues to hold, forcing the subject to act according to the route fixated by the primary repression.

Freud's words support the idea of trauma described earlier. Repetition compulsion and the repetition of trauma do not bring back the traumatic event but rather the impossibility of encountering this event. Anxiety produced in the face of impulses analogous to those experienced at the moment of danger does not have the danger itself as its object but signifies, paradoxically enough, the warding of danger. Danger is real insofar as the presence of anxiety accompanying repetition testifies to it; yet danger is absent, since there is no way of coming across the object of danger in any real way. Repetition is hence a way of presenting through an image a possibility accompanied by anxiety in face of danger, although repetition represents no danger, is opaque to danger. This is the effect of Warhol's *Marilyns*, and this is the effect of doll images in repetitive series. The doll as the effect of repetition is a doll by means of which no encounter can be implemented but the encounter with repetition itself. The series of breasts will not channel our way to fertility or sexuality, since repetition has emptied this mold of all meaning or value; yet repetition produces another value, that of an indeterminate idea, as the true referent of the repetitive form. Through the family of dolls or the dolls engaged in an orgy, nothing can be known, by simulation, about perverse sexuality, sex in groups, incest, or sexual abuse in the family. It is the imposed repetition of these doll images that posits the dolls at the place of missed encounter with all of these themes of great importance yet irrelevant to the place from which the anxiety caused by dolls emerges.

". . . [T]he archetype of taste, which does indeed rest on reason's indeterminate idea of a maximum, but which still can be presented not through concepts but only in an individual exhibition, may . . . be called the ideal of the beautiful. Though we do not have such an ideal in our possession, we do strive to produce it within us."[54] Kant's words emphasize again that the beauty assigned to presentations is the core of the aesthetic, yet this beauty is neither in the image, nor conceptually derivable, nor determinate in any other sense. The beautiful image is hence the fundamental condition of aesthetic judgment, whose function is to suggest an idea of reason that cannot be exhibited, and yet, through an exhibition in form, the image succeeds in constituting an ideal of beauty that is, by necessity, beyond the pleasing image. Beauty is attributable to the Thing, while the image we face is no more than its impossible presentation.

CHAPTER 3

Catharsis, Displeasure, and Anxiety

"But the other liking (the feeling of the sublime) is a pleasure that arises only indirectly: it is produced by the feeling of a momentary inhibition of the vital forces followed immediately by an outpouring of them that is all the stronger . . . the liking for the sublime contains not so much a positive pleasure as rather admiration and respect, and so should be called a negative pleasure."[1]

The case of the sublime introduces into Kant's critique the idea that aesthetic pleasure can arise from negative feelings. We saw in the first chapter that some sort of negative feelings can be claimed to figure as part of the aesthetic experience prior to the emergence of aesthetic pleasure. But what are these negative feelings indicated in the first chapter as being prior to aesthetic judgment in general, and which Kant notices prior to the pleasure from the sublime? Are these the only negative feelings that can arise in aesthetic experience? Are all negative feelings involved in the aesthetic experience of the same kind? Kant has claimed that pleasure is always the same, whether it is a pleasure from the agreeable or pleasure from the beautiful. Pleasure is a feeling, which Kant's entire argument makes clear is a single psychological state phenomenologically identical in all of its occurrences: "The feeling of pleasure itself is always the same."[2]

What differentiates one pleasure from another is the way cognitive powers are "balanced out" to produce this pleasure. With this commensuration of pleasures, Kant wanted to avoid the possibility that the difference between aesthetic pleasure and other pleasures will be taken to be a difference between psychological states. He emphasized the difference between the "conditions of the occurrence of a feeling of pleasure and the conditions for judgment on such a feeling"[3] that is, between the epistemic conditions under which pleasure is produced and the pleasure itself.

Can one thus infer that displeasure also is always the same displeasure? What are the conditions under which displeasure is produced? The first chapter clarified that anxiety, as a type of displeasure that also is pleasing, necessarily arises when the subject's relation to her desire is at stake. The subject's relation to desire is bound to provoke anxiety. This thesis was further investigated in the second chapter, which showed that the object judged as beautiful also entertains with the judging subject relations that may result in anxiety, or with uncanny feelings, and demonstrated that beauty does not exempt us from anxiety but rather constitutes/locates it.

Considerable ground needs to be covered to grasp the notion of anxiety, so as to justify the claim that anxiety has a necessary place in aesthetic experience, that anxiety defines the fundamental position of the subject facing a work of art. To ground this further investigation, two directions of inquiry will be pursued: first, in the present chapter, conditions under which the presence of displeasure is acknowledged in aesthetic contexts and the limits set on displeasure will be examined, and second, in the following chapter, the coordinates that define anxiety in the psychoanalytic context will be investigated. These two directions will lead us to an attempt to define the aesthetic experience as structurally imbued with anxiety, yet an anxiety that can be particularized in different modes. Negative feelings aroused in the context of aesthetic experience with art do not all involve the subject in the same structure.

The idea of negative pleasure bears obvious similarities to the ancient Aristotelian notion of *catharsis*: in both cases negative sentiments (inhibition of vital forces in the case of the sublime, and pity and fear in the case of catharsis) serve a positive purpose and form an integral, structurally necessary part of the process of arriving at aesthetic pleasure. Also, both the negative feelings that constitute the experience of the sublime and the pity and fear that precede catharsis are prior stages in a kind of "narrative of affects" that begins with negative feelings to arrive at a positive, pleasing affect. In both cases, the narrative of affects makes each affective phase causally bound to the occurrence of the other phase.[4]

This apparent closeness between the affect of the sublime and *catharsis* should not however mislead us: the pleasure from tragedy and the pleasure from the sublime refer to the ultimate phase of pleasure in dissimilar terms. The pleasure from the sublime is presented as an achievement, an outcome of the subject's reason striving to gain the upper hand over the limited capacity of the imagination facing a voluminous manifold. In catharsis, the state of affairs is different. Feeling pleasure after being exposed to the tragic events on stage is a surprisingly inappropriate response, even immoral, as some commentators have suggested. We need to study profoundly Aristotle's ethics to justify this tragic gesture. Thus the pleasure that comes after displeasure is *not self-evident in the case of the sublime,* and not every subject is assumed to be capable of attaining the relevant pleasure. The *evident advent of pleasure in the context of tragedy* is conversely viewed as awkward, especially when one attempts to integrate the ethical overtones of Aristotle's *Poetics* with the morally unbecoming satisfaction from other people's suffering (even if only on stage).

So we see that displeasure, whether requiring an effort of reason to be transcended, or requiring a moral leap to be justified, cannot simply be subsumed under pleasure, even when the former is presented as the self-evident sequel to the latter. The overall impression then is that negative feelings do not hold smooth, self-evident relations with the pleasure that ensues, that the displeasure in the experience of the sublime or the tragic needs a certain conceptual leap to be accounted for. It is in relation to this, even if tentative impression, that psychoanalytic anxiety can provide an important rectification. Anxiety in psychoanalysis is not considered a problematic state, a dysfunction that should be cured or surmounted. Lacanian anxiety poses the question not of curing it but of *crossing* it. The idea of "*franchir l'angoisse*" indeed intensely occupies recent commentaries on the notion of anxiety in psychoanalysis.[5] Crossing anxiety, rather than overcoming it, is an idea that can be associated with the displeasure in the aesthetic experience of the sublime or the tragic, as a displeasure that does not function as a temporary affect to be overcome or dissolved but rather analyzed. Something is revealed through these negative feelings that cannot be dispensed with, nor neutralized or cured.

The idea of *crossing* displeasure, that is, that negative feelings play a role that cannot be dissolved through aesthetic pleasure but rather contribute to our understanding of aesthetic experience, can direct us to two crucial coordinates shared by displeasure and anxiety. These coordinates will guide the examination of anxiety, discussed in the pages that follow: (1) Anxiety and displeasure are *affects,* not signs to be symbolized (see note 4). Anxiety and displeasure cannot be dissolved through interpretation or as carrying signification. For instance, the fact that we know that we feel pity for the tragic heroes and fear their fate is made no less potent when we note to ourselves that these characters are fictional and the events befalling them happen on stage. (2) Anxiety and displeasure carry ethical implications. Kant, for instance, points to the inadequacy between our imagination's striving to progress toward infinity and our reason's demand of absolute totality. "This inadequacy itself is the arousal in us of the feeling that we have within us a supersensible power."[6] The pleasure we feel has to do with our mind having a power of surpassing the standard of sense, and it thus requires that a (painful) sense of inadequacy be built into that pleasure as the very condition for reason to enact its freedom. We can thus surmise that displeasure has an ethical dimension, as it is by undergoing displeasure that the subject, both in tragedy and in the sublime, emerges as more excellent and worthy of happy feelings, worthy of pleasure. Freedom in the enactment of reason and happiness in not being inflicted by tragic fate are moral rewards that have displeasure at their roots. The fuller significance of the ethical implications of displeasure still remain to be grounded on the psychoanalytic notion of anxiety, as anxiety signifies the fundamental human ethics of not foregoing one's desire ("the only thing one can be guilty of is giving ground relative to one's desire"7). That is, with anxiety, displeasure is not a condition for reaching a moral state but is in itself an exhibition of human ethics.

Before considering these crucial coordinates of the various modes of displeasure, a word should be said on the affinity, or lack of one, between these modes, that is, between catharsis, displeasure, and anxiety. The first chapter dealt with the necessary place of anxiety in the structure of aesthetic judgment, while the next chapters motivate this necessity by locating anxiety (and other displeasures) in relation to human desire and (for) pleasure. By establishing the necessary, universal, and certain place of anxiety in the human psyche (a task mainly pursued in the next chapter), its association with aesthetic experience will be further grounded. That is, once the necessary place of anxiety is established, it will support the claim that art, in various ways, negotiates for the subject the relation between the realm of pleasure and the reality of the drives, between the desire of the subject and the desire of the Other, and between what is controlled and what cannot be controlled in the domain of the pleasure principle.

Returning to the question of whether all displeasures are of the same kind, it has already been implied that catharsis, displeasure, and anxiety are not synonymous. On the contrary, each of these affects presents a different way of negotiating pleasure with what is beyond the pleasure principle. To establish this nonsynonymy the concept of catharsis will first be examined, while the discussion of psychoanalytic anxiety will take place in the next chapter. The place of displeasure in the experience of the sublime will be addressed through the question, "What is the object of the sublime?," in chapter 5.

CATHARSIS: BETWEEN THE PLEASURE PRINCIPLE AND BEYOND THE PLEASURE PRINCIPLE

Catharsis is presented in the theory of tragedy as a resolution of a displeasurable emotional state. Yet "catharsis" is a word of many applications, and the relations between these applications shed light on the significance of catharsis as a state that reconstitutes harmony. Catharsis as a medical method, catharsis as a therapeutic method, and catharsis as an aesthetic affect are intuitively taken to be close in sense. Catharsis in the context of aesthetic experience is a key word in the theory of tragedy, ever since Aristotle inserted a too-short, almost enigmatic reference to catharsis into the *Poetics.* Attempts to explicate the immanence of catharsis to tragedy have to cope with the way this pleasing affect emerges from pity and fear that are thereby purged. Catharsis also figures in Freud's and Breuer's early work on cathartic treatment, in relation to which Freud later insisted that cathartic therapy is closer to analytic therapy than to hypnotic, suggestion-based therapy. Cathartic therapy, Freud insisted, aims "to bring out something."[8] That is, through a return to the psychical state in which the patient's symptom had appeared for the first time, a therapeutic effectiveness is achieved "as due to the discharge of what had previously been, as it were, 'strangulated' affect attaching to the suppressed mental acts ('abreaction')."[9] Catharsis, in various contexts and in its most straightforward sense, has to do with a relief, a relaxation of negative feelings. The idea of abreaction, of discharge, as used by Freud and Breuer, relates to the kind of relief the purgation of emotions of pity and fear brings about. This notion of catharsis in Freud, Lacan would claim later, is indicative of the optimistic view that the *primal scene* can be reproduced. That is, the view that catharsis is not the effect of repeating symbolically the impact of strangulating suppressed experiences but is an effect of actually reviving these experiences. Lacan indeed attempts to rectify this idea of catharsis as what results from reproducing a lost object in order to motivate effects of pleasure. He suggests that the effects of catharsis should be considered of the order of the symbolic, that is, as effects that derive from the presence of the signifier.

The following analysis of catharsis traces its vicissitudes in Lacan's seminar on ethics. The aim of this analysis is to highlight the ambivalent face of catharsis in relation to the pleasure principle, an ambivalence that is articulated rather than solved by Lacan. For Lacan, catharsis is involved in ethics precisely because it is produced at the limit of the pleasure principle, engaging the subject in what appears to be a contradictory state of pleasure founded on displeasure. Had catharsis been strictly defined as either pleasure *or* displeasure, it would have belonged exclusively to the domain of the good and in that would be of no interest to questions of ethics. The good, according to Lacan, is a *moral* issue within the domain of the pleasure principle rather than an *ethical* position beyond the domain of the pleasure principle. In highlighting the insoluble, ambivalent nature of catharsis, Lacan presents an approach different from the one suggested by philosophical commentaries. These commentaries, discussed later in this chapter, aim to reconcile the double face of catharsis by incorporating its apparently immoral side within the educational-moral dimension. That is, philosophical commentaries aim to reveal the justified place of catharsis as pleasure, indicating its moral nature. Psychoanalysis, however, unfolds the particular position of cathartic states as located in between the pleasure principle and what is beyond the pleasure principle, a position that cannot be solved and yet underlines the ambivalence catharsis signals in the subject.

To begin to follow Lacan's critique of cathartic treatment, we should first look at his overall conception of pleasure in his seminar on the ethics of psychoanalysis. There he refers at length to catharsis and its significance to the tragic structure. This seminar can be read as a revision of Lacan's earlier position regarding the Freudian distinction between the pleasure principle and what is beyond the pleasure principle. This opposition in Freud leans on the idea of homeostasis, as what regulates the pleasure principle (the organism demands minimal excitation to be satisfied, while excitation causes displeasure). Beyond the pleasure principle is the realm of repetition where the encumbering presence of a displeasing signifier (image, event, sign) points to what is beyond the pleasure principle, in the domain of the symbolic, or at its limit. So we have repetition on the side of beyond the pleasure principle and homeostasis on the side of the pleasure principle. In his teachings during the 1959–1960 period, Lacan modifies this distinction between the pleasure principle and beyond the pleasure principle, a change crucial to our present concerns. Following this renewed distinction, the pleasure principle is located on the side of the symbolic, and so is repetition. Beyond the pleasure principle is now beyond the signifier and is connected to the notion of *das Ding.* The difference lies in a certain withdrawal from Freud, as now Lacan maintains that the signifier is not foreign to pleasure; the repetition of the signifier and the satisfaction of pleasure are the same. It is only beyond the pleasure principle that the limit of the signifier emerges: "The Thing is that which in the real suffers from this fundamental, initial relation, which commits man to the ways of the signifier by reason of the fact that he is subjected to what Freud calls the pleasure principle, and which . . . is nothing else than the dominance of the signifier."[10]

How is catharsis to be located in relation to the signifier and to the beyond of the pleasure principle? I claim that catharsis is located in the domain of pleasure, even if an extreme one, and is thus to be distinguished from anxiety that relates to what is beyond the pleasure principle. To reveal the motivation for this distinction, we can trace, following Lacan, the way the idea of catharsis is linked to the classical thought of antiquity.

In the *Poetics*, the nature of catharsis is phrased in a manner that has yielded floods of commentaries: "Tragedy then is an imitation of an action . . . in the form of action, not of narrative; through pity and fear effecting the proper purgation of these emotions."[11] The idea of purifying rituals that appease certain uncontrolled emotions appears also in another text by Aristotle—*Politics*, a source that may somewhat illuminate what appears as a deficient reference to catharsis in the *Poetics.* There, in Book VIII of *Politics,* catharsis is related to music, which unlike other modes (such as vision and touch) has the natural power of forming the character, of affecting directly one's moral ideas. Yet music can carry a moral impact on everybody, not because it imitates moral issues but through the pleasing way in which it affects people. Music affects people and inspires enthusiasm, "and enthusiasm is an emotion of the ethical part of the soul."[12] While the affect of music on people also can be drawn to a recreational direction with no other end, Aristotle insists that the pleasing effect of music does not contradict its suitability for a program of education. Music can even please in the extreme, and Aristotle moves in Section 7 of Book VIII to describe the effect of music in the following manner:

"Some persons fall into a religious frenzy, whom we see as a result of the sacred melodies—when they have used the melodies that excite the soul to mystic frenzy—restored as though they had found healing and purgation. Those who are influenced by pity or fear, and every emotional nature, must have a like experience, and others insofar as each is susceptible to such emotions, and all are in a manner purged and their souls lightened and delighted. The purgative melodies likewise give an innocent pleasure to mankind."[13] The idea here is that besides the educational function of music, it also has something to do with a kind of enjoyment felt by those people who are prone to be influenced by pity and fear "for feelings such as pity and fear, or, again, enthusiasm, exist very strongly in some souls." Music thus can be experienced as a state of exaltation, as a Dionysian frenzy. Yet music also has its pleasing effect, whether of the enjoying, educational, or purgatory type, on different kinds of people. Catharsis here refers to the particular case in which the pleasing effect of music works in the direction of relief and relaxation.

Lacan addresses this discussion in Aristotle as what can be taken to complement the extremely meager clarification in the *Poetics* of the nature of purgation (catharsis) that tragedy brings on. Lacan, in the context of his interest in the law, and the enjoyment the subject draws from being proximate to the law, points to the fact that catharsis is attributed by Aristotle to a function beyond the realm that writers and literary theoreticians usually talk about. Aristotle's description of the effect of music stresses the side of music that has nothing to do with the ethics of education but is related to excitement of a kind that makes its participation in education problematic: "Once they have experienced the state of exaltation, the Dionysian frenzy stimulated by such music, they become calm. That's what catharsis means as it is evoked in Book VIII of the *Politics*." Catharsis effectuated by music belongs to a realm in which Lacan would like to locate the foundations of ethics, the realm of *jouissance*. Not everyone enters states of catharsis. Those prey to other passions, such as pity and fear, enjoy a calming effect of catharsis through music, the same music we can assume has a role in tragedy. And this effect of music comes about through pleasure.

Three points can be extricated from Lacan's highlighting the Dionysian side of catharsis: (1) For Aristotle, catharsis, even if not directly educational, educates by pleasure; (2) The moral function of music is not necessary for its cathartic effect to be working, as this effect is straightforwardly pleasurable; (3) This pleasurable effect of catharsis is unequivocally explained by the pleasure principle, which locates on one side pleasure (enthusiasm, purgation, relaxation, etc.) and on the other side displeasure (pity, fear, and such like emotions), with the former bringing relief to the latter.

So Aristotle locates catharsis within the domain of the pleasure principle, even if he drifts into descriptions of Dionysian frenzy, of enjoyment beyond the restrictive rule of the pleasure principle, it is yet controlled by that rule. Ecstatic enjoyment is what here reveals, according to Lacan's standpoint, the blind spot of philosophical ethics: its attempt to cover up the enjoyment involved in pursuing an ethical position. Here and elsewhere, moral philosophy, from Aristotle through Kant, suppresses the enjoying dimension there is for the subject who follows the ever-growing demands of the superego, or what Kant called the "pathological" dimension that clearly plays a role in human ethics. Despite this persistent suppression of the pathological, insists Lacan, throughout his seminar on ethics, the place of this enjoyment is marked. This enjoyment is identified by Lacan with the pleasure "to which one returns after a crisis that occurs in another dimension . . . for we all know to what extremes a certain kind of ecstatic music may lead."[14] At the core of the ethical agenda lies *jouissance*,[15] which is beyond the pleasure principle, whereas it is to the pleasure principle to which moral philosophy is officially committed (that is, to the relation between moral behavior and the pleasure or displeasure it may imply for the subject).

CATHARSIS "IS PREVIOUS TO DESIRE'S FORMIDABLE CENTER THAT SUCKS US IN"

Lacan goes even further in articulating the meaning of catharsis. He argues that Aristotle's catharsis is prior to desire, that what Aristotle suggests here is a "topology of pleasure as the law of that which functions previous to that apparatus where desire's formidable center sucks us in."[16] Once desire enters the picture, which is the case we would have to consider in order to decipher anxiety, the pleasure principle is problematized. Desire hinders pleasure, places it under restrictions, a hindrance that, as Aristotle's music reveals, is alien to catharsis. Before desire sucks us in, the pleasure connected to the calming of pity and fear, and granted by music, can hence be a pleasure of an extreme, almost transgressive kind and yet subsumed under the agenda of edifying the young. The pleasure that is possible when we desire is, however, to be grasped in a different register. Here, in the context of Lacan's earlier teaching, desire can be described as a gravitational power, and as such, it cannot produce a direct satisfaction. Desire as "the metonymy of our being" is not simply located in the modulation of the signifying chain but in "that which flows beneath it as well; that is . . . that which is signified in an act passes from one signifier of the chain to another beneath all the significations."[17]

Desire hence cannot satisfy in simple identifications. The object of satisfaction in desire is not something with which we can identify. The object of desire, unlike the object of catharsis, is indeterminate. In catharsis, however, the satisfaction attained has an identificatory aspect, as is clearly revealed in the way pity and fear are perceived as arising from the spectator's identification with the suffering characters on stage. Desire, unlike catharsis, is caught in the defiles of the signifier, and tragedy reminds us of the distance between them: "We will grasp what tragedy serves: to remind us, subject of science dedicated to the service of goods, what crossing of the limit our experience of our desire presumes."[18]

Lacan situates the affect of catharsis as prior to the law of desire in the sense that the law of desire, with the problematic satisfaction it suggests, is not yet relevant. Catharsis is straightforward pleasure before we know anything about the beyond of the pleasure principle.

Lacan's words here also point to the direction for deciphering the problem of anxiety. The appeasing effect of music in tragedy, where music is wholly given to the law of balancing out emotions, maintains the ecstatic aspect of catharsis as a reminder. Catharsis is attributed a therapeutic function, just as Freud and Breuer thought; catharsis is the solution pleasure provides to stop negative feelings. Yet catharsis stops not just negative feelings but primarily the frenzy of a prior moment, of the Dionysian overwhelming moment. Hence, catharsis, in its very structure, works as an imaginary mechanism that solves the displeasure (in pity and fear and such similar emotions) by either harnessing ecstatic pleasure to this cause or by putting a limit on transgressive pleasure. As such, catharsis works as a reminder both of ecstatic enjoyment and of the desire that will impose itself on the subject through the symbolic order of signifiers.

This way of locating catharsis can be further clarified if we consider the fact that Lacan presents in this seminar an exceptional approach to tragedy. As demonstrated in the previous chapter that dealt with beauty, for Lacan tragedy touches us because it is situated at the limit of the symbolic. Tragedy is an art that dramatizes the events befalling characters who invite no identification and are blatantly resistant to any attempt on the spectator's part to comprehend their actions: "Over and beyond the dialogue, over and beyond the question of family and country, over and beyond the moralizing arguments, it is Antigone herself who fascinates us. . . . She has a quality that both attracts us and startles us, in the sense of intimidates us."[19] This idea of the splendor of beautiful figures as being resistant to signification further clarifies, in the present context, the function of catharsis. Catharsis is a way of solving the negative feelings elicited by a false identification with the tragic hero, false because the suffering of the hero cannot be deciphered in terms of the pleasure principle, nor made sense of. Oedipus suffers for reasons that seem unjust to the spectator; Antigone suffers because driven by a conviction that remains unknown to the spectator. Catharsis works by providing the tool of pleasure for relieving pity and fear while maintaining the insoluble aspect of the ecstasy or startled intimidation as a constant reminder of there being something more, something that cannot be harnessed to the sweeping cathartic affect. The direction in which this "something more" should be looked for is provided by the psychoanalytic approach to negative feelings. As Aristotle's phrasing suggests, catharsis works *on and through* pity and fear,[20] which suggests that pity and fear are not just modes of suffering for the subject but feelings that already contain the potential of enjoyment. Pity and fear, claims Lacan, are paradoxically not felt by the tragic figure herself. Antigone fears nothing and pities no one; it is the spectator who feels pity and fear when facing this tragic yet assertive Other who acts decisively, appearing to lack nothing. The fact that the tragic figure is located beyond the human pleasing and displeasing feelings places these displeasing feelings so that they constantly function psychically as reminders of the *jouissance* of the Other, of the possibility of absolute enjoyment. Catharsis thus buffers and purges negative feelings, while maintaining in view the possibility of unlimited *jouissance*.

The notion of negative feelings that store a possibility of enjoyment also is suggested by Juan-David Nasio in his *Book of Love and Pain*. Nasio shows the great affinity between fear, pain, and *jouissance,* claiming that the mere idea of excessive *jouissance* causes great fear, and that pain is another form of suffering that is "the most evocative representative of an inaccessible *jouissance*/suffering."[21] Modes of suffering are not simple modes of displeasure but rather represent the subject's reaction to uninhibited *jouissance*. This is an idea that also underlies the following quote from Freud: "A certain amount of protection against suffering is secured, in that non-satisfaction is not so painfully felt in the case of instincts kept in dependence as in the case of uninhibited ones,"[22] that is, we suffer less when satisfaction is under check than when satisfaction appears uninhibited. This notion of suffering and its structuring in relation to uninhibited pleasure should be kept in mind when the function of catharsis in tragedy is considered.

What is beyond the pleasure principle in tragedy, claims Lacan, is what has such a radical effect on us, because it "reveals to us the line of sight that defines desire."[23] This line settles on an image, the splendid image of Antigone, which "forces you to close your eyes at the very moment you look at it." Lacan would later point out, "It is in connection with this power of attraction that we should look for the true sense, the true mystery, the true significance of tragedy—in connection with the excitement involved, in connection with the emotions and, in particular, with the singular emotions that are fear and pity, since it is through their intervention . . . that we are purged, purified of everything of that order. And that order . . . is properly speaking the order of the imaginary. And we are purged of it through the intervention of one image among others."[24]

This quote presents two points. First, catharsis as the *purgation of pity and fear is presented as a solution to the excitement involved in the encounter with the image of the tragic figure*. Second, the tragic figure is located beyond human emotions and transcends whatever human subjects, fearing, pitying, and purged, can bear or decipher. Hence, the tragic figure constitutes an image *beyond imaginary or symbolic codification*. This one central image is what elicits catharsis in order to push aside the emotional excitation, the frenzy described by Aristotle.

It is interesting to note that the Lacanian reading of Aristotelian catharsis, which for the reasons elaborated on earlier stresses the split between the appeasing effect of catharsis on negative feelings and the ecstasy that plays a role in accounting for the pleasure concerned, diverges from the position of other commentators. These latter tend to merge the two aspects of catharsis and treat catharsis as a simple pleasure, albeit a pleasure predicated in specific ways. The theme shared by the commentaries referred to later is that of *transformation*: in the context of art, whatever is painful can be transformed into pleasure, and catharsis should be understood in such terms. That is, the three commentaries presented later attempt to reconcile the negative feelings with what appears like a positive, pleasing effect of purgation, an attempt that leans on the distinction between negative suffering and positive pleasure. Stephen Halliwell, for instance, claims that the feeling arising in tragic experience is fused with aspects of understanding (or thought), a fusion that provides an account *en bloc* of aesthetic tragic experience. As the pleasure appropriate to tragedy has to do with tragedy's use of a model of mimesis (which, according to Halliwell, keeps an intricate balance between the universal and the particular/historical), pity and fear, although painful emotions, are transformed into aesthetic pleasure because of their profound dependence on tragic mimesis as a realization of tragic thought.[25]

Pity and fear and the ethical alleviation of these emotions also are appropriate to tragedy, according to Martha Nussbaum, who locates Aristotle's discussion of catharsis in his overall ethical disagreement with Plato. While for Plato "there is no use at all for pity," as "it is built on false beliefs and has bad effects,"[26] Aristotle allows good persons to be dislodged from happiness and does not regard this gap between moral actions and their consequences as false: "The reversals characteristic of tragedy can be ethically illuminating." Pity and fear for Aristotle are not ethically controversial but rather the foundations that dictate a whole range of choices: the choice of hero, type of story, causal structure, and so on. In view of the need to achieve the pleasure apt for tragedy, pity and fear are subject to the relevant mode of representation, thus contributing to the overall ethical structure of tragedy. Nussbaum summarizes her position by downplaying the ethical irregularity of catharsis, harnessing it to the same production of pleasure appropriate to tragedy and crucial for our understanding of human experience. For Aristotle, pity and fear are "genuine sources of understanding, showing the spectator possibilities that are there for good people."[27] Within this framework, catharsis is simply the process of clearing up an impediment, a clearing up that is experienced through the emotional upheaval of pity and fear that no human being, as noble as he or she may be, can fail to benefit from: "Is there anyone so good as not to need such reminders, such an emotional house-cleaning? I [Nussbaum] do not think so, and I do not think that Aristotle thought so."[28]

For Nussbaum the incompatibility between catharsis and negative feelings raised by tragedy as a result of structural demand is played down by drawing a whole ethical picture of pity, fear, and their clearing up. These are all structurally subsumed under the tragic scene of noble people to whom events that are deliberately presented as undeserved befall. That is, pity and fear experienced vis-à-vis persons undeserving of the misfortune that had befallen them, have a cleansing effect as genuine sources of understanding. Catharsis is simply the name of the effect these negative feelings bear for the spectator, thus forming a constitutive part of the edifying ethics of tragedy.

Unlike Nussbaum, Jonathan Lear subsumes catharsis under the aesthetic, rather than the ethical, purposes of the tragic drama.[29] Lear reads pity and fear in the larger context of Aristotle's conception of feelings, thereby arriving at the conclusion that Aristotle could not have meant that these emotions are simply purged. For Aristotle, emotions establish one's orientation to the world, and so "an emotion is too complex and world-directed an item for the purgation model to be of significant value."[30] It is thus self-evident that in tragedy pain cannot be transformed into pleasure. "Pity and fear are not abolished by the tragedy; it is just that in addition to the pity and fear . . . one is also capable of experiencing a certain pleasure."[31] This pleasure, according to Lear, has to do with the mimetic distance set between the spectator and the tragic events. Catharsis is neither educational nor edifying, and definitely it is not cognitive; our response to tragedy "is not what we would or should feel in response to real life counterparts. Tragic pleasure depends crucially on the belief that one is emotionally responding to a *mimesis* of tragic events. Without this belief, tragic pleasure is impossible."[32]

Lear does not conceive of mimesis as a distance in the usual sense; mimesis does not dull the emotional burden caused by witnessing the suffering that befalls distinguished men. He refers to mimesis as a *modal operator* whose function is two-faced. First, the pity and fear felt in view of the events of the drama are not dimmed in comparison to the emotions that strike the spectator in real life. Nevertheless, it also is misleading, claims Lear, "to say that tragedy restores the appropriate feelings to our already existing beliefs,"[33] that is, that tragedy revives the feelings that should have been attached to our unavoidable belief that tragic events *could* possibly befall us, feelings that we tend to suppress. The modal operator of mimesis maintains pity and fear in its usual sense, otherwise people would not go to the theater to watch other people's predicament. Rather, the role of tragic plot is to awaken us to this possibility, which we tend to suppress in real life, although it raises in us the very same negative emotions we attach to this possibility in real life.

Yet, the modal operator also functions as a safety bound, as "it is crucial to the pleasure we derive from tragedy that we never lose sight of the fact that we are an audience, enjoying a work of art."[34] Why does the mimetic operator entail pleasure? How should we understand the pleasing effect of this realization? Suffice it to locate our relief in the fact that the world in which good men fall does not deteriorate into chaos. Tragedy, according to Lear, does not occur in a world that in itself is ultimately chaotic and meaningless. A comforting assurance of this kind enables the mimetic safety bound to inspire pleasure while maintaining negative emotions in its usual intensity. We can note at this juncture that such an interpretation of Aristotle's intentions with catharsis is common. The pleasure in tragedy is taken to be an aesthetic operation by many—a formal pleasure managed by a form of representation.[35]

The philosophical commentators attempt to reconcile the cathartic pleasure with its negative source by approaching catharsis as an ethical, aesthetic, or cognitive requirement necessitated by the very presence of negative feelings. Catharsis in a way branches from the ethical or aesthetic platform that pity and fear constitute in tragedy. I claim that catharsis should indeed be understood, along the Aristotelian lines, as a mode of relieving anxiety, a mode of alleviating pressure and various negative feelings that, within the domain of the pleasure principle, create too much tension. Unlike anxiety, which occurs beyond the pleasure principle, tragedy is a dramatization in the moral dimension; that is, it symbolizes dramatic action within the domain of the good and the maxims of the Law. Thus the spectator's response to pleasure requires an alibi for this allegedly immoral act: "From the origin of moral philosophy, from the moment when the term ethics acquired the meaning of man's reflection on his condition and calculation of the proper paths to follow, all meditation on man's good has taken place as a function of the index of pleasure."[36] But this is no contradiction, as the moral dramatic event is complemented by the spectator in that the catharsis reveals what the moral act always camouflages, that is, the other side of morality that has to do with excess, with an overwhelming enjoyment that cannot be controlled. The alleged immorality of catharsis should be renounced not by subsuming in rational terms the cathartic effects under an overall significant ethical or aesthetic picture but by pointing out that catharsis is precisely the other side of the moral answer that tragedy provides. The catharsis felt by the spectator is the suitable complement where the concealed side of moral action is revealed. In tragedy, the overwhelming power of *jouissance*, of what is beyond the pleasure principle, is under control.

Lear's notion of mimesis as modal operator is reminiscent of Kant's mode of dealing with the possibility of feeling the dynamic sublime of nature when the powers embodied by nature on such occasions also could have carried an intimidating, fearful effect: "The sight of them [threatening rocks, thunderclouds piling up in the sky and moving about accompanied by lightning and thunderclaps, volcanoes with all their destructive power, hurricanes with all the devastation they leave behind, the boundless ocean heaved up, the high waterfall of a mighty river] becomes all the more attractive the more fearful it is, *provided we are in a safe place*."[37] The fact that the spectator must find himself or herself safe in order to "feel this exciting liking" was taken into consideration by the great painter of the sublime, Caspar David Friedrich, who depicts the wanderer above the storming sea, sheltered by height and distance from the intimidating scene (see Figure 3.1).

"A distance from what?" one may ask, and the answer to this query will be addressed in the chapter on the sublime. At the present stage, we can note, however, that the displeasure to which Kant refers is displeasure from the fact that while at a safe distance "we found our own limitation when we considered the immensity of nature and the inadequacy of our ability to adopt a standard proportionate to estimating aesthetically the magnitude of nature's *domain*."[38] That is, displeasure, when facing the sublime, is not the displeasure of threat or danger but rather the suffering, when safely secured, from the inability to sensibly grasp the magnitude of nature. It is the impossibility to contain what the subject cannot grasp sensibly, the impossibility to control the magnitude of the Other of nature that brings about displeasure; it is not the displeasure in the sense of suffering from physical or actual danger that is at stake.

At this point we can indicate the emergence of two different senses of displeasure: the displeasure in negative feelings (pity and fear before tragic events, or fear before the threat from a powerful nature); the displeasure to which art provides a modal operator as a solution, the safety zone of mimetic distance. This is the type of displeasure that catharsis or the distance from the menacing scene alleviates. Yet there is also the displeasure in the inability to comprehend the object, the displeasure before an object that cannot be subjected to imaginative or symbolic powers. Kant, in other words, refers to displeasure in a different sense than the moral one: for him, displeasure, the same as the satisfaction that will follow in the experience of the sublime, can commence only once the threat of actual menace is set aside. We can again refer in this context to Nasio's idea of pain: "Pain, considered as a traumatic excitation,

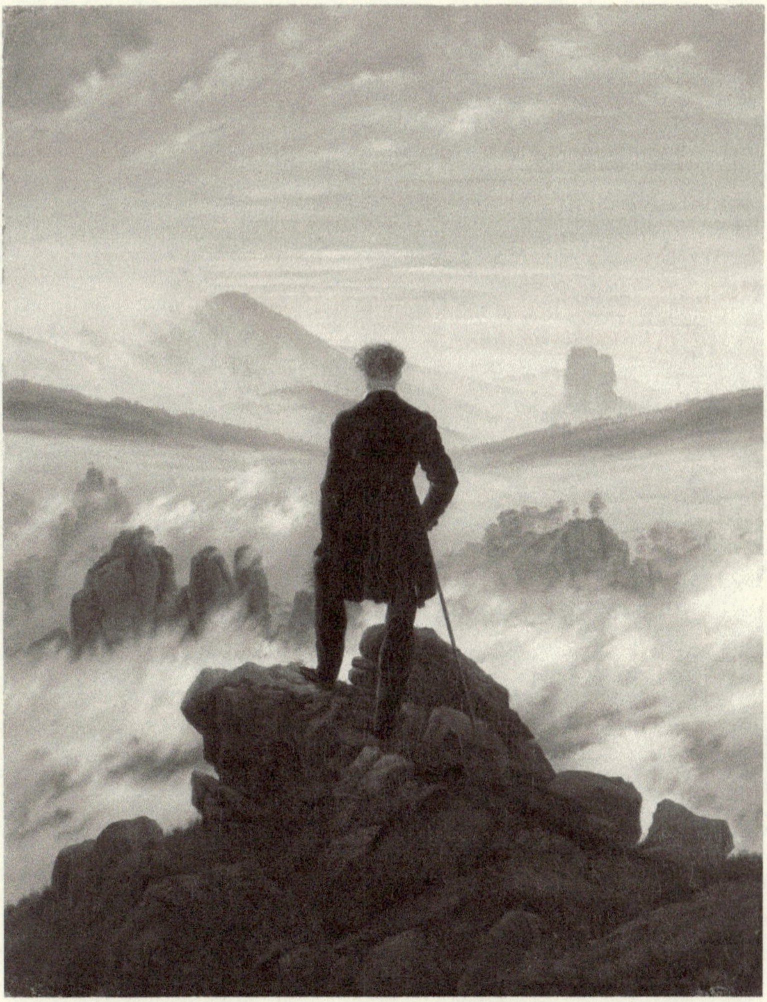

Figure 3.1. Caspar David Friedrich (1774–1840). *Wanderer Above the Sea of Fog (Der Wanderer über dem Nebelmeer).* Ca. 1817. Oil on canvas. © bpk, Berlin.

does not belong to the criteria of pleasure and unpleasure. Certainly, it is an unpleasant affect, but it has a very different quality than unpleasure. We recall that the occurrence of pain means that the pleasure/unpleasure principle that regulates the functioning of our psyche has been abolished. . . . Whenever there is pain, we are beyond the pleasure principle."[39] It is this kind of displeasure that brings us closer to the notion of anxiety.

CHAPTER 4

Toward Two Principles of Aesthetic Functioning

ANXIETY: THE ACCESS ROAD TO THE REAL

If catharsis is a *solution*, then anxiety is a *cause*. Saying that anxiety is a "cause" means that, unlike catharsis, its universality cannot be detached from the particularity of the subject.[1] In this chapter, the fundamental picture of anxiety as a cause will be unfolded through Freud's article "Inhibition, Symptom, and Anxiety" and through Lacan's seminar "Anxiety." It should be noted that both Freud and Lacan modified their approach throughout their writings, and that each stage in their thinking reveals another dimension of anxiety. Accordingly, anxiety should be unraveled differently than by conceptualizing it as part of a hermetic theory. Anxiety is viewed as a mode of exploring the subject's position in relation to the Other and to desire. The following statements will direct this task of unraveling anxiety:

1. Anxiety is a signal of a possibility, and not a possibility actualized.
2. Anxiety is an affect and not a signifier.
3. Anxiety has a certainty rather than an authenticity or a truth.
4. Anxiety in the subject is related to the cause of desire.

These aspects are derived from the diverse and versatile approaches of psychoanalysts to anxiety, and to Lacan's 1962–1963 seminar dedicated to it. They reveal those dimensions of anxiety that will contribute to the present attempt to constitute anxiety as fundamental to the very structure and nature of aesthetic experience.

Following the presentation of anxiety in the four subsections that follow, I further consider its relation to the aesthetic experience by analyzing anxiety's place both within neurotic and psychotic modes of creation. I show that the various parameters in terms of which anxiety is approached reveal two modes of locating anxiety within aesthetic experience. That is, anxiety in the aesthetic domain will be articulated first in terms of the various parameters through which psychoanalytic thought has established the place of anxiety in psychic reality, and, second, through the idea that anxiety in aesthetic experience can be located either in the neurotic or psychotic registers. It will be shown that these two registers of anxiety formulated as two modes of creation (the neurotic and the psychotic)[2] correspond to two facets of Lacan's discussion of anxiety in his 1962–1963 seminar: anxiety can emerge around a *fundamental lack* when it signals a danger of the cause of desire not being marked, and anxiety can emerge around *an object of excess* when the cause of desire, the locus of *jouissance,* is suggested by some element in the work of art.

Anxiety is a Signal of a Possible Danger, not a Possibility Actualized

Freud refers to anxiety as a signal of a possibility of danger: "Anxiety arose originally as a reaction to a state of *danger* and it is reproduced whenever a state of that kind recurs."[3] This is the main change in Freud's conception of anxiety, as he had first thought of anxiety as being caused by insufficiently discharged sexual libido (which is the cause of anxiety neurosis), or by the return of suppressed sensations (which appear through repetition compulsions). After 1925, Freud associates anxiety with a traumatic situation of separation, and as of this stage he believes that anxiety is modeled on the event of birth, which is the prototypic experience in which the sensation of anxiety is bound to innervations due to the traumatic separation from the mother. Later situations of danger reproduce the prototypic one and are those of loss of the object of love, castration, and so forth.

Yet anxiety states throughout a subject's life, Freud notices, do not reproduce the situation of danger at birth in economic terms (that is, in terms of increase of excitation and discharge at extreme levels) but maintain a different relation to the constitutive model of birth. When the infant finds by experience that anxiety from nonsatisfaction can be put to an end (by a substitutive object of satisfaction), the content of the danger the infant fears is displaced from the economic situation (the danger that stimulation will rise to an unpleasurable height without possibility of discharge) and on to the condition that caused that situation, that is, to the *possibility* of a loss of object. At this point, as soon as the *possibility of danger* arises, the infant gives a signal of anxiety before the dreaded economic situation has even set in.[4]

In locating anxiety in what caused the situation of danger, Freud distinguishes the moment of anxiety as a signal from the phenomenon or state of anxiety. According to François Leguil, Freud's notion of anxiety as a signal implies that anxiety is a moment actually reduced to a pure and simple *punctuality of commencement*. Anxiety, to be thought of, has to be reduced, circumscribed, and restrained.[5] This distinction between anxiety as signal and the situation of anxiety also is manifested in Freud's discussion of the relations between anxiety and the symptom, where anxiety is thought of as the *cause of the symptom*, while the symptom itself is formed in order to relieve anxiety. This is the difference between anxiety as a cause, and anxiety as symptomatology. "Symptoms are created in order to remove the ego from a situation of danger. If the symptoms are prevented from being formed, the danger does in fact materialize."[6] For instance, if we prevent an obsessional neurotic from washing his hands after having touched something, then he will have an anxiety attack. The anxiety state is a symptom that relieves anxiety as a signal of danger.

Leguil draws further implications from the fact that for Freud the function of anxiety is that of "preluding the formation of the symptom." As the essence of anxiety is its being a formal function, a pure sketch, the expression of this essence in the commencement of the formation of symptom (which is the clinical realization of that essence) may appear *antithetical* to the actual manifestation of anxiety. We can add to Leguil's assessment by pointing out that it is immanent to anxiety that it always will lead to the formation of a symptom that is apparently inappropriate or disproportionate to the anxiety effectuated. Indeed, Freud himself refers to this possibility when he notes that an anxiety is neurotic when in face of a real danger: "The anxiety in regard to it is over-great, greater than seems proper to us."[7]

This inopportune, inappropriate essence of anxiety also permeates the animal kingdom, as can be illustrated in the flight of animals when sensing the trembling of the earth, or the escape of mice from the sinking sea vessel. For Freud, the anticipatory flight from a menacing danger "appeared to him to represent a sure response to a modification of the surrounding, a modification that profiles another place, announcing the opening of an elsewhere there, where a familiar homogenous surrounding reigns."[8] Something happens in the animal's *Umwelt* that suggests an immanent change, although the change itself has not set in. The anxiety state and the over-great response corresponding to it regain their balance when the cause of anxiety is taken into account beyond the minor change or feared change in the surrounding.

This idea is clearly related to Freud's uncanny (discussed in chapter 2): anxiety is not a response but, rather, it brings about a change in otherwise perfectly uninterrupted circumstances. It is anxiety that turns a set of neutral numbers recurring accidentally into a premonition or bad omen. Likewise, in the context of a familiar, well-known surrounding, the subject acts anxiously (that is, with an uncanny sensation), thus turning his or her world into a world of menace. Anxiety hence operates as a cause, as what creates an opening of an elsewhere, as what brings about the need to find relief from anxiety. An antithetical structure is hence immanent.

Furthermore, Leguil points to another crucial point regarding anxiety: in its function as a signal, it is hardly registered. Miller also elaborates on this point in his introduction to Lacan's seminar and likens anxiety to the second movement in the phantasm of "A Child Is Being Beaten," as analyzed by Freud.[9] There, according to Freud, the core of the phantasm, that is, the repressed part of the situation in which "my father is beating me" (a movement that should have replaced the rather impersonal version of the first movement, "A Child Is Being Beaten," that consciously appears), is precisely the movement that cannot be remembered nor made present as a situation to which the subject of the phantasm can relate as involving him or her. In clinical experience, this missing movement in the phantasm is similar to the presence of anxiety as a cause in a given situation. That is, anxiety itself connotes the move from reality to the real, from the presence of external danger to the danger as psychically registered, causing the hidden face of the situation to appear.

We can say that anxiety as a cause is neither the somatic signs that ensue nor the transformation of a given situation into a state of danger but, rather, is the formal operator responsible for this change itself. Anxiety is a way of crossing reality into the domain of the Real, which is why it is correlated to what Miller calls a "faintness of the signifier." Anxiety, in other words, is already beyond (or, rather, prior to) the limits of the signifier, as it cannot actually be articulated but only inferred.

Again, we can find support for this faintness of the signifier in Freud who, according to the Lacanian reading of his text, modifies the status of the initial choice of *birth* as a primordial episode that creates a prototypical model for anxiety into a formal function. Since the episode of birth has no psychic content in itself (i.e., one cannot say what in the vast disturbance in the economy of the fetus' narcissistic libido deserves the sign of danger situation),[10] it is clear rather that the episode of birth serves Freud as a kind of myth, as a formal scheme. *Birth is a formally localized event that can constitute the human subject as universally anxious*, as a subject in whom a moment of real danger (and not a danger in reality) that produces anxiety is registered.

But how is anxiety to be identified, if it is only faintly registered? How do we recognize the presence of anxiety in the prototypical episode or its subsequent incurrence in analogous situations? This is hard to tell, apart from a series of somatic signs of discomfort associated with an anxious disposition or state. In this sense the specific attribution of model status to the episode of birth does not amount to much. Even in the reality of birth, anxiety is not registered as an interpretable signifier. It is in the structure of the episode itself, in the way in which birth already functions as the signal of crossing the reality of the opening event of our life into the real of its psychic registration, that anxiety can be localized. So anxiety cannot be identified with a state of anxiety nor reduced to a set of formal features shared with the prototypical moment of birth.

The originality of Freud was to mark anxiety as a cause, a cause for the subject who is its answer; the signal of anxiety in the subject is hence to be distinguished from the status of anxiety as a cause. A soft wind from the sea and a cyclone are both winds; their consequences are yet not identical.[11] With these two winds one can nevertheless distinguish between the cause and the signal. An experienced sailor can observe with fright a small cloud in the sky that looks banal to the passenger, whereas for him it announces the approach of a hurricane. Changing the direction of sailing or fleeing is a measure antithetical to the trifle that functions as a signal but corresponds well to the cause. Likewise, a subject can transform a minor thing into a signal of agony. That is, she turns a difference in intensity into the real function to which she responds as a subject taking measures by treating the event as a possibility of a possibility, a possibility of a possibility of an unbearable displeasure. While the signal is the registration of anxiety, it reveals nothing regarding the anxiety itself, an anxiety that as a cause will only show its face through the excessive nature of the anxious situation that ensues.

So anxiety is a signal, functioning as an opening mark and antithetical to its manifestation; anxiety also is a cause whose presence in the psychic real signals that anxiety crosses reality and is beyond the symbolic order of the signifier.

The notion of anxiety as a signal stems, as shown in this section, from Freud, who associates anxiety with a danger of separation. By an illustration or, rather, a suggestion, as to how these theoretical-clinical conclusions psychoanalytically drawn regarding anxiety can be related to one's experience with art, I refer to the excessively decorated artwork created (1910) by Klimt under the title *The Park* (Figure 4.1).

This illustration shows to what extent anxiety is decisively present in one's encounter with art and can be qualified as a cause, although it cannot be said to register in any specific signifier. In the face of this green thicket, the observer's anxiety is raised, thereby creating an "elsewhere" in the apparently innocent depiction of a park. Anxiety is the signal raised before a landscape drawing, thereby producing an excessive, inappropriate affect. Anxiety, however, is not in the drawing and cannot be located in any signifier. What is the cause of anxiety? Is it in the lighter opening in between the trees? Is it in the almost surreal extension of the thicket that may be perceived as hiding something? What is it that assigns the thicket its menacing look and causes the spectator to become anxious? It is only natural to locate anxiety as the cause of the cause, as what resides in the spectator as subject, and creates, as a consequence, an initial observing position that is anxious. Actually looking at the picture or attempting to locate the manifestations of its attraction

Figure 4.1. Gustave Klimt (1862–1918). *The Park.* 1910 (or earlier). New York, Museum of Modern Art. Oil on canvas, 43½ x 43½ (110.4 x 110.4 cm). Gertrud A. Mellon Fund. Digital image © 2007 The Museum of Modern Art, New York / SCALA, Florence.

in any of its components already functions, as any signification, as a way of relieving anxiety.

Anxiety is an Affect, not a Signifier

In the beginning of Lacan's seminar on anxiety, anxiety is claimed to be *an affect, not of the order of the signifier.* The notion of anxiety as affect was originally presented in Freud's essay, in which he claims that anxiety is an affective state, although we are "ignorant of what an affect is."[12] Anxiety is hence something we sense, yet because of its instinctual source we have no determinate notion of it, it is not an object of knowledge, "for analysis shows that to the known real danger an unknown instinctual one is attached."[13] The indeterminate notion of anxiety as affect, then, is motivated in Freud by the fact that anxiety originates from the drives.[14] We do not know what affect is, because the reality of the drives is unknown or inaccessible to us. As demonstrated in the previous section, anxiety is a cause in the subject that becomes a signal directed to the Other: "Instinctual impulses are determinants of external dangers and so become dangerous in themselves."[15] So the unknown instinctual danger signaled by anxiety is translated by the subject as involving an external danger (coming from the Other, to use Lacan's later formulation), despite the internal source of the cause of anxiety. The danger attributed to an external source is that of losing an object of love or of pleasure, or of being separated from it.

This brings us to one point on which Freud and Lacan radically differ. Lacan argues that it is the *lack of separation* rather than the *danger of separation* that causes anxiety in the subject. Lacan claims that it is inconceivable to think of birth as the beginning of separation between mother and child; the cut between them can already be discerned in the prespecular level (before the mother has turned into an object-image of the child's demand). Separation is present as early as the embryonic stage, where the fetus, within the body of the mother, is like a foreign body, encrusted by envelopes (the chorion, amnion, ectodermic lamina).[16] The potential of separation is hence between the embryo and these envelopes that, before birth takes place, form a part of the embryo's own body. When the fetus is detached from the mother's body, it emerges with its envelopes, and this is the real moment of separation. Freud's notion of the instinctual danger is indeed internal, yet it should relate to an object, an organ, that stands for the impossible relation between the dependent child and the always already foreign, distant Other. It is not the separation from the Other that is at issue but, rather, the separation from an instinctually cathectic object that is part of the subject's body yet falls off it at the moment of birth. This body part, the organ, carries the burden of separation, even when the fetus is still apparently part of the mother's body. The enjoyment of enveloping the fetus already registers the danger of separation that is real, even if inactual. The membrane is an object functioning as the organ of life that is neither of the child nor of the mother and is yet both of the child (as body part) and of the mother (as enveloping it). It is through the organ that the paradoxicality of separation is hence illustrated by Lacan in this seminar, and this paradoxical object of separation receives the signifier of *object a*. Later moments in life, such as being carried by the mother or being held by the hand, manifest ways by which the subject locates her or his *object a* in the Other, thereby warding off the danger of separation from *object a* as part of her or his own body.

Lacan believes that the act clinically defined as "acting out" is a way by which the subject aims to designate in the Other her or his *object a,* thus warding off anxiety. Dora slapping Mr. K.'s face can illustrate this relation constituted in acting out, as this slapping of the Other's face locates for the subject the question of her sexuality in the Other. When Mr. K. says to Dora, "My wife is nothing to me," when this wife of his has functioned for Dora as the ultimate object of feminine sexuality, Dora must register the question of sexuality by acting out. The question of sexuality, the question of whether she may have the thing that can make her an object of desire for the Other, is a question to which Mr. K. turns a blank face with his remark. The anxiety before the deaf Other is dealt with by acting out, by forcing *object a,* the unknown secret of sexuality, unto the Other to avoid anxiety. Anxiety as a cause is hence located in the subject's own body, and by being projected onto the Other, anxiety already finds its (at least partial) relief. Acting out, either by slapping the Other on this occasion or by dropping the child who holds one's hand, is a way by which to guarantee separation, thus relieving anxiety.

Lacan's position regarding the prototypical moment of separation suggests an extraordinary conception of the relation between the instinctual excitation in the subject and the Other. For Lacan, the separateness from the Other works to relieve anxiety, since it is this separation that allows the subject to locate the object attached to the instinctual source *in the Other.* Fear of separation is hence already a warding off of the cause of anxiety in the possibility of inseparateness between the subject and *object a,* the object of total self-satisfaction. It is because Dora acts to situate herself as object implicated by the desire of the Other as Other that she can appease her anxiety through acting out. The subject needs to be separated from the Other so *object a* can become tangible, to reveal its essential relation to the subject's desire by way of the Other. We will see later that *object a* in this context of anxiety, the object that in the episode of birth Lacan identifies with the body's envelopes, is the object-cause-of-desire. At this point, it could be claimed that *object a* is the object that drops from the subject, thus revealing something forever lost for the subject. The possibility of that object not being lost, of there being a subject immersed in a totality of *jouissance,* is *a* possibility that anxiety warns against.

The subject has two ways to ward off anxiety. First, anxiety can be ward off by succeeding to locate the object cause of desire in the Other through an act, which was, for instance, Hamlet's maneuver in staging a play, a maneuver that failed. Similarly, Dora locates the question of her desire in the Other by acting to expose the desire of the Other as implicating her as object. Second, anxiety can be ward off by identifying completely with that object, when the subject merges her or his desire completely with the desire of the Other, thus turning herself or himself into an object (this, as Lacan shows later in the seminar, is the solution the pervert opts for). Whereas the first option depends on locating the lack in the Other ("What does Mr. K. want from a woman?" asks Dora), the second option depends on blocking the lack in the Other, camouflaging this lack completely. In both cases, however, anxiety arises in front of the possibility of the lack lacking, that is, of the object of loss being lost from view.

Thus anxiety, according to Lacan, is not a signal of a danger of being separated from the Other; rather, it is a signal of the danger of not being separated from *object a,* of not being able to situate oneself in relation to the desire of the Other as separate. *Object a* here is the object marking the perfect happiness of prenatal totality inside one's envelopes and is hence an object that cannot drop from the infant's body, cannot be marked as separate from that body, unless separation from the Other occurs. Note that the prenatal situation of *jouissance* is in itself a myth or metaphor accounting for the cause of the cause, that is, for the cause of anxiety.

Anxiety as affect reveals the unknown danger that *object a* will not drop from the subject, will not appear as cedeable, as being let to drop: "the function of anxiety is prior to this ceding of the object."[17] In referring to the object as thus fallen, Lacan calls it *le déjet*—which combines the object with its fall (*objet déchu*). It is in reference to this cedeability of *object a* that Lacan suggests that the child is dropped, rather than separated, from the mother's body, which requires that in subsequent situations the subject also must be able to guard her or his *object a* as separated from the Other. This object marks the element foreign to the body of the mother and cedeable in the subject, the object that defines the subject's own particularity, her or his lost part. The moment of anxiety, Lacan therefore claims, is the moment when the subject fears that separation is denied, that, being enveloped by the all-enveloping mOther, the separateness of her or him as subject will not be marked; *object a* will not appear, and the subject will lose touch with desire.

"In anxiety," Lacan further claims, "the subject is affected by the desire of the Other. He is affected by it in a nondialectizable manner."[18] The earlier discussion makes it clear that the desire of the Other determines and regulates the whole dialectic between the subject and object-cause-of-desire, so in what sense is the Other nondialectizable? Anxiety arises in the face of the danger of the subject not appearing as separate, which is why Lacan would say that *object a*, the object-cause-of-desire that marks the subject's separateness, is what falls from the subject in anxiety. Although anxiety as affect cannot be reduced to intuitive psychological states, we can refer again to the dreamer in Freud's work on the uncanny, who, finding himself again and again on the same strange street, feels a fit of anxiety. This situation can clarify the notion of anxiety as signaling the danger of being devoured by the Other (the dreamer is drawn to the place as if by a power stronger than him) and yet of not being marked at all in a totally opaque situation in which the subject and his desire are left unregistered. The fit of anxiety guarantees then that the object-cause-of-desire will "show its face." Another mode for the subject to react to anxiety is by developing a symptom in order to find rescue in the signifier, to find a way to signify *object a* with a symbolic substitute. Both an anxiety state and a symptom (as much as the acting out described earlier) are hence ways of registering the object-cause.

So in anxiety, according to Lacan, *object a* falls from the subject, as anxiety signals the danger of losing the loss from sight, the danger of inseparateness from the object that is at the root of absolute *jouissance,* the object-cause-of-desire. When anxiety is raised, in other words, its appearance suggests this object of cause. Since desire is, however, structurally constituted vis-à-vis the Other, the possibility of losing sight of the loss is located in the Other, so that the Other, being primordially separate from the subject, does not appear in its separateness, thus sealing out the object of desire. Anxiety hence arises in front of an Other that is absolute and indifferent to the subject, that is, an Other that threatens to devour the subject in its separateness. This notion of anxiety as the affect of an absolute Other, an affect that arises when the subject is confronted with the desire of the Other not knowing what object she or he is for that desire, or how this desire is situated in relation to the desire of the Other, can explain the previous quote from Lacan, claiming that in anxiety the desire of the Other affects the subject in a nondialectizable manner.

This notion also provides a further explanation of the Freudian insistence on the instinctual element in anxiety. Anxiety has to do with an Other as absolute, an Other that has no need of the subject and in its enjoyment raises the possibility of annihilation of the subject. It is the annihilation that in Freud's theory of drives is related to what is beyond the pleasure principle, to the death drive, or, in other words, to the absolute enjoyment of a primordial Other. The subject in relation to the Other is anxious when the Other appears to suggest absoluteness in relation to which the subject has no place, having access to only partial manifestations of satisfaction. Locating the object-cause-of-desire, the totality of instinctual satisfaction in the Other, both annihilates the subject and causes pain: "The mere idea of excessive *jouissance* causes great fear. Now, pain is also a suffering. . . . From this point of view, pain is the most evocative representative of an inaccessible *jouissance*/suffering."[19]

Anxiety, as distinct from fear, pain, and other affects, thus has to be articulated in terms of the subject's position vis-à-vis the Other. The way the subject is positioned in relation to the possibility of absolute *jouissance* should be the key to the affect of anxiety. Generally speaking, the danger to which anxiety alerts the subject is indeterminate, because the subject does not know what the Other conceals.

Anxiety is the affect of the route taken by the subject in search of her or his object of desire, the route where anxiety is perceived to alert the subject to the possibility that she or he has no place in the Other. This "route of desire" can be illustrated by Lacan's attribution of anxiety to a necessary link to the order of the image. For Lacan the priority of the image is not there to underline the visual, as opposed to the verbal, but rather is related to the constitutive role the image plays regarding the desire of the subject (as exemplified in his notion of the "mirror stage"). The subject's desire is always constituted in the field of the Other, as materialized in the image that returns to the subject, as if from the field of an Other responsible for producing it. "Desire" here means that the subject looking at her or his image wonders, "What is it in me that returns this image of me from the Other as the way of representing what I am for Him/Her?" In other words, desire is the way to describe the subject's demand from the Other incarnated in the image that always leaves this demand unanswered. These relations of the subject to the image are exemplified in the visual terms of the mirror stage but also can be illustrated in the verbal field.

So how are we to understand the relations between an Other that is nondialectizable and an Other that through the image of the self negotiates for the subject her or his desire? The following analysis of the difference between an affect and a signifier will elucidate the difference between two modes of relating to the Other, the latter necessary for explaining the emergence of anxiety. The notion of "signifier" materializes the logic of the subject's desire as being the desire of the Other. The signifier stands for a differential *dialectic* between S1 (that represents a subject) and S2 (that stands for all other signifiers that come from the Other). The subject in the field of the Other is represented by a signifier (an image, a name, a description, a mere sound), one from among the treasure of all signifiers. This signifier does not necessarily make sense for the subject (the mother can use a nickname or a sound to call her child of which the child cannot make sense), yet it is by the attribution of this signifier that the subject locates herself or himself in relation to the Other in whom the sense of this signifier is stored; it is the signifier that the subject hence takes to be locating/identifying her or him in the domain of the Other. The subject is dialectically tied to the signifier. The signifier represents the subject in the field of the Other (of language, of identities), yet the signifier also misrecognizes the subject and is unable to represent the subject's particularity (the signifier that stands for the subject is always misrecognizing the subject, as the mirror image misrepresents the baby as self-sufficient and ideally whole).

Anxiety as an affect is, however, produced in a *nondialectic* manner. Anxiety as affect is a nonsignifier, which means that in anxiety the subject fails to see himself or herself represented or registered in the Other. The

Other of anxiety is impervious to the subject's lack or fear of loss. This can be demonstrated in the Freudian paradigmatic birth event, where the infant does not know what it is in this event that produces consequent anxiety states. The signifier "death" has a significance that the subject cannot access, yet it affects her or him through anxiety.

Anxiety confines the subject to a domain outside of any signifying dialectic, where the Other appears as a function that is not in need of the subject, thus hampering the dynamic of desire as the desire of the Other. Anxiety is imposed on the subject from the realm beyond the attribution of sense to the Other; as such, as a *primordial affect*, anxiety does not deceive. These are Lacan's words regarding anxiety, and he refers to the nondeceptive nature of anxiety in order to indicate that anxiety as affect is not a product of interpretation, not something addressed to the Other; rather, it appears in the subject as what cannot be attributed sense, but whose presence is certain.[20] In anxiety, therefore, the Other is nondialectic in the sense that its position or desire cannot be made sense of, cannot be symbolized, not even erroneously. Somewhat paradoxically, it is this trait of anxiety as being outside of a possible negotiation with signifiers that attributes certainty to it. Roberto Harari, one of Lacan's interpreters, describes this absolute domain of an Other that cannot be made sense of, a domain imposed on the subject through anxiety, in the following terms: The desire of the Other is what turns back, ungovernable, toward the subject, thus arousing anxiety. A dimension of devouring is thus manifested and lurks behind anxiety.[21]

This observation, that *anxiety is not a signifier but an affect*, can be illuminated with the example Lacan provides of the praying mantis, a voracious insect, often devoured by its female after mating: "Since I did not know what kind of mask I was wearing you can easily imagine that I had some reason not to be reassured, in the case where by chance this mask would not have been unsuitable for drawing my partner into some error about my identity, the thing being well underlined by the fact that I had added that in the enigmatic mirror of the ocular globe of the insect I did not see my own image."[22] The subject figured as a praying mantis, yet unable to see its own image, is affected by anxiety not because of its desire being dialectically linked to the desire of whatever stands in front (a desire represented by the doubt that can be phrased as: "What is it in me that can make the Other desire me?"); rather, the subject is affected by anxiety because *wholly given to the unknown desire of the Other* threatening to devour the subject. Anxiety emerges in the subject and so marks the closing distance between the subject (as image) and the unknown, yet unequivocally all-devouring desire of the Other, a desire that is *prior to any judgment*, as the subject cannot tell what would count as an "error of identity" for the Other, whether male or female.

The subject, masked as insect, cannot control what is to come by being ward off as evil or inconsiderate. Such complaints would clearly be irrelevant. The Other in this case is not given to any law, nor controlled by any morality or appropriateness of behavior. The nondialectizable, uncontrolled, indifferent desire of the Other that the subject faces serves to elucidate the notion of "affect."

The primordial Father whose demand for satisfaction knows no constraint, the devouring praying mantis that does not flinch at the possibility of an error of identification, or the artistic composition that gives the observer no hold is a construction that manifests the possible elsewhere of absolute jouissance that the occurrence of anxiety signals and brings about. The anxiety before the enveloping presence of the Other can be illustrated in those artistic works and installations constructed with the idea of erasing signs of separateness between the artwork and the viewing position of the spectator. This is one reason the much-discussed genius painting by Velázquez, *Las Meninas,* which presents a scene in relation to which the outside spectator holds an ambiguous position, can be said to raise anxiety. Furthermore, cases of *trompe l'oeil* can also maintain the subject in a position from which the installation remains opaque. Let us look at the way Arthur Danto describes an installation created by Swiss artists Fischli and Weiss, presented in the Sonnabend Gallery in New York: "One walked into the Sonnabend Gallery expecting to see an exhibition and instead saw the sorts of gear whose presence one might associate with the installation of an exhibition: spools of tape, Elmer's glue' mat knives. . . . There were stepladders, ashtrays, buckets of paint and plaster. . . . One immediately assumed one had come either too early or too late, but in fact this *was* the show! The objects were in polyurethane, carved and painted by Fischli and Weiss as sons of Parahesios."[23] *Trompe l'oeil* neither supports the possibility of the object presented being genuine nor the possibility of utter deception. The fact that the objects are made of polyurethane further emphasizes the work being beyond the truth/fiction divide. It is in such contexts, where the observer is averted from dialectizing the image implanted in the domain of the Other in terms of truth or deception, for instance, that anxiety typically arises. A similarly structured subversion of the observer's point of support in the picture can be found in the works of artists such as Matisse or J. Edouard Vuillard, who undo the distinction between inside and outside, figure and ground, and setting and scene. Vuillard, in Figure 4.2, while using the contours of a traditional perspective composition, upsets the viewer's ability to make sense of the composition by striking out all signs of relative importance or salience by positioning, coloring, highlighting, and so on. Facing such a picture, the viewer finds it hard to relate to the question of the artist's desire: What is the object of salience or desire for the artist?

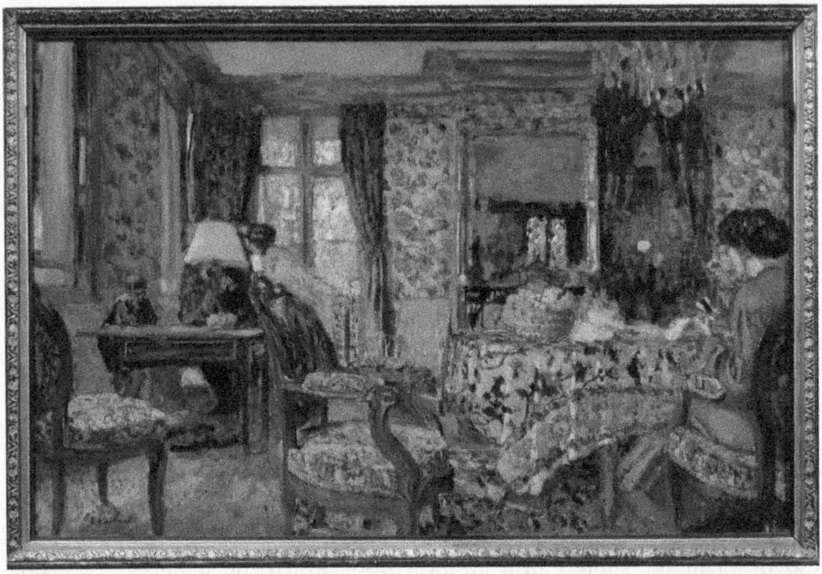

Figure 4.2. Jean Edouard Vuillard (1868–1940). *Interior.* Moscow, Pushkin Museum. © 2007 Artists Rights Society (ARS), New York / ADAGP, Paris. Photo © SCALA, Florence.

Anxiety Is Certain Rather Than Authentic or True

Freud made numerous references to the problem of anxiety. The last major reference to this subject appeared in the *New Introductory Lectures,* where he describes the appearance of anxiety in hysteria in the following way: A quota of libido remains after the idea that had to be repressed is sufficiently distorted, and this quota is transformed into anxiety.[24] This understanding of anxiety in economical terms of utilized and unutilized libido has accompanied Freud's notion of anxiety throughout the years. Yet in this text Freud makes the final move in completely separating anxiety from the pleasure principle (the first substantial move having been made in "Inhibitions, Symptoms, and Anxiety") when he claims that a traumatic moment may arise in mental life without reference to hypothetical situations of danger. That is, the fact that the traumatic moment repressed brings about excitation that "paralyzes the function of the pleasure principle" has further consequences of enabling anxiety to arise as a signal of dangerous excitation with no evidence for there being reasons for the signal of danger to arise. Anxiety occurs as a repetition of prior moments of danger with no evidence of the prior moment being economically locatable at all. This move, within Freud's notion of anxiety, already determines that the certainty attributed to the emergence of anxiety does not result from the specific object of anxiety, previously understood by Freud as a traumatic moment of danger, nor does the certainty of anxiety have to do with a prior interpretation of the given situation.

What, then, is the "crushing degree of certainty" that Lacan attributes to anxiety, a certainty caused by anxiety being "the only connection of the subject to the Real"?[25] It should be briefly noted that in its certainty, as in the other aspects used here to describe anxiety, anxiety constitutes a unique affect in psychoanalysis. The nondeceptive dimension of certainty does not occur with any other affect, from love to melancholy or anger.

In Freudian terms, it is the insistence of the drive beyond the pleasure principle that causes anxiety, and this insistence will be reformulated by Lacan when referring to anxiety as a signal of the Real. But why does the relation to the drives posit anxiety as an affect with a crushing degree of certainty? The fact that for Freud anxiety eventually is seen as not requiring any particular situation of danger (and the model of such a situation, birth, functions more as a mythical empty form, as was shown earlier), and that it arises in terms of the pure movement of the drive, shows that anxiety is not subject to interpretation, as it is not a concept. Here we are almost on Kantian terrain: anxiety, just like a judgment of taste, cannot rely on a concept. "No one can use reasons or principles to talk us into a judgment on whether some garment, house, or flower is beautiful. We want to submit the object to our own eyes, just as if our liking of it depended on that sensation. And yet, if we then call the object beautiful, we believe we have a universal voice, and lay claim to the agreement of everyone."[26] This analogy suggests that anxiety stands the Kantian criteria of aesthetic feelings (the pleasure in the beautiful also being certain beyond conceptualization or empirical proof) and enables us to further use this analogy in order to take a step farther in studying the nature of aesthetic experience. Just as Kant pursues the cause for this certainty in the cognitive constellation that leads to the certainty of the subject running an aesthetic judgment of the beautiful, so in anxiety psychoanalytic theory is interested in accounting for this certainty in terms of the nature of anxiety as a cause.

For Heidegger, too, anxiety is certain, a certainty that is of an ontological rather than an epistemic nature.[27] Anxiety is ontological, and thus it always involves a certain indeterminacy—once it becomes an object of introspection, anxiety disappears. Anxiety, for Heidegger, exposes something in the ontological dimension of Being, yet despite this apparent affinity for the psychoanalytic anxiety and the certitude assigned to it (in both cases it is independent of epistemic and symbolic considerations) one crucial difference distinguishes Lacanian anxiety from Heideggerian. Heidegger does not think of anxiety as a cause in the sense that for Freud and Lacan a primordial trauma produces particular anxiety states. Anxiety in Freud and Lacan can be universalized in its structure but not in its instantiation. Anxiety in psychoanalysis is not an object of introspection (it is an affect and not a signifier), yet it is wholly particularized in every subject. Psychoanalysis attributes anxiety to the Real because it is a *cause*, a particular cause in every subject, and as such it cannot be *presupposed*. Heidegger, however, considers the status of anxiety as *prior to the subject speaking or acting*. *Sorge* and *Angst* are "about everything, about the one, about the omnitude of the human everyday."[28] Anxiety in Heidegger is presupposed before the subject acts, as a condition of being.

"In anxiety, the subject is affected by the desire of the Other . . . in a nondialectizable manner, and it is for that reason that anxiety, within the affectivity of the subject, is what does not deceive."[29] We return to this quote because it unequivocally expresses the idea that anxiety does not deceive. This nondeception can be related to the fact that everybody knows what anxiety is, without being able to interpret it or to attribute sense to it. Everybody knows what anxiety is, although not everybody is anxious. This idea of the universality of anxiety is of a particular nature. *We know what anxiety is, although anxiety is not an object of knowledge. We know what anxiety is, although we may be exempt from the displeasure it brings us.*

Freud, for whom anxiety almost completely overlays with neurosis, does distinguish "realistic anxiety" from "neurotic anxiety." Realistic anxiety is triggered and motivated by an externally known danger, while anxiety neurosis arises from an instinctual source.[30] With this distinction, Freud indicates that there are other symptoms with no anxiety, just as there are anxieties without symptoms. That is, although for Freud anxiety is the prevalent affect in neurosis, anxiety should be limited in its scope; it disappears with the advent of the symptom, and not all psychic structures are affected by anxiety. So what is certain about anxiety? To clarify the kind of universalization involved, Leguil presents a pastiche in the context of his reading Lacan's seminar. He brings an Alexandrine describing animals in the plague: "They did not all die from it but they were all afflicted with it."[31] That is, everyone is informed of anxiety, but not everyone put it to the test. What is the status, asks Leguil, of this recognition of an intimate experience that one possesses, even if exempted from it? What is the nature of this universal knowledge of a nongeneral experience that is yet to be put to the test of truth?

Lacan, in his unfinished seminar *The Names-of-the-Father*, summarizes the seminar on anxiety from the previous year, claiming that anxiety does not deceive because it is "a direct transformation of the libido." That is, the subject knows when the reality of the drives is lurking in a dangerous manner, even if this danger is not located universally in a given event or object. Similarly, for Kant, aesthetic pleasure is not an empirical fact shared by all subjects in front of a given object, and yet the conditions that enable the subject to sense such pleasure are universal. Anxiety should be thought of in similar terms.

Anxiety is universal, although not everyone is afflicted with it. It is certain and nondeceptive, yet is neither true nor authentic. We know what anxiety is, as it introduces itself with absolute certainty. We sense anxiety in our ego, as Freud insistently repeated; that is, anxiety is not the domain of the unconscious, and it is not repressed. Kant has acknowledged the possibility of a subject who makes an erroneous judgment of taste while being certain of the conditions under which the judgment is executed (taking these conditions to secure separateness between the beautiful, the agreeable, and the good): "Whether someone who believes he is making a judgment of taste is in fact judging in conformity with that idea may be uncertain; but by using the term beauty he indicates that he is at least referring his judging to that idea. . . . For himself, however, he can attain certainty on this point."[32] Anxiety, however, cannot deceive; it is not true, yet it is put to the test of truth. To follow this complex of attributes and their negation, I trace the difference between certainty and authenticity in this context first through the way the subject of certainty is addressed by Lacan in the seminar of the following year, 1964–1965.

The Cartesian *cogito* is dealt with extensively by Lacan in Seminar XI, where Lacan refers to the Cartesian subject as the true subject of the unconscious and, as such, as a subject of certainty. The Cartesian subject gains his or her certainty in the single point into which his or her inaugural beliefs (in common knowledge) were reduced through doubt.[33] That is, the *cogito* as materializing a moment of certainty cannot be reached unless all knowledge is radically put in doubt. Although certainty is materialized in the punctual signifier of the subject who says "I think," it does not rely or refer to any outside knowledge. This moment of certainty is achieved epistemically and should be understood as an epistemic gesture, although emerging from the undermining of knowledge with doubt. It is the subject who *knows* that he or she thinks or doubts what he or she knows, who stands as a cause for the certainty of the *cogito*. The certainty to be found in anxiety, I would claim, is not of such an epistemic nature, even if this certainty also is exempt from outside knowledge and does not refer to truth as substance.

Why should the certainty in anxiety be distinguished from the certainty of the *cogito*? While Lacan reconsiders the Cartesian *Cogito* as heralding the subject of the unconscious, the unconscious *can deceive*. The unconscious deceives, as Freud himself noticed, when, for instance, the subject dreams something that answers what she or he takes to be the analyst's demand from her or him, that is, as part of transference. But anxiety does not deceive, which means that its certainty goes beyond the certainty of the *cogito*. The certainty of anxiety goes beyond the certainty of the subject, who knows that she doubts.

To clarify this difference, let us refer back to anxiety as affect. In Freud's *Introductory Lectures,* we find the following reference: Anxiety is "the subjective state into which we are put by perceiving the 'generation of anxiety' and we call this an affect."[34] This self-referential punctualization of anxiety as affect is one source of its certainty, but this is not all. Freud later says that affect is the repetition of some significant experience, and that "this experience could only be a very early impression of a very general nature, placed in the pre-history not of the individual but of the species."[35] Anxiety as affect is prior to any knowledge of the subject. This is the true nature of the universality of anxiety that is both wholly dependent on the particular experiencing of it and yet exceeds or precedes any knowledge. Anxiety has to do with the preservation of the species and not of the self; it is hence related neither to a preestablished knowledge nor to any epistemic relations to knowledge, even if knowledge is under the shadow of doubt.

On Lacan's interpretation of the *cogito,* Descartes leaves the dimension of truth outside certainty and will need to bring God into the picture in order to restore a relation between the subject's certainty and truth. Descartes, who says "I think," knows that certainty, even if a minimal one, must be epistemically restituted, that is, reconstructed as true knowledge. Knowledge is only temporarily rejected. Any restored knowledge would, however, maintain its doubtful status with regard to truth, unless an external authority is brought in.[36] We need Freud to know that the Cartesian subject is analogous to the subject of the unconscious: the latter can be certain, although his or her fundamental position in what concerns the content of the unconscious is that of being uncertain, of doubting.[37] It is the subject being constituted by what she or he does not know that makes her or him, according to psychoanalytic thought, a subject of the unconscious. It is this doubt, the lack of certainty in the content of the "I think," that constitutes the subject around a point of certainty. If, however, anxiety is prior to knowledge, then knowledge cannot be regained through an Other, be it God or the analyst, nor can the relation of knowledge to truth be assigned to such an external function. The relation of anxiety to certainty and truth must lie elsewhere.

The relations between certainty, truth, and authenticity are extrapolated by Leguil in the following manner. Religion views anxiety as revealing the truth of a question that has to be built into certitude. Psychoanalysis sees anxiety not as true but as being put to the test of truth. That is, the certainty of anxiety is prior to true knowledge because it relates to the cause of truth. This assertion can be interpreted in the following manner: The certainty of anxiety reveals the presence of a truth, a truth that emerges from anxiety itself, which makes it a truth that does not pass by way of knowledge.

Anxiety is the cause of truth; its certainty does not gain substance through the dialectic relation with the knowledge of the Other. While anxiety is the cause of truth, it is also inauthentic. Leguil claims that had anxiety been authentic, it would not have lended itself to the theatricalization so consubstantial and constant with it. Through theatricalization the anxious subject makes an effort to contain anxiety in the scene in which it manifests itself, as if he or she wanted to avoid the threat that anxiety will extend to the entire world. The idea of the theatricalization of anxiety within the confines of the theatricalized scene can be illustrated in the case brought by Leguil of a subject who practices a very dangerous kind of sports, his life dominantly turning around it. At a moment of crisis, one day the subject starts feeling anxiety, an anxiety that is explained neither by the danger in which he puts himself nor by his feeling of ignorance as to the reasons that drive him to a practice of such risks. The subject can be said to theatricalize something through his sportive practice, thus underscoring the inauthentic nature of the anxiety that accompanies this practice. The subject, through the sportive scene, attempts to restrict a danger that pertains to the whole species (a danger associated with sexual drives) to one image with which he is faced, in this case the image of great physical danger.

Anxiety is hence inauthentic in that it calls for theatricality to interrogate a phantasmatic junction. Yet this inauthenticity is intimately related to the certainty in anxiety, and to the fact that it persists outside of the domain of knowledge. Had the subject known, says Leguil, that anxiety is the pursuit of a phantasm by alternative means, then he would have understood that his energetic vivacity is sexual. So the subject incurs a very dramatic kind of danger that the fit of anxiety further erotizes. The subject engages in an instance of fascinated desire before an image, and in the anxiety that entails, truth appears outside of any knowledge or signification, and not subject to any. Anxiety is no compensation, as it does not make one know more. When anxiety is relieved, one is happier, but this is due neither to fact that anxiety has embanked repression nor that it signifies a gain in knowledge. Anxiety furthermore does not reflect a subject who has triumphed over the real or has discovered truth (as a consequence).[38]

Anxiety is a fear from the fear, which means that the phenomenon manifesting danger makes the subject fearful only as an idealized, reduced reminder of what the subject phantasmatically fears. It is a fear from what cannot be known but only enacted, revealing an elsewhere. We can further infer from these relations between anxiety and truth that anxiety, in its inauthentic theatricality, shows itself to be extensively related to the visual order, or to scopic structure. Yet the function of the image in anxiety is exactly the opposite of its function in the "mirror stage": in anxiety, the image has an indicative function in relation to the Real, which makes it neither superior nor compromised by the visual phenomenon itself. In the mirror stage, the subject faces a unified impressiveness of the body image in the mirror, an image superior in relation to the fragmentation of the body in the real. In anxiety, the image appears as failing and yet not in what regards its representational function.

Anxiety signifies the entry of certainty into subjectivity by suffering.[39] The anxious subject is hence facing something that knowledge cannot relieve, and that representation cannot screen out. Anxiety is the connection of the subject to the Real, not a way of camouflaging the Real with an image or a sign.

To go one step farther in coming to grips with the certainty in anxiety, I examine the notion of cause as it figures in Lacan's seminar on anxiety. It is the notion of anxiety as cause that can illuminate the idea of anxiety's certainty outside the domain of knowledge. To claim that anxiety is cause, prior to any symbolization, outside any given knowledge, and dependent on imaging that connects the subject to the Real, is to accept that "the cause always arises in correlation with the fact that something is omitted in the consideration of knowledge, something which is precisely the desire which animates the function of knowledge."[40]

So the certainty of anxiety has to do with its correlation with desire as the cause of knowledge. The question of the cause of knowledge is of a long history in philosophy, from Plato (who places it in the "Sovereign Good") to Nietzsche (who also places it in desire). Lacan refers to the myth of the origin of knowledge, which often takes the form of a questioning that touches on what a domain of knowledge believes it is obliged to forge as the final cause. Every leaning on the signifier to constitute knowledge means an articulation of desire into knowledge and, as in every phantasmatic articulation, it necessitates a "syncope of the function of *object a*."[41] That is, the phantasmatic articulation of cause entails the aphanisis (disappearance) of *object a,* and it is in this object that we should look every time we find ourselves confronted with this final functioning of the cause. Every system of knowledge locates something else as the ultimate, even if irreducible, cause. Yet what gives various essentialisms their certainty "is the shadow of something else, of another certainty," and this certainty should be recognized in the anxiety that is linked to the approach to *object a*. In other words, the certainty attributed to any essential cause of knowledge (e.g., reason, God, Being) is simply a manner by which to avoid the certainty of *object a,* the object-cause-of-desire, whose approach is the only thing we can be certain of in any articulation of knowledge: "The only certainty, which is founded, unambiguous, is that of anxiety; anxiety precisely insofar as every object escapes it. And the certainty linked to the recourse to the primary cause and the shadow of this fundamental certainty, its shadowlike character is what gives it this essentially precarious aspect . . . which is surmounted by the essentialist argument."[42] The certainty involved in any essentialist theory of knowledge, the certainty of cause, is a displacement, a secondary certainty relative to the primary certainty of anxiety.

Thus anxiety signifies the entry of certainty into subjectivity by suffering; it signifies the moment prior to the doubtful domain of the signifier and the articulation of knowledge. The picture by Zurbarán (Figure 4.3) demonstrates the notion of anxiety as a theatricalization that locates anxiety, although it appears as if the picture evades this possibility by placing under shadow whatever may be identified as the cause of anxiety in the articulation of the image.

The play of light in this picture paradoxically works to undermine the specular dimension (the specular domain for Lacan is where the subject appears signified in an image of himself, in an image simultaneously oneself and other[43]), although it manipulates the visual field in an effective manner. Unlike a typical Caravaggio, for instance, the spot of light does not fall here to highlight the dramatic potential of the picture. The folded hands, the side of the body, and the nose receive the visual accentuation that may bring on the affect of anxiety. Just like another one of Zurbarán's pictures, St. Agatha holding her breasts on a tray, in this picture, the nose, missing from the skull, is highlighted in St. Francis's face. The picture dramatizes in St. Francis the indeterminacy of the lack in the visual sphere: his face that should have been highlighted as the ultimate expression of devotion is obscured, while the missing organ, the nose, appears as part of the depicted figure yet as a disconnected, alien body part. This picture illustrates the way anxiety is a cause that connects

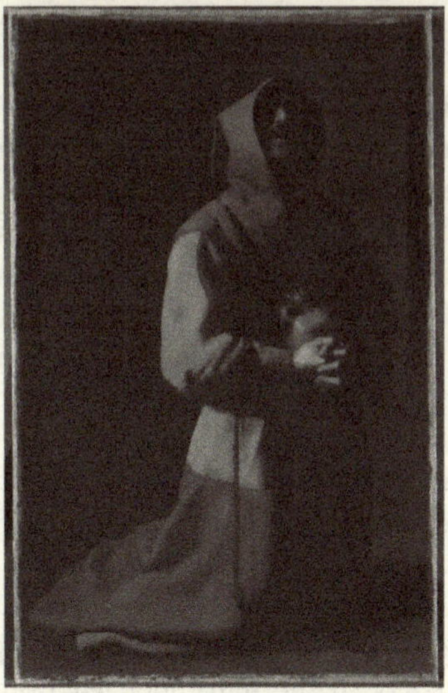

Figure 4.3. Francisco de Zurbarán (1598–1664). *Saint Francis in Meditation.* 1635–40. Oil on canvas. Photo © 2007 The National Gallery.

the subject to an object that cannot be specularized, cannot appear as part of the image, and the picture dramatizes this impossible specularization.

Anxiety in the Subject Is Related to the Cause of Desire

In "Inhibitions, Symptoms, and Anxiety," Freud warns against putting too much emphasis on castration as a decisive cause for anxiety neurosis. "I have shown elsewhere how little girls, in the course of their development, are led into making a tender object-cathexis by their castration complex. . . . All we need to do is to make a slight modification in our description of their determinant of anxiety, in the sense that it is no longer a matter of feeling the want of, or actually losing the object itself, but of losing the object's love."[44] As a determinant of anxiety, concludes Freud, the loss of love plays much the same part in hysteria as the threat of castration does in phobia and other neuroses.

It has already been suggested that anxiety plays a role that can only partly be located in the Other, as its relation to the object of the drive, to the object-cause-of-desire, puts it beyond any dialectical relation to an Other. This means that anxiety, while emerging as a signal to the Other, cannot be considered a message to be deciphered by signifiers that come from the Other. Anxiety is both addressed to the Other and circumvents this function, an ambivalence that should be clarified through the notion of cause.

Here I present an argument developed by J-A. Miller in his introduction to the reading of Lacan's seminar, that anxiety occurs outside of the Oedipal drama. Through this argument the idea that anxiety's object is the object-cause-of-desire, and the fact that this object becomes tangible to the subject as both associated with the Other and as foreclosed from the Other, will be elucidated. The Other to which anxiety is addressed both refers to an Other as lacking and to an Other as foreclosed; this two-headed function of the Other has to be articulated for the logic of anxiety to be explained.

Miller, in his introduction to reading Seminar X, claims that, for Lacan, anxiety is the access road to the real, that is, an access road to that part of the object that cannot be signified, and that has to do, in the work of art, with that part of *jouissance* that art envelops.[45] Anxiety as such is not a signifier, which prevents it from being considered a concept.[46] Since anxiety is the access road to the real, Lacan delineates the route of anxiety to the real in a somewhat dialectical manner. Thus the seminar should partly be read as a critique of the scopic structuring of *object a* (a structuring that finds its ultimate exemplification in the mirror stage) and partly as an attempt to trace the object of anxiety in the remainder left from the signifier/image, a remainder that Lacan finds in the subject's body. The object of anxiety, for Lacan, is an organ and not a signifier, Miller claims, which is why this object cannot be exhausted by the order of the image, of the signifier.

Thus part of the seminar is occupied by a critique of the scopic field and its object, an object that in this part of the seminar is still taken to be articulable, and with the decomposition of this order. In the context of the scopic field, the seminar revises Lacan's early conception of the mirror stage by pointing to the misrecognized strangeness of *object a*, the object most masked in the image yet perceived as the object that the desire of the Other is after (as the earlier illustration of the praying mantis indicates). The second part of the seminar refers to an altogether different object, an object that remains after the signifier. This is an object desymbolized and deimaginarized. This last part manipulates and crushes the signifier in its scopic form.

"It is also this connection between anxiety and the real of *jouissance* that Lacan stresses as the certainty of anxiety, and which contrasts with the doubtful character of the signifier—the signifier is never certain."[47] This is why, Miller claims, in this seminar, Lacan makes extensive use of the phenomenology of obsession, as the obsessional is the subject who smashes the signifier in the attempt to reach the origin, that is, the object-cause-of-desire.

The seminar first confronts the reader with a decomposition of the specular level so the reader has access to an object not of the kind she or he is used to, to the extent that the paradigmatic mode in which objects are perceived leans on a visual model, and the prototypical way of accessing this world of objects is through the reader's own image. It is this imaginary dimension of the mirror stage that is decomposed. In asking where *object a* can be trapped, Lacan shows that it is not there where the bait should be located. Anxiety is in the net of signifiers, but it is precisely there, in sense, that anxiety does not let itself be caught. This critique of the specular dimension, it must be acknowledged, follows two important notions that tie anxiety to the specular dimension. First, Lacan's claim that the specular field is the field where the subject is most secured with respect to anxiety, and therefore it is the field in which it is most difficult to grasp *object a*.[48] The second notion is that anxiety, which was previously thought of by Lacan as referring to the desire of the Other, is later provoked when the subject does not know how to locate *object a* with regard to the desire of the Other. These are the two aspects of the specular domain that Seminar X both presents and undermines. This can be manifested in the case of the praying mantis with its voracious desire, in which the scopic field does not reveal where in the Other the subject is located. No common factor links the subject to the Other, who remains opaque and undecipherable.

To trace "the moment of its constitution" of *object a,* one has to look at a level different from that of the scopic one. It is an object that signals the first form of desire: "It is indeed to the object that there is appended the first form of desire, insofar as we elaborate it as desire for separation . . . it is clear that the function of cause that I give to the object is manifested in the fact that the form of desire is turned against the function which introduces the *object a* as such. For it must be seen that this object is here already given, already produced."[49] Anxiety is linked to the first form of the object that signals the primary rupture of the link with the Other. The object of anxiety is hence the cause for future desire in reverse form—for the desire of the Other to constitute the subject's desire, the first form of desire should be that of separation from the Other.

Lacan attempts to show that the object at the root of anxiety as cause is paradoxically neither of the subject nor of an autonomous object. This can be represented in the baby's first meconium, since it is an object of negotiation (bestowed, so to speak, by the nursling to the mother or midwife in ancient times) with the Other, yet also the object marking the separation from the Other.[50] The object-cause-of-desire should be likened in this respect to the function of the meconium.

According to Lacan, this is why he opposes the structure of relations-of-desire in the Hegelian sense to the desire of the Other; in the former, desire is defined within the dialectic of assigning the cause of one's being, the cause for self-consciousness, to another. Finding comfort in the existence of a being for whom the subject's cause is not foreign is a way of eluding the fact that it is impossible for the subject, at the level of desire, to find in himself or herself as subject his or her cause. The idea of object-as-cause places anxiety, in a way, outside the realm of the Other: "It is not of the Other, it is not the link to the Other that has to be broken, it is at the very most the first sign of this link."[51]

Lacan once again illustrates this idea of cause outside the link to the Other with Hamlet. We have seen that Hamlet causes anxiety, because his desire remains unplaced. As a subject, he cannot make use of the Other to locate the object of his desire. But what is the cause of this inability? What is the cause of this cause? We should trace the cause back to the fact that Hamlet does not mourn his mother, which brings Lacan to surmise the roots of Hamlet's lacking desire: "The desire is lacking because the ideal has collapsed."[52] Hamlet, lacking such an ideal (a fact Lacan demonstrates through the way the mother is only negotiated for Hamlet through the image of his ghostly father), loses the power of desire, and it will not be restored "until the vision outside of a mourning, a true one, with which he enters into competition, that of Laertes for his sister, for the object loved by Hamlet, and from whom he had found himself suddenly, through lack of desire, separated."[53] As long as Hamlet was provided with images of beloved objects as supplied by an Other, his desire could not be restored. Mourning is a way of negotiating—through the link to the object narcissistically chosen as an object of love, an image of the ideal ego, the place of the masked object, *object a*, the veritable object of the relationship, for which, subsequently, a substitute may be provided. *Object a* is usually masked behind the ideal ego of narcissism, the image of the self in the mirror. It is precisely for this reason that the scopic field of the mirror stage, where the object of fascination is always misrecognized in its substitutes, has to be crossed so the true cause of anxiety can be revealed. Hamlet, we can surmise, failed to enact this crossing.

Thus while Lacan in the first part of the seminar considers a Hegelianism of a subject misrecognizing himself in the Other, a subject that dialectically awaits to find his cause in the being outside himself (in the image), Lacan in the second part of the seminar replaces this object with something "*qui ne se prête pas à la dialectique, ne se prête pas au signifiant*."[54] What does not lend itself to the dialectic of the signifier is the remainder. That is where anxiety is—in the remainder that introduces an obstacle to symbolic dialectic and to the logic of the signifier, as this remainder remains insoluble. Anxiety is consequently an alternative road to Hegelian *Aufhebung*. The seminar moves in the first lessons from the glitter of the signifier, a glitter that turns out to be completely deceptive, just like the imaginary, to the final lessons, which take anxiety away from the imaginary and from the symbolic (and from the concept).

With anxiety there is a crossing of reality. Anxiety is placed outside the limits designated by the subject of the signifier. In that, Miller claims, this seminar succeeds in pointing to the cause of desire outside of castration anxiety, outside of the Oedipal drama.[55] It is not the threat of the father that brings on anxiety. Castration constitutes an anxiety (what Freud referred to as castration anxiety) that has to do with a signifying object—a lacking object in the mother is signified by the phallus, the signifier of castration, the signifier of a lack. Castration anxiety is raised in front of the image of lack and could be differentiated from anxiety proper with the example of the object signifying castration in Little Hans's case (a case extensively discussed in Lacan's fourth seminar on object relations).[56] The object of lack here is attributed significance (like the horse for Hans), and it hence presents the *Aufhebung* of anxiety by phobia. The anxiety of castration is replaced by a misrecognized object, thus bringing a symptom (a signifier) as a solution to castration anxiety. The relation with the signifying object, however, always leaves a remainder; phobia does not abolish anxiety completely. There is something that remains, and only in the present seminar (X), this remainder is desymbolized and deimaginarized. Here we face a new structure of lack, a nonsignifying structure conveyed by topology, releasing a new status for the body.

In this seminar that deals at length with the mirror stage, we face a different notion of the body—no longer a body susceptible to signification but a body that implies the function of split and cannot be made to signify. Until the seminar on anxiety, the theory of castration anxiety rested on the signification of the phallus. Freud, too, anchored castration anxiety in feminine privation. Until the seminar on anxiety, privation was conceived as a real hole, which bears on a symbolic object. In Seminar IV, an imaginary damage, insofar as there is a defect in satisfaction, can bring about the real object. Castration is conceived of as a symbolic debt that bears on an imaginarily lacking object. The paradigmatic object of frustration is the mother's breast. Sucking from the breast, the whole world drinks with you, sucks with you. With castration, we already have the law, and the law sublimates everything that beforehand appeared as contingent, accidental. The law intervenes like an operator of the lost object. It is because of the law that whatever is conceived as privation or frustration becomes a debt.[57] We see here how Oedipus inspires Lacan in his early teaching as an essential articulation of the development of sexuality. This is because Oedipus brings along the law and interdiction by the voice of castration that bears on the imaginary phallus. The menace of castration, virtual or real, basically implies the effect of the Other.

In the seminar on anxiety, nothing of this mechanism remains. Lacan refers to the mechanism of castration to bring the opposite of this lack, the presence of the object there where it cannot be grasped. Miller reads Lacan's seminar along these lines. The seminar presents frustration beyond the phallus, by traversing the idea of phallic frustration. This frustration is presented as imaginary in the scopic field. The imaginary phallus is an image of power, and this illusion of power should be traversed. The phallus in Seminar X is *désignifiantisé et désimaginarisé* (designified and deimaginarized).[58] Lacan leaves aside the unitary specular form in order to interest himself in the anatomic particulars of the organism; in place of the signifier, we encounter the organ itself refound. The veil of the signifier has been lifted, and the body, the splendid body of the mirror, finds anew its organs. The body is barred, but this carries a totally different function than the signifying cut. In this seminar, Lacan speaks of revival of the dialectic of desire, because the dialectic articulated in terms of the signifier produces no more than dead desire, desire that is constituted metonymically through a signifying chain and cannot account for libido. Before Seminar X, desire is like the signifying *Aufhebung* of the libido. In Seminar X, the libido is something different. Libido remains in all of Lacan's teaching as a kind of enclave that is not completely grasped, whose myth inspires Plato's Banquet. But in Seminar X and Seminar XI, libido is not a signifying remainder but a paradoxical organ. The remainder is now an organ, a remainder *jouissance* and not desire, an organ that rebels against the idea of dialectic, of *Aufhebung*.

To follow Miller's overall conception of the seminar, we now reach its conclusive point. The phallus in Seminar X is not the signifier of imaginary-symbolic castration but an organ. In a way, Lacan paradoxically points to this idea with Oedipus himself as person, the one "who could not have had an Oedipus complex." Oedipus exemplifies the cause of anxiety, because he is precisely the one who wants to see "what is beyond the most complete satisfaction of his desire."[59] The object Oedipus is after is not the one that can be symbolized by castration and is completely opposed to its imaginarization as power. This explains why Oedipus's debt cannot be symbolic and Oedipus must pay with the organ of knowledge, his eyes. Lacan does not use as an image of *jouissance* in this seminar the organ of enjoyment in its moment of power but in the detumescence that strikes the organ at the moment of *jouissance*. The moment of detumescence is precisely the moment that exhibits the organ of *jouissance* as an organ that cannot be symbolized, or imaginarized.

The object of this seminar is distinguished in essence, nature, and structure from the signifier but is also irreducible to a signifier. It is only in this seminar that the distinctness of *object a* is revealed. The fact of the detumescence of the organ reflects the moment of its lack, the dying out of the phallic function in the sexual act. This is the cause of anxiety. On the level of the organ, the Oedipal drama is effaced; there is no Other that threatens. Anxiety is not inscribed in Oedipus.

Object a in this seminar is hence prior to desire, to the object of desire, prior to the law, and prior to phallic symbolization, prior to the constitution of the paternal function. Anxiety is a road that permits access to what is prior to desire and its object. The phallus of this seminar is the only body organ that cannot fulfill a metaphorical function. The body organ is a remainder of a signifier, and not a signifier itself. In this notion of the object, we have reached the conclusive point in Lacan's development of the logic of anxiety. We have crossed the object of reality, its image and signifier, and we have found our access to the Real.

Anxiety is both cause, outside the domain of the signifier, and affect, that would have been located in the field of the Other had the Other been lacking. Anxiety is in this sense both referring to the moment of cause striving to remain separate from the Other and to the affect that locates the subject vis-à-vis the opaque, absolute Other that marks the danger of losing sight of the object.

CAUSE------------------- ANXIETY---------------- OTHER

ANXIETY AND CREATION

In the last section of this chapter, the notion of anxiety as it emerged from psychoanalytic discussions will be located within a picture of aesthetic experience. As indicated throughout, anxiety is an affect associated with the displeasure of the neurotic subject, but anxiety also is related to psychotic suffering.

In his seventh seminar on ethics, Lacan claims that all creation emerges ex nihilo, that is, that the object of art is built on the foundation of a *lack*.[60] What, then, motivates creation? Miller refers to Lacan's theory of art by claiming that there is in Lacanian psychoanalysis reference both to creation of the neurotic and to creation of the psychotic.[61] In the neurotic, whose very structure is that of the void, it is easy to see how creation correlates with that structure. Lacan claims that castration incarnates a subject, and the object of the neurotic is created from this void to contain it, to assign this void a place. This type of creation can be formulated so that the sign $-\varphi$, which is the sign of castration, is what incarnates the subject and creates the object to envelop it (the void). This is the formula of creation that grounds itself on castration, and it is, for instance, what guides Freud in his study of Leonardo da Vinci,[62] as constituted around the fundamental lack of the mother object.

Psychotic creation appears under the sign of *foreclosure*. The subject is incarnated through the Ideal of the ego, which is that of an Other who lacks nothing. This place of the Ego Ideal is the place left vacant by the law, since the creator of the law, the Other, is regarded by the psychotic as disloyal to the world, as one who cannot be trusted.[63] The psychotic creation hence should be understood as creation that takes place where the object of art is created in order to occupy the place left vacant by the name-of-the-father. The signifier marking the place of the Other is vacant, and this is where the psychotic work of art is produced, to replace the place of the foreclosed name of the father.[64]

This distinction between neurotic and psychotic creation can clarify why anxiety in the aesthetic experience can wear both varieties. In a way, this distinction corresponds to the two parts of Lacan's seminar on anxiety, elaborated on earlier. Neurotic creation creates neurotic anxiety when, in the order of the scopic, the possibility of losing sight of the loss, the object of desire lacking in the subject, threatens. This is the subject of castration who needs the lack to be registered in order to have the certainty of a subject. Psychotic creation creates psychotic suffering where *jouissance,* uninhibited by the law, threatens to invade the subject completely. The analysis of Lacan's seminar should have clarified how anxiety should be understood as actualizing both structural causes, thus incarnating the very foundations of an aesthetic experience in its intimate correlation with psychic structures of particular subjects.

Having articulated the two modes of creation and consequently the two domains in which anxiety can emerge, I refer to two examples from Zurbarán's art, the one, St. Francis in meditation, referred to earlier, and the other, St. Agatha, with her breasts on a tray. These two works of art can elucidate the difference between anxiety that refers to the failure of the image, its failure in imaging the object of lack, and anxiety that refers to the object of *jouissance* that escapes the signifier and eludes the image, that object Miller identified as non-Oedipal. Note that in both cases anxiety is indeed associated with the object-cause.

Looking back at St. Francis, we can stress the fact that not only does the image "fail" to picture the main object of picturing, that is, the devoted person of the monk, but the picture, as already suggested, subtracts the face of the monk from its "natural" place in order to duplicate it in the skull. The uncanny affect of the picture can underline the fact that the anxiety raised in front of this picture is not only related to the image losing hold on the desire of the subject (by presenting it as blanked out), but anxiety also is related to the way the object of the ecstatic *jouissance* of the monk is not given in the image but is displaced into the object the monk holds in his hands. This transition not only stresses the fact that the object in reality (the face of the monk) has become an object in the Real (the "face" of the skull), thus bringing the observer into an elsewhere, but that one has already crossed the bounds of the signifier and is in the domain of the object-as-organ. In this picture, one faces an object that transcends any symbolic function, or any power of imaginarization.

This dimension of the picture is further illustrated with the case of St. Agatha, a picture that, like the object of sexual *jouissance* embodied in the detumescence of the phallus, presents that object of enjoyment as absolutely identified with the organ (Figure 4.4). The subject, St. Agatha, reduced to

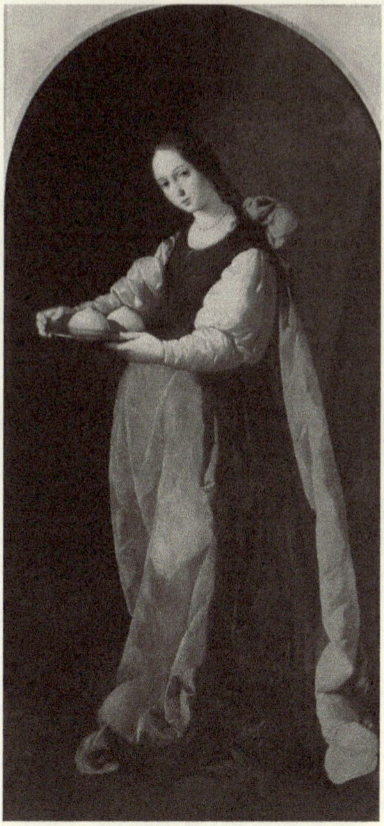

Figure 4.4. Francisco de Zurbarán (1598–1664). *St. Agatha*. Oil on canvas. Photo © Musee Fabre, Montpellier, France; Lauros / Giraudon / the Bridgeman Art Library.

the organ of her enjoyment, thus raises our anxiety in front of an object that completely belongs to the order of the Real: it is the vibrating organ of pure *jouissance* in front of which the observer is affected by anxiety. St. Agatha's composed countenance serves in this context to highlight the very fine line that converges, rather than separates, suffering and *jouissance.* In contemporary art, anxiety in front of an image of this sort is prevalent. I mention in this context the self-incurred surgery and suffering of Orlan, who theatricalized her suffering with a grinning, ecstatic face, thus turning her whole body into an organ of *jouissance*. Similar creative acts are made by Lars von Trier's movies.

I have demonstrated the ways anxiety is involved in the very constitution of the subject, as a speaking, enjoying being, and that anxiety signals universal forms of encountering the real. Between Freud's uncanny and the distinction between neurotic and psychotic structures of creation these chapters have examined the various ways in which the structure of anxiety, in its relation to the subject's desire, becomes manifest.

CHAPTER 5

Beyond the Sublime

This chapter and the following exemplify the two dimensions of anxiety that emerge from *neurotic creation* and *psychotic creation*, as these modes of creation relate to two cardinal issues in aesthetics: the *sublime* and the *genius*. The phenomenon of the sublime, which is of central place and importance in aesthetic theory, brings into the limelight the question of the *object that causes the sublime,* and by concentrating on the object that causes the sublime, the relation between the sublime and anxiety can be clarified. Anxiety pertains to the encounter with the sublime, first because in the sublime the subject goes through a necessary phase of displeasure, as Kant himself remarked. Second, the sublime raises with particular force the intriguing question of the object causing it. The case of the sublime will exemplify that the anxiety associated with aesthetic practice has to do with an elsewhere occluded by what is given in a presentation. This object is not unique to the case of the sublime, yet in the aesthetic judgment of the sublime the judgment is explicitly inapplicable to the object in reality. As Charles Shepherdson writes in relation to Kant's "ideal beauty," the ideal brings into play "a dimension of infinity, a rupture with visibility, an 'ideality' that in fact only genuinely finds its place . . . in the analytic of the sublime."[1] In our Kantian-Lacanian reading, the sublime is associated with the occlusion of the object-cause-of-desire, an object constituted through Kant's negation of concrete objects as possible objects for sublime judgments. The effect of this occlusion of the object that causes desire from the visual field is that of highlighting the lack in the image. While the object of *desire* will be pointed to as the object of the judgment of the sublime in the present chapter, in the following chapter the notion of genius in aesthetic theory will be established in order to exemplify the way creation can put an object of *jouissance,* an object that eludes the symbolic function of castration and lack in the domain of imaging, in this place of vacancy. The following chapter will hence reveal that genius is the name of the creation that evades the symbolic order, evades meaning yet brings the observer/reader to the Real, to her or his utmost anxiety.

THE SUBLIME AND THE OBJECT OF NATURE

What is the sublime? A sentiment? A mental event? An affect? A cognitive state? In the part called "Analytic of the Sublime" in the third critique, Kant explicitly distinguishes the judgment of the beautiful, whose object is the purposefulness of form, from the sublime that has no object, not even an object in nature, let alone an object of art. "For what is sublime, in the proper meaning of the term, cannot be contained in any sensible form but concerns only ideas of reason. . . . Thus the vast ocean heaved up by storms cannot be called sublime. The sight of it is horrible; and one must already have filled one's mind with all sorts of ideas if such an intuition is to attune it to a feeling that is itself sublime, inasmuch as the mind is induced to abandon sensibility and occupy itself with ideas containing a higher purposiveness."[2]

Whereas with regard to the beautiful, a subjective state can be associated with an object, thus entitling us to call the object beautiful, the situation is fundamentally different with the sublime, as we cannot say that the object itself is sublime, but it is rather terrifying, intimidating, and so on. Furthermore, while there is something in the object of beauty that makes it appropriate for our aesthetic judgment, which is its purposefulness of form, no *forms* of nature can be found appropriate for the predication "sublime." In what we call sublime, there is an utter lack of conformity between forms of nature and objective principles that regulate and account for these forms' occurrence: "That it is rather in its chaos that nature most arouses our ideas of the sublime, or in its wildest and most ruleless disarray and devastation."[3]

So as much as sublime terminology has been widely adopted by art criticism (with regard to abstract art, for instance) as a way to describe works of art, for Kant the sublime cannot be attributed to an object. Moreover, those objects that elicit in the observer ideas of sublimity resist the status of *cause* of the experience of the sublime. Kant goes even farther on this point and finds the attempt to find sublimity in an object of nature futile, not to say ridiculous. "Who would want to call sublime such things as shapeless mountain masses piled on one another in wild disarray, with their pyramids of ice, or the gloomy raging sea?"[4] While it is unlikely that Kant ever had a chance of actually envisaging the sight of the stormy ocean or the menacing masses of ice from his home in Konigsberg, he indulged no illusions regarding the true nature of grandiose objects of nature. Kant decisively warned against confusing the wild object of nature with the affect of the sublime that is in fact aroused when the mind "contemplates these without concern for their form" and then "abandons itself to the imagination and to a reason that has come to be connected with it—although quite without a determinate purpose, and merely expanding it."[5]

Kant's formulations raise the unremitting question regarding the association between the experience of the sublime and the object eliciting it. Were generations of critics and art lovers whose hearts melted in front of Caspar David Friedrich's solemn paintings or when facing the enigmatic sublimity of Turner's hazy scenery, all in error? Were they putting too much weight on the puissance of nature revealed before the observer dwarfed under this grandeur? True, for Kant, the beautiful also is judged as being such not because the object itself is cognized as beautiful but only in relation to the powers of cognition whose play justifies one's judgment. Nevertheless, in the case of the sublime, the association with the object seems particularly weak. This loosened tie with the object of aesthetic judgment raises a true difficulty, because the judgment of the sublime is aesthetic according to all parameters established by Kant as the conditions of an aesthetic judgment.

This difficulty increases when we examine the relations between the sublime and the artistic object that will elicit sublimity rather than the natural one. While beauty in nature can be analogously extended to produce rich insights regarding beauty in art, it is clear that the sublime that appears in the observer's encounter with an unbounded phenomenon of nature cannot be analogously extended to the domain of art. The work of art, as much as it faithfully represents unbounded nature, is characterized by that annoying Platonic feature: it still remains too distant from the idea to be represented. Consequently, there is a burden of explanation of how, standing in front of nature as depicted by Friedrich or reading the biblical "Song on Crossing the Red Sea," we experience the sublime as Kant had envisaged. The problematic relation to the actual object does not figure uniquely in Kant. The Greek temple that serves Heidegger as a central example also is a case in point (even if Heidegger does not use the term *sublime* at any point, probably for the same reason he rejects traditional aesthetic concepts). "A building, a Greek temple, portrays nothing. It simply stands there in the middle of the rock-cleft valley. The building encloses the figure of the god." "The temple's firm towering makes visible the invisible space of air. The steadfastness of the work contrasts with the surge of the surf, and its own repose brings out the raging of the sea."[6] The temple—between the thing, the equipment, and the work—is to be identified with neither. The object enables a happening of truth that could not have occurred without it, and yet truth does not reside in the object itself.

If we follow the steps outlined by Kant, then are we bound to claim that the sublime has no object? How could we think the sublime in art or link ideas of the sublime with the artistic form? If the sublime has no object, then how can the sublime be related to a text or a picture? Is it not absurd to claim that art can exhibit the sublime? The circumstances under which the sublime is experienced in nature are such that apprehension of the object cannot be unified; these are tied by Kant to the type of affect the sublime produces in the observer—displeasure that later gives way to pleasure. "But our imagination, even in its greatest effort to do what is demanded of it and comprehend a given object in a whole of intuition, proves its own limits and inadequacy. . . . Hence the feeling of the sublime is a feeling of displeasure that arises from the imagination's inadequacy, in an aesthetic estimation of magnitude."[7] To the conflictive set of questions regarding the sublime formulated earlier we can add Kant's insistence that the dissociation of the sublime from an object of intuition, or at least the problematic relation of the sublime to the object, is what constitutes the condition for an experience of the sublime. The experience of the sublime is distinct from the experience of the beautiful concerning which the aesthetic experience is only pleasurable. For Kant, the imagination's failure in intuiting a sublime object is constitutive of the experience of the sublime as displeasing, and yet by making "intuitable for us the superiority of the rational vocation of our cognitive powers over the greatest power of sensibility,"[8] the experience of the sublime also is pleasurable.

The necessary link between the lack of object to be considered an object of the sublime and the displeasure accompanying the sublime feeling suggests the direction this chapter will take in order to solve the problem of the sublime. The object of the sublime and the reality of its occurrence should be unearthed so that the pain and suffering ascribed to the sublime can be linked to anxiety. The kind of object eventually ascribed to the sublime will motivate the identification of the affect of the sublime as anxiety. In pursuing this aim of clarifying the object of the sublime, the Lacanian notion of anxiety, that it is "*not without an object*," it will be viewed as crucial to understanding the cause of anxiety and the cause of the sublime.

The previous chapter explored the idea that anxiety is a cause, and not a resulting state. The question of what is the cause of this cause, what is the object linked to the emergence of anxiety, was examined from the point of view of psychoanalytic thought. Our present concern, however, is to tie the previous discussion of anxiety as cause to a specific problem that is constantly on the agenda of the aesthetic paradigm of thought: the problem of the sublime and its object. Anxiety is felt by the subject as a result of the subject's encounter with the Real, with an object that is not the object actually met with in reality. By reconsidering the question of the object of the sublime, following Kant and his commentators, and in light of psychoanalytic references to the "not without an object" of anxiety, the place of the object-as-cause will be articulated in connection to the sublime. The Kantian insistence on the pain endured during the experience of the sublime will thereby gain its precise location and justification.

It should be mentioned before moving on that the Lacanian construction of "not without" is a typical negative construction that he uses in various contexts. Lacan refers, for example, to the masculine condition as being "not without having it" (i.e., the phallus) and to the feminine one as being "without having it." Harari mentions this construction as what indicates the "obscure, imprecise condition of the object at hand," thus pointing to psychoanalytic thought as being uninvolved in the philosophical opposition between being and nothingness but involved in the opposition between being and having.[9] The subject is anxious because in her or his desire she or he is barred from the object that caused desire. That is, the "not without an object" not only points to the gap between what the subject desires in reality and the object that caused this desire but also to the necessary asymmetry between the subject's being identified with the object of desire and the subject having that object. Thus the subject in the male position *has* the phallus but *is not* the phallus, while the subject in the female position does *not have* the phallus and *is* yet the phallus. On Harari's interpretation, then, the "not without an object" of anxiety refers to the fact that the subject's being is determined by an object that she or he cannot have, or vice versa: she or he has an object that can only be located in the being of the Other. Anxiety is hence raised either when the subject loses sight of the object with which she or he is identified in her or his very being or when she or he approaches (and recoils) before the possibility of having that object.

Let us return to the "not without an object" of the sublime. Facing a picture of Friedrich, we see that some of his works contain an inside observer (e.g., *Two Men Contemplating the Moon,* 1830, or the well-known *Chalk Cliffs in Rugen*, 1818) *and* some do not (e.g., *Sunrise on an Empty Shore*, 1837–1839). The paradigmatic, even if occasional, use of an inside observer first suggests the idea that the object of the sublime *constitutes the observer*, that the sublime concerns an object both desired and prior to the desiring glance of the subject. In more general terms, the observing subject internal to the pictures made by Friedrich indicates the intricate relations between the subject observing the scene and the object observed; the observer is both part of the scene and excluded from it. This marks something in Kant's approach to the sublime, which is essential to what concerns the object of the (dynamically)[10] sublime in art: it is an object not feared directly but embodied in a solemn, powerful nature, somewhat removed from the observing subject. A certain distance from the actual scene of nature enables, rather than weakens, the experience of the sublime. The sublime is not experienced when immediately facing the fearful object, nor does it require complete separation from sublime nature. This measured position of the observing subject suggests that *the sublime demands optimal conditions for the cognitive power of the imagination when facing the object of nature*. In such a case, one could ask wherefrom emerges the inadequacy of the imagination described by Kant as the source of displeasure?

Given what was claimed after Gasché in chapter 1, that is, that "productive imagination transcends nature as it is given to us, by reflecting on it in a manner analogous to the way reason reflects on the manifold empirical laws,"[11] the displeasure associated with the sublime cannot simply be associated with imagination's inadequacy in confronting the power of sensible nature. The failure in attempting to grasp the object cannot simply be understood as a failure of the imagination to unify the manifold perceptions associated with the powerful nature, a failure that produces displeasure. In view of the approach to imagination, as being a faculty that in its very standing within the judgment of taste exceeds nature as it is given to us, the displeasure mounted in the encounter with the sublime cannot be simply attributed to displeasure from a failing imagination. Furthermore, if the imagination is supposed to fail in the attempt to exhibit the object sensibly, then why has Friedrich chosen to present the object of nature as optimally arranged for the subject to see yet not fear? Friedrich's pictures seem to suggest a very different structure.

The introduction of the observing subject into the sublime scene is puzzling on two accounts.[12] First, the subject observing the scene is cognitively equipped with more than sensible intuition, a fact demonstrated in the way the subject observing the scene looks self-composed and absorbed enough rather than sensuously seized. Second, the subject is positioned to overcome the incomprehensible measures of the phenomenon of nature, as he is markedly positioned at an adequate distance, neither intimidated by nature nor detached from it.

I claim here that the imagination fails with regard to an object other than the object of nature, and it is in the encounter with this other object that the experience of the sublime can be claimed to cause anxiety. A more precise grasp of the object of the sublime will be needed to account for this failure, which at the same time amounts to success in reaching the aesthetic experience of the sublime.

To grasp the core of the problem of the sublime, the fluctuations of this concept beyond Kant must be considered. The sublime is a concept that appeared in Western thought in the second half of the seventeenth century, when Longinus's "On the Sublime" was translated from the Greek, and later, in the work of Burke and Kant as part of the aesthetics of the eighteenth century. The notion of the sublime, not necessarily as an authentic aesthetic feature but as an experience that touches human Being, reappears in Schiller (*On the Sublime*) and later in Nietzsche. At the end of the twentieth century, the sublime undergoes a veritable renaissance when it finds a dominant place in the work of Lyotard, Derrida, and other postmodernists. These historical vicissitudes regarding the idea of the sublime are beyond the scope of this book in themselves, yet within the postmodernist context, a revived interest in the object of the sublime takes shape parallel to a similar revival in the context of analytic aesthetics. The latter, for many years, treated the sublime as a marginal concern in Kant's aesthetics.[13] While a marked change in the importance assigned to the sublime is evident in aesthetic discussions from the 1980s onward, a parallel interest in the sublime is noticeable in post-modern theorizing.

In general, the postmodern interest in the sublime is formulated as a question regarding what cannot be said or represented and yet is included in representation. The sublime serves Lyotard, for instance, as the ultimate case of the unpresentable which, in its postmodern version, is put into presentation itself to mark the "lack of reality," which is the raison d'être of any modernism.[14] The sublime is thus the mode appropriate for modernism, as it has to do with Ideas "of which no presentation is possible. Therefore they impart no knowledge about reality. . . . They can be said to be unpresentable." In this one can recognize the axioms of avant-gardes in painting "inasmuch as they devote themselves to making an allusion to the unpresentable by means of visible presentations."[15] For Lyotard, in order to understand the artistic systems of a sublime vocation, one should relate to these practices as originating in the incommensurability of reality to concept, implied in the Kantian philosophy of the sublime. That is, Lyotard takes the Kantian sublime as a metaphor for the entire postmodern agenda. But how can this incommensurability of reality to concept be structured in less general terms appropriate for the sublime? What are its unique coordinates?

THE SUBLIME IS NOT WITHOUT AN OBJECT

Whether the Kantian sublime, as it has come to play a leading role in postmodern discourse, is truly compatible with the aesthetic thought of the eighteenth century is beside the point.[16] What does pertain to the issue at hand is that postmodern philosophers take the sublime, as presented in Kant, to be linked to "derealization," and with innovative ways of making the Idea of the unpresentable presentable (by the use of pictorial techniques, in the case of painting, and of textual techniques, in the case of literature). There is ostensibly something of the impossible in the sublime and in its exhibition in and through signifying structures.

To explain this idea of the sublime, we can refer to Derrida's conception of the unpresentable as stemming from the necessary presence of a *limit* in every signifying system. Limit in this context is equated with a framing, a delineated boundary, with the margins of a discourse. In the context of his study of the truth in painting, Derrida concentrates on the Kantian notion of the "colossal" that appears in the analytic of the sublime (in connection to the mathematical sublime). The colossal is sublime for Kant, as it is almost too great for presentation, too great for one's faculty of perception. The colossal, says Derrida, is an image of something, "a presentation of something which can be taken without being able to be taken, in hand or eye."[17] From then on the sublime "crushes you, throws you down while elevating you at the same time, since you can take it in view without taking it in your hand, without comprehending it."[18] For Derrida, the aesthetic evaluation of "beyond measure" reaches its subjective maximum, which constitutes an "absolute reference," and it is this idea of the absolute that elicits the experience of the sublime. The "colossal" thus serves Derrida in order to point to the referent of the sublime as being present in the image that is split between the presentation and between what is too great, almost too great to be presented. The colossal, claims Derrida, is unlimited in the very thing that comes to appear or to be presented through the colossal.

The colossal, although not deriving from art or from culture, nevertheless has nothing natural about it. "The *cise* [a neologism from Derrida] of the colossus is neither culture nor nature but culture and nature. It is perhaps, between the presentable and the unpresentable, the passage from the one to the other as much as the irreducibility of the one to the other."[19] The colossal has a sublime quality because it comes to stand for the limit itself, for what is most authentically unclassifiable in terms of presentation.

Derrida links the presentation to what is unpresentable in the colossal, and this duality of what is measured without measure has to do with the splitting effect that the colossal has on any schematization. The rupture that the colossal introduces into the signifying notion of size serves Derrida as the center of his discussion of the sublime. It should be noted in this context that, for Kant, the colossal and the monstrous are not cases of the pure sublime, as the case of the colossal is that of exhibiting a concept, a concept "almost too large for exhibition," whereas the sublime is a case that has "no purpose whatsoever of the object as the basis determining it."[20]

Derrida points to the object of the sublime as an object inhabiting, by its being a mark of a limit, the split between the apprehendable, and what evades apprehension. The object of the sublime is the object designated by the "almost too," by the rupture between being presented and being too great for presentation. With Derrida as a point of departure, we can come closer to grasping the significance of aesthetic anxiety being "not without an object." It is interesting to mention in this context Alenka Zupančič's claim that Kant himself, in the third critique, develops the four moments of the judgment of taste as evolving around four signifiers of lack: "Beauty is 'liking without interest,' 'universality without concept,' 'purposiveness without purpose,' and 'necessity without concept.' Kant's basic operation in these definitions consists in what one might call essential subtraction; in each of the definitions Kant deprives the first notion exactly of that which is considered to be its essential characterization."[21] Both Derrida and Zupančič refer to the object of aesthetic judgment as being in between presence and absence. The evasive object of aesthetic judgment lures us in the "Analytic of the Beautiful" as much as it eludes us in the "Analytic of the Sublime."

Kant himself, as we saw earlier, rejected the idea that the object of the sublime is the object of fierce nature encountered without mediation. And yet the sublime, even if not caused by an actual scene of nature, must have an object in front of which the limitedness of the imagination would become evident and painful. Likewise, the object of anxiety is not an object in reality, yet anxiety is not without an object. This observation can be clarified through the distinction between *anxiety* and *fear* originally made by Freud, and later revised by Lacan. Freud, in "Inhibitions, Symptoms, and Anxiety," claims that anxiety is "about something," and at the same time "it has a quality of *indefiniteness and lack of object*." We use, however, fear rather than anxiety when "it has found an object."[22] Freud hence distinguishes between fear that has an object and anxiety that has an object, yet such an object that has the quality of indefiniteness.

Lacan, unlike Freud, distinguishes fear from anxiety by claiming that fear has no object, while anxiety is "not without an object." In his seminar on anxiety, Lacan gives the example of a story by Chekhov called "Frights." A young boy riding his sled along a plane, suddenly apprehends in the distance a church tower, at a range that could reasonably make the details discernible, and from the tower erupts an inexplicable flame. It is on a very high story of the church tower, which he knows there is no way anyone can gain entry into. Moreover, he cannot attribute the flame to any effect of reflection, and after having made a short reckoning of what could or could not account for the fire, and having excluded every kind of known cause, he is all of the sudden gripped by fright. "What he is afraid of is not anything that *threatens* him; it is something which has precisely this character of referring to the unknown."[23] Fear does not refer to an object but to something unknown; fear has no object, which is why reacting to fear by running away is irrelevant. This may indicate in preliminary terms why the sublime cannot correspond to fear, why Friedrich's young man surveying the storming sea does not look fearful. Being intimidated by the waves of the ocean, being terrified by an imaginary unknown threat, and dreading the familiar object or figure that suddenly appears as strange and menacing are experiences that do not involve the same object. It can be said that *fear camouflages the object that affects the subject, while anxiety exposes it.*

To clarify this point, I refer to the psychoanalytic approach to *inhibition.* Inhibition is defined by Freud as the decrease in a function, such as the function of walking or of writing. Inhibition, Lacan claims, is in its very essence a way to suspend or disguise desire.[24] Inhibition grips the subject in an inverse desire, the desire "not to go," for the hysterical subject whose legs become paralyzed, or the desire "not to write" for the writer suffering a block. Inhibition hence suspends and disguises the fact that the leg or hand is already seized in another desire, aiming to retain this other object of desire by inhibiting the action. So inhibition that appears as an impediment to action is in itself an act, which camouflages its relation to the object of desire. Inhibition, by presenting the object that causes desire (related to walking or writing) as if it was an object of fear, succeeds in removing it from sight by preventing action. Thus it could be claimed that just as desire could be structurally occluded behind inhibition, so anxiety could be structurally occluded behind fear. The act executed by inhibiting an action is that of occluding the object-cause-of-desire. The affect raised by the object-cause-of-desire is occluded by a fear seemingly directed to an object, which has in fact an unknown source.

It is for this reason that an act can be considered countering anxiety, just as in the case of acting out, discussed in chapter 4. We fear and flee something, we act as inhibited or detained in our action, and in that we camouflage "another field" in which our desire is realized, a field that causes the subject's anxiety. When an action inscribes the gap of desire, that is, when "there is manifested in [the action] the very desire which is supposed to have been designed to inhibit it,"[25] then we speak about an act as a defense against anxiety. The artist desires to produce a work of art but is inhibited in her or his actions (i.e., she or he has writer's cramp or painter's block). The artist's hand being captured in the desire that aims to retain the object (the hand itself has become an erotogenic object of satisfaction) is inhibited in its action, and it thereby camouflages the cause of anxiety which, according to Lacan, has to do with a certain relation of the subject to the object-cause-of-desire. As long as the cause of desire is camouflaged, anxiety is blocked out. Anxiety is raised in front of the possibility that the object produced is cedeable, that it can be dissociated or lost from the Other, a possibility that an act of inhibition can circumvent. By inhibiting action, yet acting on another level, the subject retains the object, thus enabling him or her not to face the possibility that the object is let to drop. The artist blocked in his or her creation, suffering from an inhibition, thus retains the object and avoids anxiety. It is in similar terms that the fear, as if directed to a definite object or event, can camouflage the "not without an object" of anxiety.

So Kant, in his ambivalent dependence on the object of nature, Derrida, with the "almost too" of the colossal, and Lacan, in his formulation of "not without an object," supply sufficient ground for further developing our investigation into the object of the sublime. There is an object to the sublime, yet this object is occluded by the impressive apparition of a fearsome nature.[26]

THE OBJECT OF THE SUBLIME

Derrida has shown that the sublime does not appear where the object has stopped being relevant, nor is the sublime produced when the subject has encountered an object of immensity. Rather, the sublime is the consequence of a certain relation that exists between the presentable and that which cannot be exhibited. Two examples will illustrate the sublime in art, examples that reveal something crucial about the object of the sublime, although they cannot be said to refer to a magnitude in any sense. They do, however, answer the conditions under which Kant identifies the affect of the sublime.

The first literary example is from James Joyce"s story "The Dead."[27] One crucial and typical aspect of Joyce's writing is that the characters in his stories undergo *an epiphany*, a moment of enlightenment or revelation. These epiphanies, however, occur around extremely mundane, trivial, common events. There is something about this apparent insignificance that exposes or reveals another truth that the literary character faces at an unexpected moment, and precisely through this flat insignificance of the scene the moment of revelation can materialize.

In "The Dead," toward the end of the story, the reader is told of an accidental moment when the hero, Gabriel, standing at the bottom of the staircase at the end of the annual party at his elderly aunt's house, an insipid situation by any standard, is looking up the staircase, watching his wife, who is unaware of his presence and regard.

> He was in a dark part of the hall gazing up the staircase. A woman was standing near the top of the first flight, in the shadow also. He could not see her face but he could see the terra-cotta and salmon-pink panels of her skirt which the shadow made appear black and white. It was his wife. She was leaning on the banisters, listening to something . . .
>
> She was standing right under the dusty fanlight and the flame of the gas lit up the rich bronze of her hair, which he had seen her drying at the fire a few days before. She was in the same attitude and seemed unaware of the talk about her. . . . A sudden tide of joy went leaping out of his heart.[28]

The story accentuates the lack of continuity between the standard mental moving along in which Gabriel is usually engaged with his calculations, his prosaic occupation with details, and so on and the present outburst that seems to arrive from nowhere, causing a radical turnabout (stylistically and essentially) in the hero's position. This outburst, which seems to gush from a certain gap opening in the mundane scene, is very typical of Joyce's writing.

The second visual example is in fact a response to a visual example. Lacan's final work, written before his death, was dedicated to the work of a French artist, one of Lacan's acquaintances. For the occasion of an exhibition of François Rouan, the artist, Lacan wrote an intricate, rather enigmatic text, dedicated more to topology[29] than to Rouan's art, yet through which allows for a preliminary glimpse of the psychoanalytic sublime. Although in his last work, Lacan had already written about the art of painting. Well known are his references to Holbein's *The Ambassadors* (Seminar XI), Velásquez's *Las Maninas* (Seminar XIII), Caravaggio's *The Sacrifice of Isaac* (seminar on "The Names of the Father"), Jacopo Zucchi's *Eros and Psyche* (Seminar VIII), and Munch's *The Scream* (Seminar XII). It is curious to note that with regard to Rouan, perhaps because here he is dealing with a case of a living rather than a dead artist, Lacan has some suggestions for improvements.[30] Lacan's basic claim is that Rouan paints *bands,* while he should have painted *braids*. Lacan compares these two modes of painting, indicating that in a scheme of bands "the little holes do not exist. The bands are married."[31] The twists of the braid, however, constitute a Borromean chain. In the case of bands, the flatness makes no use of the dimensionality effect, while braids are a projection of three-dimensionality, determining its own limits and producing unexpected and impossible spaces when topologically analyzed. Thus it could be said that the braid allows the impossible object to appear, a fact shown by Lacan through the topological possibilities of representing the braid and its twists. Lacan shows how the shift from three-dimensionality to two-dimensionality brings on a radical change, although it is difficult to locate this change. For instance, the way of untying the braid changes (how the braid unties when one of its knots is loosened). When the braid is flattened, its whole structure changes, and it becomes decomposed (Figure 5.1). Rouan, according to Lacan, misses the object represented, does not allow the object to appear and, in this sense, we can argue, does not create the possibility for an aesthetic experience (Figure 5.2).

In these illustrations we can see Rouan's original composition and Lacan's way of representing it when "redone" as a braid.

Both examples exhibit the idea of the object as appearing in the place of a rupture or split, in the discrepancy between what is exhibited of the object and the "almost too great" for exhibition. To further explore this notion of object, both in the critique of Rouan and in Joyce, and to develop the

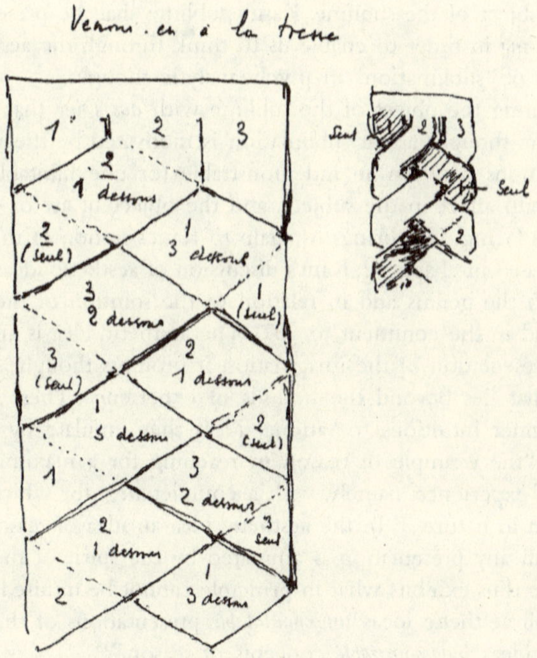

Figure 5.1. Jacques Lacan. Drawing from Catalogue de l'exposition François Rouan. 1978. © Musée Cantini, Marseille.

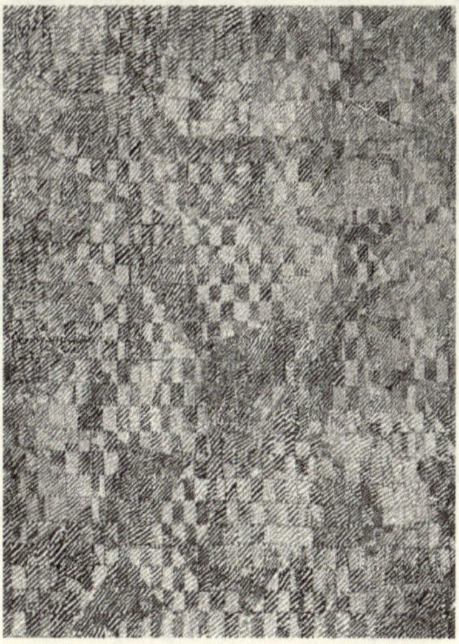

Figure 5.2. François Rouan (b. 1943). *Tressage quatre toils, gris, bleu et blanc.* 1967–1969. © 2007 Artists Rights Society (ARS), New York / ADAGP, Paris.

idea of the object of the sublime, Kant's sublime shall be presented vis-à-vis Lacan's *das Ding* in order to enable us to think through the aesthetic sublime and the idea of "sublimation" in psychoanalytic thought.

Associating the object of the sublime with *das Ding* that figures in the psychoanalytic thought about sublimation is motivated by the need to structure the relations between an indemonstrable (or unexhibitable) object that causes a certain affect in the subject, and the object of art or of nature that the subject is facing. This brings us again to Kant's notion of the *aesthetic idea*, already discussed in chapter 2. Kant's discussion of aesthetic ideas appears both in relation to the genius and in relation to the solution of the antinomy of taste (§49 and in the comment to §57). The aesthetic idea is an idea because through a presentation of the imagination it prompts thought, strives toward something that lies beyond the bounds of experience. These are ideas also because as inner intuitions to rational ideas they emulate by means of the imagination "the example of reason in reaching for a maximum . . . beyond the limits of experience, namely, with a completeness for which no example can be found in nature."[32] In the aesthetic idea an idea of reason that cannot be intuited in any presentation is animated by the spirit of the imagination. The aesthetic thus exhibits what in principle cannot be intuited by the senses: "We may call aesthetic ideas *unexpoundable* presentations of the imagination, and rational ideas *indemonstrable* concepts of reason."[33]

Although aesthetic ideas are not mentioned as part of untying the intricate case of the sublime, the notion of *aesthetic idea* yet posits at the heart of Kantian aesthetics an impossible object: an imaginative form that aims at the impossible task of exhibiting something of a concept of reason. Thus while *magnitude* can be given in the a priori intuition of space,[34] absolute magnitude, with which the sublime is concerned, cannot be given in such an intuition, and yet absolute magnitude is somehow exhibited in one's experience of the sublime. Aesthetic presentation, as practiced by the poet or the genius, is a way of intuiting an object in a form that can exhibit an Idea to which no presentation is adequate.[35] The aesthetic idea that figured in Kant and in the work of his commentators and followers also has served Thierry de Duve in his attempt to account for the modernist object of art after Duchamp, in terms of the *indemonstrable.* This use of the aesthetic idea is mentioned here because de Duve succeeds to stress in his approach to art after Duchamp how the indemonstrable idea of reason can figure in the certainty of a judgment of taste, although the object of judgment cannot be said to exhibit anything in particular, that is, a work of art that cannot be said to exhibit anything imaginative (a bicycle wheel, for instance) yet brings with certainty to this presentation an idea of reason—the idea that "art is a proper name" (rather than a concept). This point concerning aesthetic ideas will prove crucial to our present concerns. In reference to the antinomy of taste in Kant, de

Duve formulates the solution of the antinomy in terms of the discrepancy between art as a determinate concept of understanding (to which we can find examples in the field of experience) and as an indemonstrable Idea of reason, which no particular instance can exhibit, to further think of the modernist object of art after Duchamp.[36] An idea of reason cannot be theoretically proven, since it is "inexponible," and it cannot be empirically shown, since it is "indemonstrable," "but it can be exemplified analogically at the hand of any object designated by the word 'this' in the sentence 'this is art.' Therefore, by referring to Duchamp's urinal as 'this is art,' I endorse a certain Idea of modern or avant-garde art that is not only indeterminate but stands for its own indeterminacy."[37] With this move, de Duve stresses the fact that at the heart of Kantian aesthetics, no less than at the heart of modernist art, there stands an impossible object, an object that demonstrates the indemonstrable by exhibiting a crucial Idea of reason presented with spirit in a sensible form that resists theorization.

De Duve mediates the object of art that apparently lacks distinctly aesthetic qualities with the fact that a Rembrandt, just as much as Duchamp's urinal, constitutes spirited presentations of a rational idea that require the work of genius to be demonstrated. In that he reveals through the solution of Kant's antinomy that at the heart of the third critique we encounter an object qualified as the *supersensible substratum*, whose relevance to aesthetic judgment can only be suggested through the presence of an actual object or image that fails in its imaginary function.

This brings us to the psychoanalytic notion of "the Thing" (*das Ding*), an object called for to explicate the mechanism of sublimation. I will show that sublimation can be applicable to the dilemma regarding the object of the sublime. Sublimation in psychoanalysis pertains to the relation this object maintains with objects of nature (or art), on the one hand, and with an unexhibitable Idea of reason, on the other hand. The psychoanalytic thought around the real object named *das Ding* can be shown to be congruent with Kant's thought about the object of aesthetic judgment. The aforementioned presentation of aesthetic ideas, particularly in the way they figure in de Duve's approach to modernism, can indicate that aesthetic judgment, whether of the beautiful or of the sublime, equally faces an object that raises the problem of the unexhibitable and the unexpoundable. The notion of "aesthetic idea" suggests an object that cannot be exhibited by the imagination (and is hence not identifiable with the artistic or natural image), nor explained in signifying terms (and is hence not identifiable with a theoretical concept of reason). Aesthetic ideas play a role in every aesthetic judgmental act, functioning as a kind of bridge between the image seen and the Thing thereby exhibited.

It is in this direction that Derrida's reading of Kantian sublime can be diagnosed, and it is in this spirit that Gasché orients his reading of Kant's

Critique of Judgment.[38] Gasché does not hold a canonical position among Kant's commentators, some of whom establish a view of the sublime as strictly relating an act of judgment to an object of direct experience. Guyer, for instance, claims that Kant was mistaken in thinking that no particular object can function as a grammatical subject in a judgment of the sublime: "Kant seems wrong to suppose that the formlessness of that which makes us aware of sublimity disqualifies it from being the grammatical subject of an aesthetic judgment."[39] The vastness of an object of nature, even if ungraspable by the imagination without the aid of reason, "is certainly as objective a property of as ordinary an object (or collection of objects) as the delicacy of a flower or the regularity of a frieze."[40] There is no substantial difference between the force of a storm or the extent of the mountain and the delicacy of a flower in this respect. Guyer has strong reservations regarding the distinction made by Kant between the beautiful and the sublime in terms of the causal link between the aesthetic judgment and the object in reality. Guyer finds that Kant errs in presenting a difference in phenomenology (an appearance of unlimitedness responsible for the feeling of sublimity raises a feeling that allows one to pick out the proper object) and grammatical practicability as an ultimate difference in ontology.[41] The fact that we cannot tie the feeling of the sublime to a particular object means that the object of the sublime does not possess the same purposive form as the beautiful object (its purposiveness is indeterminate); it does not mean that aesthetic judgments are of two kinds: the judgment of the beautiful has an object, while the judgment of the sublime does not. According to Guyer, considering the judgment of the sublime in ontological terms diverts us from the domain of reflective judgments in which the subjectivity of experience leans on a necessary link with the purposiveness of the form of an object, even if this purposiveness is not conceptually determined. Our pleasure in the dynamical sublime "depends upon the way in which physically fearsome natural phenomena turn our thought to the indestructible moral personality which lies within us. The physical properties play a causal role in this reflection," even if the property of sublimity should be attributed to our own moral character.[42]

While Guyer reconstitutes the concrete object of nature as an object of sublimity, Gasché adopts a very different approach. He shows how the absence of form in the object of sublimity is what enables a judgment of taste rather than what hinders it. This must be a formlessness of a certain kind, since where form is merely lacking, the judgment of taste is excluded as aesthetically irrelevant: a merely formless thing is found ugly and in no way suggests sublimity. The sublime has an essence of its own. The formlessness proper to the sublime is one accompanied by the thought of totality. "Boundless chaos is not enough to suggest sublimity; it must be such that it allows thinking to add totality to it."[43] Gasché adds that had Kant's terminology not prohibited it, one would have been inclined to say that *"boundless formlessness must have the 'form' of a whole, in order for it to be sublime."*[44] To answer the question of how totality can be added to absence of form, Gasché returns to the objects of nature as constituting the domain where judgments of the sublime are executed. The sublime relates to reason and morality not only because it is a presentation of an Idea of reason but because the sublime is a case in which the thought about totality (i.e., about an Idea of reason) is *added* to the presentation of intuition. Hence, the aesthetic judgment of the sublime is, according to Gasché, moral on more than one account or, more precisely, also on account of the overall intricate structure of this aesthetic judgment. How can this morality of judgment be demonstrated?

Absence of form in this presentation, in this exhibition, is so far reaching that it defies all attempts at subsuming it under the powers of cognition. "By finding totality in boundless formlessness, a representation that is infinitely rebellious against all cognition is nonetheless found to agree with the faculty of reason."[45] Hence, the presentation of the sublime takes place at moments when a given thing not only cannot be subsumed under given concepts but refuses even to be a presentation of the powers of cognition in general. Gasché builds the intricate case of the sublime so that *both negative pleasure and the resistance of the given thing to cognitive totalization are taken to be irreducible in the final operation of the judgment of the sublime.* The agitation and turbulence characteristic of the sublime hence constitute the essence of the sublime, since this agitation testifies that "even though the formless object thwarts the powers of cognition, it does not bring the mind to a final halt . . . it is the pleasure involved in feeling that the mind is still in business at all."[46]

Gasché concludes that judgments of the sublime are not *about* the formlessness of nature, because these judgments defy "aboutness"—that is, objectification—by their very definition. "What is judged sublime is the mind's capacity to form an apprehension of something that thwarts even the possibility of minimal objectification."[47] Paradoxically, it is the defiance of objectification that constitutes the condition for judgments of the sublime. By demonstrating the necessary link of the sublime to formless totality, Gasché indicates that the sublime is not a way of going beyond the object but rather of going through the object. Only an object that defies any objectification, even the most minimal one, can be associated with the judgment of the sublime. The sublime is produced beyond any imaginary relations between presentation and the forms of nature; it is not about these forms. It is where the object of nature, the wide ocean disturbed by a storm in its horrible magnitude, defies totalization and is yet totalized by the supersensible faculty of reason.

Gasché emphasizes the place of the object defying measure for which a totalizing thought must be found. Thus he directs us back to Kant and to the link between imagination and reason in the experience of the sublime. Instead of interpreting the sublime as the moment in which reason gains the upper hand, after imagination has failed to totalize the manifold of apprehensions, Gasché claims that the sublime resides in this very failure of imagination in its agitated state, not in overcoming this failure by the power of reason. The power of reason is not a mode of compensation for the limit of imagination. Indeed, the phenomenon of nature that has caused imagination to fail brings on the recognition that reason, as an intellectual measure, can achieve what imagination has lost on another register. Yet the moment of negative pleasure, of pain in the experience of the sublime, is not motivated by failure. Gasché does not aim to rescue the prestige of the imagination but rather attempts to show that pain does not result from the failure of the cognitive faculty of the imagination. The pain suffered by the imagination in its not being up to the task of intuiting a given magnitude into a whole is a pain that can be felt only because imagination obeys the laws of reason from the very outset. "In its failed quest for a fundamental aesthetic measure, the imagination already seeks to realize the law of reason.... This pain is therefore not simply pain; it is inextricably linked with the realization of the imagination's supersensible destination."[48] The pleasure in the sublime is not a pleasure in the removal of inadequate imagination, nor is displeasure a reflection of this failure. The affect of the sublime is in its very essence caused by the constitutive bond between reason and imagination. We cannot but surmise that the formlessness of the object that elicits sublimity should not be overcome or eliminated by the idea of totality that reason offers. This would be a totally misleading picture of the place of the sublime in the cognitive play of faculties.

Gasché's method of approaching the paradoxical relations between sublimity and the formless phenomenon of nature can be simply added to Kant's repertoire of illustrations for the sublime, which include man-made objects such as St. Peter's Cathedral and the pyramids, as well as events of nature. Kant, we know, illustrates the sublime with examples from both domains, although he explicitly insists that the sublime can only be reasonably associated with a wild nature.[49] A purposive use that the imagination makes of the presentation of nature both leans on the formlessness of the object (whether of nature or of culture) and transcends the object's lack of purposiveness. To apprehend the case of the sublime, we need to analyze the structural relations between the object that lacks form, and the thought about totality, so that through this structure, the object we may call sublime (the paradoxical object of totalized formlessness) can emerge. In the context of the sublime, the need to examine the relations between the object in reality and the Idea of totality must send us through the phenomenon of nature or culture, yet to an object that cannot be identified with either of these phenomena. The thought about totality is impossible without the phenomenon of nature or culture. Gasché, in other words, succeeds to anchor the idea of the sublime in an irreducible object that possesses a real presence, and upon which the emergence of the thought about totality is dependent.

SUBLIMATION AND THE TOTALITY OF THE THING

What does psychoanalytic sublimation have to do with the aesthetic sublime, beyond what seems like an arbitrary similarity in sound? Freud associated sublimation with the reality of drives, the very same domain Kant saw as pathological, and as a domain that should best be suppressed wherever the power of reason is at issue. How can we still justify describing the object of the sublime in terms of the object of the drives?[50]

Sublimation enabled Freud to discern, in what concerns the drive,[51] the *aim* of the drive from the *object* of the drive. The *aim* of the drive is always satisfaction, but although this aim is unchangeable, the path to satisfaction can vary. The drive, Freud acknowledges, may be *inhibited in its aim*, and yet this inhibition does not prevent satisfaction. The *object* of the drive is that in regard to which satisfaction is achieved. The object, peculiarly enough, is not originally connected to the drive but is assigned to satisfaction as what befits the satisfaction sought. The object, moreover, "may be changed any number of times in the course of the vicissitudes which the instinct undergoes during its existence; and highly important parts are played by this displacement of instinct."[52] The drive can change its object, it can merge with another drive in one object, or it can be fixated on one object. All of these options equally point to the simultaneously necessary and contingent relation between the drive and its object. Freud further claims, regarding the object of the drive as it is employed in defense modes, that although the object of drive can be located in a body organ of the subject, the object is in fact always different from that organ.[53]

In his essay "On Narcissism" from 1914, Freud distinguishes *sublimation* from *idealization* in the working of the drive and claims that in sublimation it is not the object of drive that is at issue but only the aim of the drive that is diverted from sexual satisfaction, directed to an aim "other than, and remote from, that of sexual satisfaction." In the case of idealization, the object "without any alteration in its nature is aggrandized and exalted in the subject's mind."[54] In idealization, the change is in the overvaluation of an object; in sublimation, satisfaction is achieved but in an inhibited way, through an alternative, inhibited path. Sublimation is hence one of the defense modes against the drives.

The concept of sublimation in many ways remained preliminary with Freud and was much expanded and developed by Lacan, especially in his seminar on ethics, in which Lacan investigates these two possible moves of the drive: idealization and sublimation. It will be claimed here, following the psychoanalytic analysis of sublimation, that the sublime comes across its object even if this object must be precisely qualified. It is an object that is not a substitute for an inaccessible, indemonstrable object but an object that is *itself* elevated to the place of the Thing, an object that exhibits the impossible totality (of reason for Kant; of the drive for Freud and Lacan). No empirical object, no representation, can present the Thing (the supersensible Idea), but the sublime is an object in which one can experience this very impossibility.[55] That is, the significance of the object of the sublime, the thing posited before one's powers of cognition, is that this object is not a partial representative of a totality, but rather the object of the sublime is precisely what stands as the signifier of this very totality. In line with Gasché's reading, I claim that the object of the sublime is there in its immeasurable magnitude, itself irreducible and indispensable: "Only when it [the mind] is unsuccessful at aesthetically comprehending an object of nature does the imagination become aware of another, nonsensible standard for measurement in the mind; and the phenomenon of nature that caused the imagination to fail then becomes the indirect presentation of that standard."[56] This entails, claims Gasché after Kant, that the sublime does not lie in the magnitude of the natural object that the imagination vainly attempts to comprehend aesthetically but rather in the "supersensible substrate" that is awakened in the mind during the attempt at estimating this magnitude. The magnitude and its totalization are to be attributed to an object to which Kant referred as the "supersensible substrate," that is, what underlies nature is the object of theoretical reason given through the capacity of cognition to exhibit sensibly. This object is determinable yet is great beyond all standards, hence is not determined. It is in this way that the representation of unbound nature can give rise to an object of reason. Sublimity, we can conclude, suggests *elevation of unbound nature to the order of reason.*

It is in view of this analysis that the satisfaction in the sublime is bound to the "almost too great for the standards of sense," characterizing sublime scenes of nature, and hence is also bound to the pain felt in this experience. It is additionally evident that as much as the object of the sublime defies objectification, the sublime is not without an object. While judgments upon the sublime are not "about" nature, they arise "in response to spectacles that inhibit all possible objectification."[57] This intricate relation of nature's spectacle to the judgment of the sublime is our concern here and will be described later in relation to sublimation.

Had Rouan painted braids, the topological form that cannot be intuited would have appeared in the braid itself. The braid is not a replacement, not a partial substitute, but is what exhibits the very rupture that topology reveals to us in its dealings with impossible shapes. Nor should we think of Joyce as creating a linkage between flat moments and moments of revelation, of enlightment. Just as the braid itself exhibits the impossible shape of topology and is thus elevated to the status of a topological form, so the trivial moment is itself elevated to the status of epiphany. It is through such objects elevated to the position of *das Ding* that the "not without an object" of the sublime can be clarified. How is this braid, this trivial moment of everydayness, this chaotic nature, elevated to the place of *das Ding*? What is the nature of the totalization suggested by the Thing?

In Seminar VII, Lacan notes that Freud himself had already denied the possibility of unifying the drives.[58] The network of drives (the oral and the anal), appears to be unified at a certain moment, in what is called the genital organization. However, this unity or totality is mere fiction. Drives, being extremely versatile and plastically related to one another and to possibilities of satisfaction, cannot be unified. Inhibiting one drive can result in the satisfaction of another drive; one drive can replace another drive, and so on. Sexuality, or total satisfaction of the drive, is present in every motion of a drive but never as absolute or complete. Partiality is the fate of every satisfaction, although it does not imply lack of satisfaction, or that satisfaction itself is reduced or substitutive. Satisfaction will just take a different route than the original one between drive and aim and yet will always attain its goal.

Sublimation is related to this plasticity of the drives, and sublimation therefore cannot possibly be complete. "There is something that cannot be sublimated; libidinal demand exists, the demand for a certain dose, of a certain level of direct satisfaction, without which harm results."[59]

Sublimation, then, as what serves the plasticity of the drives in their insistence on satisfaction, even if inhibited in its aim, does not cover completely its instinctual source. That is, the psychic mechanism of sublimation allows satisfaction through an aim different from what the drive was striving for originally, yet something of this original aim retains its real presence.

Furthermore, "Sublimation is represented as distinct from that economy of substitution in which the repressed drive is usually satisfied."[60] Although the drive is able to find its satisfaction elsewhere than in that which is its original aim, this is not attained through a compromise formation. The satisfaction of the drive, then, paradoxically occurs elsewhere than where its aim is, and yet the libidinal source of the drive remains irreducible and unchanged. The primary wishes of the child, from his mother, for instance, create a core that cannot be decomposed, no matter how much one insists on representing these wishes or demands through acceptable social structures. The libidinal investment of the drive hence cannot be totalized in terms of genital sexuality, whether male or female. These are but forms of satisfaction we have adopted in our mature body, yet something of the primordial libido of the drive and its original aim remains through all substitutive formations or symbolic representations we use. Sublimation is what refers to this irreducible original drive through its inhibited aim. While the drive can settle on different goals, different partial, substitutive objects, the object of the drive has a different status. Whether we drink cola or spring water is only a matter of substitutive relations, yet the object of the drive, *the totality of satiation*, is an object that cannot be inhibited in its aim, and it retains its presence as the *Thing* signifying the original aim of the drive. The object elevated to this place of the Thing is the object, therefore, that rather than functioning as a substitute, it retains something of this irreducible, libidinal investment in the "original" object of satisfaction.

This irreducibility of the object of the drive also is marked by Freud in "Three Essays on Sexuality," where he observes that the activity of the sexual impulses does not cease even during the period of latency, though energy is diverted, wholly or in great part, from sexual use and directed to other ends.[61] "This enables excessively strong excitations arising from particular sources of sexuality to find an outlet and use in other fields."[62] Since during this period sexual impulses cannot be utilized, and would in themselves seem perverse (as do impulses that arise from erotogenic zones and derive their activity directly from the instincts), they arouse unpleasurable feelings.[63] It can be seen that sublimation does not change the sexual nature of the drive, nor does it change the essence of the satisfaction it requires. Sublimation has an immediate relation rather than a displaced one with satisfaction (conversely, satisfaction in a symptom can be displaced, for example, from masturbation to a hysterical paralyzation of the hand). In sublimation, substitute satisfaction is not possible, and for this reason *sublimation touches the very source of sexual drives*. For Freud, the force of creativity (in art, history, and other domains) has to do with this mechanism of inhibiting the drive that settles on socially and culturally valued objects while retaining the libidinal source of the drive. Works of art therefore constitute direct, rather than compromised, formations, and the satisfaction they allow, although sublimated, retains something of its instinctual source, which is the inevitable cause of displeasure in sublimated satisfaction.

How does the object of social consensus lead to direct satisfaction? This is a crucial point the answer to which can support Gasché's approach that the pleasure in the sublime is not to be conceived as a circuitous later phase in the experience of the sublime. The libidinal core retained in every sublimation can be the psychoanalytic answer to this problem, as it shows that the *satisfaction (pleasure) in the social structures, the satisfaction derived from sublimation, is bound to the displeasure associated with the irreducible libidinal source.*

The case of narcissism can illustrate this point. Narcissism marks the phenomena of love to an object as dependent on the object-of-love replaceability with the image of the ideal ego. The case of narcissism is intimately related to sublimation, as Freud himself ties sublimation to the power of visual fascination, to the imaginary hold of the image on the subject ("Visual impressions remain the most frequent pathway along which libidinal excitation is aroused. . . . It can however be diverted, 'sublimated,' in the direction of art").[64] The distance between the image of the ego and its constitution in an external ideal as an object of love is where sublimation appears, that is, in the diversion to an ideal, imaginary object that retains something of the autoerotic impulse toward the image of the ego.

Lacan also refers to the mirage of the relation between the ego and its external ideal; it is an imaginary mirage because the ideal gives form, within the subject, not to the ego but to another object to which the subject henceforth submits. "It is through this mirage relation that the notion of an object is introduced. But this object is not the same as that which is aimed at on the horizon of the instinct. Between the object as it is structured by the narcissistic relation and *das Ding,* there is a difference, and it is precisely on the slope of that difference that the problem of sublimation is situated for us."[65] Sublimation provides the drive with satisfaction different from its aim, because sublimation has a relationship to *das Ding,* to the Thing as distinct from the object. It is precisely this relation to the Thing that places sublimation, as well as the aesthetic sublime, beyond the pleasure principle, where anxiety in front of the Thing is imbued with satisfaction.

Sublimation is located between the narcissistic object and the Thing. At its foundations, sublimation retains the primary loss, the culturally imposed loss of an object, which is why in sublimation one cannot distinguish the Thing from its social-cultural imaginary adaptation. The imaginary object in sublimation—whether in the form of the ideal ego, in the image of the lady of the knights in medieval culture, or in the formless sublime object of nature—constitutes a place of momentary repose in the company of *das Ding,* a moment in which the subject attains the domain of instinctual satisfaction by means of imaginary schemes.

So for Lacan the Freudian *das Ding* can be recruited to locate the object of sublimation, to show that sublimation is not without an object, and yet its object cannot be identified with the imaginary presentation. Sublimation creates forms, various forms such as those made in art, forms that correspond to socially accepted values. Sublimation is hence located in between the imaginary object of social recognition and appraisal and the aim of the drive that moves as it pleases, directing itself to satisfaction, even if inhibited in its aim, because fundamentally, the object in the diverted path can satisfy directly.

After Freud, the drive knows not of moderate satisfaction, nor of a partial one. It is only symbolically, through substitution that regulates man's relation to his social surrounding, that moderation can be imposed. This is why Freud claimed with regard to perversion that extreme perversions and socially acceptable ones, even if the former are much more disgusting and seemingly abnormal than the latter, equally demonstrate the sexual bend of the instinctual path.[66] The paradoxical fact is that the drive, the instinctual source of a subject's moving along, the drive that gives this moving along its necessary perverse bent, can be satisfied through sublimation, through an aim other than its original one. The drive inhibited in its aim is not diverted, it does not substitute *das Ding* (unlike the signifier or the symptom as compromise formations) for another object, but only "the object is elevated to the dignity of the Thing."[67]

Satisfaction is hence possible not because the aim has become desexualized, as Freud was erroneously interpreted to have claimed, but because sublimation satisfies the drive elsewhere than where its true nature is constituted. Sublimation holds a critical relation to the Thing, to the Thing that an imaginary object has been elevated to its dignity. At a concrete historical moment, an object that is culturally valued as ideal—an ideal of the ego, an ideal of love, an ideal of satiation—is elevated to the position of the Thing. It is in terms of this relationship between the object that satisfies and the Thing that psychoanalysis explains paradoxical moments in which a work of art is elevated to the dignity of a masterpiece (a work of genius), the Lady is elevated to the dignity of the ideal Woman, and a cola bottle is elevated to the dignity of a cultural symbol (the ideal of satiation). These elevated objects are all imaginary places of satisfaction where the subject, within a socially appraised domain, can find satisfaction in the company of the Thing.

To return to Kant, we can say that the sublime in a text or a picture is where the imaginary object succeeds to exhibit the unpresentable, the Ideal object that cannot be demonstrated yet allows an imaginary stand-in to fulfill its instinctual function. Thus the sublime elevates an image or a sign to the dignity of the Thing, so the Thing can be presented in its unpresentable totality, thus causing the subject in art both anxiety and the deepest satisfaction.

CHAPTER 6

The Subversion of the Genius and the Dialectic of Creation

> "What does the enigma consist in? In an art which I would term between-the-lines, to refer to the cord. It is not clear why lines which are written should not be knotted by a second cord. Writing: it's an interest of mine . . . the writing of little letters, little mathematical letters, is what supports the real.
>
> "Beauty is connected to something other than the obscene, in other words, the real. There would be, in sum, nothing but beautiful writing—why not?"[1]

These words of Lacan refer to writing, in particular to the writing of Joyce. Joyce, the author of the following lines, writes: "riverrun, past Eve and Adam's, from swerve of shore to bend of bay, brings us by a commodius vicus of recirculation back to Howth Castle and Environs."[2]

The reader, any reader, in her or his encounter with a writing that already in the first paragraph (of Joyce's last novel) confronts her or him with an incomprehensible flood that has the appearance of an "into-the-midst-of-things" opening, undergoes a certain traumatic experience. Joyce, a genius of twentieth-century literature, whose writing has many ardent fans but is hard to love, presents the reader with an insurmountable challenge of understanding, yet is consensually believed to be a revolutionary of modernism. He presents an enigma that is twofold: *the enigma of writing*, of an art that should be called "between-the-lines," to use Lacan's phrasing, as it does not convey a meaning by way of words, and *the enigma of genius*, the enigma regarding the cord that knots together the letters, making them a work of genius, which, according to Lacan again, means that the knot is what connects us, the readers, to the real. I examine in this chapter the way in which a writing of beauty, a writing of "between-the-lines," a writing that hardly makes sense in the symbolic terms of the Other, a writing that needs a knot to the real, a cord we may call "genius" or "Joyce," is a writing that affects the reader with anxiety. The anxiety in the work of genius is not, however, unilaterally displeasurable. Anxiety, beyond the pleasure principle, satisfies by way of pain. The work of genius raises anxiety, because genius is the one who evades the dictates of the Other, whose writing lacks a hold in the domain of signification. But genius also is the one who fills up with her or his creation the place the Other left vacant, and in that, the creation of genius brings something else to the domain of art, something that has to do with the *jouissance* of writing, and hence with the *jouissance* of the reader. Hence, anxiety is raised before the work of genius for two reasons. First, anxiety emerges when the support of common meaning is absent, as the genius "ventures to give sensible expression to rational ideas of invisible beings . . . in a way that goes beyond the limits of experience, namely, with a completeness for which no example can be found in nature."[3] The genius exceeds the limits of one's experience and creates an expression of one's own for which no given meaning can account. But it is not only the subversion of the "meaningful" or the "limits of experience" that elicits anxiety. Second, anxiety emerges where an excess of *jouissance* is present. In the act of genius we are presented with an enjoyment in the act of creation unmediated by the Other, as genius is positioned in the very place of uncastrated *jouissance*. Here I correlate these sources of anxiety with the Kantian genius. Genius elicits an inevitable discomfort vis-à-vis the *school* in relation to which he is an exception. Genius also is taken, however, to constitute a new, albeit indeterminate, law of nature, which can explain, according to Kant, why the products of genius elicit in us (the observers, readers) the pleasure in the beautiful and the pain inflicted by the undecipherable.

THE ENIGMA OF UNPARTICULAR PARTICULARITY IN JOYCEAN WRITING

What does incomprehensibility have to do with genius? What does beautiful writing have to do with genius? How can the incomprehensible work of genius be met with the reader's dismay and anxiety and yet be taken as beautiful?

Let us further articulate the problem of genius both in aesthetic and psychoanalytic terms. Kant, in his aesthetics, warned against "original nonsense," yet he also described the genius as one whose creation cannot be deciphered by others, nor even motivated by the genius himself. Toward the end of his seminar of 1976, dedicated to Joyce, Jacques Lacan conclude, "Not only is the Joycean text teeming with enigmas, but it could be said that he played on that, in the knowledge that there would be Joyceans for two or three hundred years. These people are occupied uniquely with resolving the enigmas—namely, at least, why Joyce put it in that way."[4] Although Joyce's writing offers no foothold for the interpreter, its unreadability, rather than having a voiding effect, appears to carry particular literary interest for generations of critics. Joyce, with his unique artistic practice, can indeed epitomize the paradox of the genius as it looms in philosophical aesthetic discussion. Well acquainted with artistic traditions, Joyce employs forms that are part of the training of artists (figurative language, narrative structures, etc.), yet at the same time, he activates material that transcends all known concepts and schemes of understanding, and in *Finnegans Wake,* he even transgresses the confines of any known language.

And yet Joyce is historically and artistically distant from the genius as understood by Kant in the context of eighteenth-century aesthetics, and thus the question that inevitably arises is, how can Joyce realize the paradox of the genius as it is formulated by Kant? The genius produces the impossible thing that is both determinate in form and indeterminate in "material" as, according to Kant, the genius furnishes "rich *material* for products of fine art"; however, "processing this material and giving it *form* requires talent that is academically trained."[5] This distinction between form and matter, "quite unusual within the whole of the Third Critique,"[6] can suggest ways of applying Kant's notion of genius also to modernist contexts. Kant claims that the act of genius is free of the rules that apply to our world of experience, yet a meaningful rule, unknown before, dwells in the genius' act to be revealed by others. This other rule combines the imaginative material of an original talent with an academic training in forms, without which the genius will be no more than a charlatan. The paradox of the genius of modernism was formulated by Thierry de Duve, a contemporary Kantian, in terms analogous to those of Kant, terms that can accommodate the case of Joyce: Joyce, while composing a text that breaks all known laws of syntax and semantics, thus implementing the modernist imperative of "do whatever" with language or paint, also creates an exemplary work that meets the mandatory "impossibility of the making" (to use Duchamp's phrase) of the modernist artist. He exhibits the absolute mandate in a particular object, that is, an absolute mandate to use whatever material in absolute freedom is met by the ultimate constraint of form thus producing the idiosyncratic act of the genius as an act bound to be producing something. The something produced by genius (and not even necessarily made by him, as in the case of the ready-made) is never a thing-in-general, and as a particular thing this something becomes exemplary/consequential for the world of art.[7] The genius of modernism thus knows how to exhibit through a particular form, any form, the Idea of reason of "absolute freedom in creation." The genius of modernism, just as the genius of classical times, hence uses her imagination to demonstrate what is impossible to demonstrate, and in that the modernist demand to create aesthetic ideas proves to be just as trying as it was for an artist of the Renaissance.

However, can Joyce be considered a modernist genius in the spirit of Kant? If we follow the implications of Lacan's depiction of him, Joyce also may seem to undermine, or at least to problematize, some of Kant's fundamental tenets. Concerning artistic geniuses, Kant primarily stresses the idea that the original indeterminate law with which the genius acts can be eventually codified into a communicable rule for the school of artists following her. From what is reflected in Lacan's words quoted earlier, the hiatus between whatever directs the genius creative act and the attempt of Joyceans to understand or put his example into action is unbridgeable. Joyce is not likely to be understood, no matter how much time goes by, no matter how many critics toil over deciphering his work. Joyce's almost unreadable language suggests meaningfulness to his readers, to the extent that his writing has fueled the fervent desire of critics to codify this material into a set of determinate, familiar rules; yet the critics' quest would be futile. Thus while Joyce is a Kantian genius who creates something previously unknown to the readers of literature, he is non-Kantian if we follow the general orientation of commentators on Kant's aesthetics, in the sense that Joyce, not being decipherable, cannot become exemplary. But is it indeed so? Does the exemplarity of the work of genius entail turning the unknown rule of nature into a communicable rule of art?

Joyce was a writer who could predict in a way what kind of desire his writing would elicit in others, yet he is unique in his form of address to readers, in that he tricks them into looking for meaningfulness in the "wrong place." We would claim that even in that, Joyce represents something typical of the genius. Had the endeavor to "translate" the genius' work into a meaningful message or to trace the genius' resources succeeded, the uniqueness of the work would be missed, and the fervor of the critics would extinguish. Thus Joyce's case points to the fact that the genius' exemplarity, the aptness of his work to serve as a model for others, does not involve comprehending or deciphering this work.

This, claims J-A. Miller, in his attempt to codify the rule of Lacanian teaching, deciphering of the work of this latter genius for the more general public of interested followers, this disruption between the particular creation of the artist and the critics' tools for deciphering it, is caused by the fact that the only truth there is about a subject is a truth arising from the subject's relation to language, and that relation is always traumatic. In other words, the subject's relation to language is particular to that subject (a trauma is not a type of event in reality but, rather, a type of psychic registration of an event in reality—actual or imaginary) and, hence, cannot be made sense of in generalized terms, which explains why the interpreting effort of critics is bound to fail.[8]

It was the genius of Joyce, or of any genius for that matter, that enabled him "to articulate the trauma he received in his encounter with language, and in that he succeeded to cause the university a trauma."[9] No form or concept that comes from the Other of language (i.e., from language as a universal arsenal of signifiers into which the subject is introduced to become a speaking subject) can account for the particular trauma of a subject—there is nothing generalizable about it. I claim here that the rule of genius must be kept indeterminate, uninterpreted, for the uniqueness of genius to be sustained. It is in relation to the domain in the Other, which remains impervious to meaning, that the subject senses anxiety. This thesis can be elucidated in preliminary terms if we consider the fact that the subject is determined by language and speech, from which it follows, says Lacan, that the subject in the beginning is in the locus of the Other. The subject appears in the locus of the Other as a signifier for another signifier. Yet which other signifier? "[S]uppose that in the desert you find a stone covered with hieroglyphics. You do not doubt for a moment that, behind them, there was a subject who wrote them. But it is an error to believe that each signifier is addressed to you—this is proved by the fact that you cannot understand any of it," and yet each of these signifiers is related to each of the others.[10] When the signifiers that come from the Other cannot be understood, the subject finds herself unregistered in the domain of the Other, which is why the opaque nature of the genius' creation is bound to leave the subject anxious. It is this ambivalent position of genius in the field of the Other that will clarify the genius' gesture and the anxiety she brings on in the subject experiencing art. Genius is the name of the creation that evades the symbolic order, evades meaning yet brings the observer/reader very close to the *jouissance of creation*. It is on these two accounts that the work of genius is accompanied by the affect of anxiety.

Joyce's art is unique. Joyce, claims Miller after Lacan, wants "to wake literature up in order to signify its end, to awaken it to something of its structure, its truth, beyond phantasms, beyond idealization. It will be like crossing the literary phantasm, toward the real of writing, which is the pure relation to language."[11] How can the particularity of Joyce's traumatic encounter with language, which leads to the pure relation of this subject to language, be integrated within the universal call of taking literature *beyond personal phantasm*? That is, if the subject Joyce has a particular encounter with language, then how can this encounter transcend the personal phantasm of this subject? This is precisely where the uniqueness of Joyce's genius lies. His traumatic encounter with language, which is particular to him and hence cannot be universally deciphered through the interpretive endeavors of so many critics, takes on the form of a "pure relation to language." That is, Joyce's writing constitutes a formal envelope of the trauma emptied of its traumatic content, of the specific connection between the personal trauma and the subject's phantasm. In that, Joyce's encounter with language can carry a meaningful weight for others, although beyond the literary phantasm of joint, shared experiencing. The formal envelope of the trauma, unique and unknown before the genius, is something that is purely of the subject, yet can elicit the interest of the reader.

This dialectic of the particular and the nonparticularizable presents the psychoanalytic approach to the problem of genius in a nutshell and suggests a productive way of characterizing genius and of addressing the central exegetic contention in Kant's discussion of genius in the third critique, that of "exemplary originality." The dialectic of the particular and the universal in the genius creation also is exemplified in the case of Joyce and thus can reveal and highlight some of the profound dilemmas around Kant's idea of genius. It will be shown that at the heart of the Kantian discussion of genius lies the paradox of the particular subject in her traumatic encounter with the language of the Other. It is an encounter that paradoxically stages the genius' unconscious knowledge (as the genius herself does not know wherefrom her creation emerges) of how to create this encounter in forms that others can relate to, yet will always remain "other" to them. The work of the genius' creation can never be "translated" into a systematic, determinate new rule, since at its kernel, the particular trauma can never be articulated in its own terms, but only through an indirect formation, that is, the subject is constituted through what cannot be directly represented, which is why a subject, within psychoanalytic thinking, is necessarily a subject of the unconscious.

Note that the genius is described here as a subject, although it is not clear in Kant whether "genius" is a way to describe a specific cognitive disposition and ability, or a way to motivate a judgmental reaction on the part of a judging subject. According to the latter conception, "genius" in Kant is a way by which the subject of judgment rationalizes her aesthetic decision, for example, "This is beautiful! It must be a work of genius!" (This will be further discussed later).

While I raise here the question of "genius" in order to demonstrate the structure of "psychotic creation," as eliciting anxiety, the case of Joyce as genius requires a double perspective on the question of anxiety. As will become clear later, the anxiety felt by the reader when the symbolic register falters requires that Joyce be regarded as the Other of the judging agent/subject. This does not contradict, however, a second perspective from which the possible sufferings of the creating subject himself are examined (however, the intricate question of the suffering of the psychotic will not be discussed here).[12]

Joyce was chosen to illustrate the fundamental Kantian dilemma of "*exemplary originality*" because this link between Kant and Joyce is supported by Lacan's approach to the case of Joycean writing. Joyce can illustrate the problem of the genius and not a particular subject who happens to be a genius on the basis of Lacan's approach to his case. Lacan, who dedicated a whole seminar to one writer (making almost no generalization about artists through this case of Joyce), resists diagnosing him, refusing to treat Joyce as a case. Joyce is a particular writing case and a nonparticular one at the same time, hence cannot be diagnosed, as *diagnosis aims to name a subject's particular truth.* Joyce's writing, while going beyond any specific local meaning of any imaginary interpretation attributed to it by critics, and in that is totally unique, refuses to be particularized, *subjectivized*. Diagnosing Joyce, that is, turning him into a subject of a particular unconscious, would have undermined the possibility of relating to him as a genius.

The following section concentrates on the Kantian dilemma of exemplary originality and its interpretations before returning to the question of Joyce, his genius, and the enigma of his writing.

KANT, GENIUS, AND THE PARADOX OF ORIGINAL EXEMPLARITY

"[F]ine art cannot itself devise the rule by which it is to bring about its product. Since, however, a product can never be called art unless it is preceded by a rule, it must be nature in the subject that gives the rule to art; in other words, fine art is possible only as the product of genius."[13]

The artistic trade-off between an "autistic" originality and a communicative relevance to the actual artistic scene of given forms and images, between "the originality of talent" and the mechanics of "academic correctness" (to use Kant's words in §47), appears always to have been on artists' minds and has found various expressions over the years. Although a world of a difference seems to separate the Homeric bard from the Romantic free associationist, the modernist doctrinaire of "everyone is an artist" from the postmodernist whose originality lies in a collage of allusions, the conflictual structure of genius appears to constantly underlie every artistic production. Some time ago, in a gallery talk of a contemporary Israeli artist, a refreshing formulation of this artistic trade-off was made by the artist who talked about "being expressive in a non-whimsical way."[14] This is just another way of phrasing the eternal dilemma detected by Kant, between uniqueness, on the one hand, and conformity to forms, on the other hand.

This is the dilemma of every artist, and its highest instance is to be found in the practice of the genius, clasped between creation and imitation. The genius produces objects that are conceptually classified as fine art and as having an artistic purpose, yet at the same time, his products go beyond anything that could be implied by the concept of art at a given moment. The genius produces objects that present before the imagination material that is free from all guidance by rules yet also creates a rule in this very production. The genius produces what is characterized as ultimate originality, not leaning on any external model, yet serving as a model for imitation by others.

Kant's notion of genius thus has an air of paradox. Genius is granted an originality that amounts to an exceptional gift and a uniqueness that cannot be generalized. Genius is led by nature to create her art; it is through her that nature gives the rule to art. Furthermore, nature appears through the genius in the special talent of producing something for which no determinate rule can be given. The genius' endowment is not a skill that can be acquired by following a rule but is described by Kant as an exceptional, extraordinary talent of the poet who "ventures to give these sensible expression in a way that goes beyond the limits of experience. . . . And it is actually in the art of poetry that the power of aesthetic ideas can manifest itself to full extent. Considered by itself, however, this power is actually only a talent (of the imagination)."[15] The genius' faculty of the imagination is exemplified in a presentation that exhibits a concept yet provokes thought to the extent that it can never be comprehended within a determinate concept. The imagination is creative in the genius' case, and it makes reason think more. Genius is not only endowed with a special gift but also is ignorant regarding the nature of this beyond-the-ordinary gift. Genius is a spontaneous faculty that resists being understood or explained.

"But no Homer or Wieland can show how his ideas, rich in fancy and yet also in thought, arise and meet in his mind; the reason is that he himself does not know, and hence cannot teach it to anyone else. . . . Moreover, the artist's skill cannot be communicated but must be conferred directly on each person by the hand of nature. And so it dies with him, until some day nature again endows someone else in the same way."[16]

The creativeness of genius is a faculty that demands and can receive no interpretation or understanding. Kant's attempt here is to specify the nature of uniqueness, to articulate the particular endowment of the genius, in order to account for the creation of beautiful art. In this, Kant reveals the paradoxical air around the genius, when uniqueness is juxtaposed to the other side of the genius' picture. Kant requires that the genius be trained in the purpose and concepts of art, and that his creation become exemplary for others. Genius is a talent for art, and as such it "presupposes a determinate concept of the product, namely, its purpose."[17] Presupposing the purpose of art means that the exceptional faculty of imagination with which the genius is endowed is controlled by the demand to exhibit the concept of understanding associated with art, even if in ways that exceed the determinate nature of this concept. The genius acts guided by a conception of the desired outcome and the steps to be taken in order to achieve that outcome.[18] Furthermore, genius is not only required to know about the purpose of art but to be acquainted with a repertory of forms. The rich material provided by genius for products of fine arts has to be processed by "giving it form," which "requires a talent that is academically trained."[19] To stand the test of judgment, the work of genius must be academically correct rather than renouncing all rules of academic constraint.

The genius is not only disciplined by his training and given knowledge, but his work is restrained by another factor—it must have relevance to others. The most difficult passage regarding this requisite appears in §47: "Since the artist's natural endowment must give the rule to art, what kind of rule is this? . . . The rule must be abstracted from what the artist has done, i.e., from the product, which others may use to test their own talent, letting it serve them as their model. . . . How that is possible is difficult to explain."[20] With these words, the genius turns out to be a paradoxical entity, both dwelling outside the domain of rules (a natural transgressor of the rule or concept) and inside the restraining domain of rules, as the genius realizes, with this very same act of creation, a rule to be abstracted by others. This "air of paradox" is what has mostly preoccupied commentators on Kant concerning the theme of genius. The question is, what is the unknown rule of nature that directs the genius' creation to be somehow transformed into a determinate rule in order for the work of genius to become exemplary? How is exemplarity to be realized without compromising the unique, indeterminate achievement of the genius, or, where does the particularity of genius lie?

If we take the example of Joyce, then the question is how can a language that comes from the Other be used to produce a uniquely enigmatic expression, which amounts to the unprecedented work of genius, and how can the particular use the genius makes of language be made communicable to others? In other words, in order to think of genius as exceptional vis-à-vis ordinary human beings, the unique/original (and hence undecipherable) core of her creation must be maintained, while her work is to be received as meaningful (rather than nonsensical) for others.

The products of genius also must be models, that is, they must be *exemplary*; hence, though they do not themselves arise through imitation, still they must serve others for this, that is, as a standard or rule by which to judge.[21]

The degree of incompatibility involved between "originality" and "exemplarity" is open to interpretation and ranges from referring to this double demand as paradoxical, as propounded by Gammon,[22] to finding no contradiction at all, as suggested by Guyer.[23] In any case, this double demand is in need of some explication.

The function of exemplarity, which the work of genius must fulfill, raises two difficulties. The first has to do with the association of genius to a set of rules: although the genius' practice should be the embodiment of freedom from law, this freedom is subsumed under a number of constraints of taste controlling and disciplining but also enabling the creation of the work of genius. The second difficulty has to do with the determinate nature the work of genius must assume in order to become relevant to others. This difficulty stems from the fact that the originality of the genius not only gives rise to an aping practice in the genius' followers, but it cannot be established as an original work of genius without it. Originality and exemplarity, although described by Kant as equally weighing demands from the art of genius, appear to pose contradictory stipulations that dwell in the same entity, the genius, and account for the power that leads the genius artist along the road of creation. Genius is led from the forms and rules dominating the field of art (and exemplified in the genius' necessary training) to the realization of her natural capacity to freely use her cognitive faculties, and further to the eventual usefulness of her creation for others. That is, genius arises from the field of art, leaves it behind, so to speak, through her exceptional capacities, and returns to this field through exemplarity.

The work of genius is constituted as being outside of the domain of the rules of art (but within the domain of nature), and at the same time, the work in some sense stores a potential rule that will later be articulated by others. Philosophical commentaries on Kant propose different strategies for coping with this complex condition of "exemplary originality." One strategy takes the path of reconciling these two apparently contradictory demands through the character of the genius, while the other strategy is that of separating originality from exemplarity, attributing each to a different agent. I examine these two paths of reconciliation in order to later distinguish them from the psychoanalytic one.

Guyer claims that exemplarity refers to the "impulse to originality," and not to the actual product of the genius, thus paving the way for reconciling the "individual's need to define his aesthetic autonomy by originality and society's interest in preserving its integrity by readily communicable traditions."[24] This clash, claims Guyer, is reconciled in Section §50, where Kant obligates the genius to discipline his rich and original ideas since "it is necessary that the imagination in its freedom be commensurate with the lawfulness of the understanding."[25] The requirements of taste thus "clip the wings" of the artist, obliging him to sacrifice some imagination and spirit so that understanding and taste can be held tight. Originality is thus located in the impulse of the artist, while exemplarity has to do with the requirements of taste that compromise that impulse, so that the understanding remains unimpaired. Kant's emphasis on the scholastic, cultural demands from the artist that discipline his impulse is taken to be the grounds for viewing the artwork of genius as a locus of compromise. In a more recent publication, Guyer refers to §50 as a shift in Kant's approach, and he stresses the fact that while genius invents aesthetic ideas, these satisfy the exemplary demand in their being universally pleasing. That is, exemplarity is primarily linked to Kant's notion that successful art has an element of contingency or novelty, yet one that is pleasing in ways valid for all.[26]

Contrary to this idea of reconciling originality and exemplarity within the genius' person, "exemplary originality" is described by Gammon as the making of grounds newly discovered—familiar.[27] That is, the absolutely original opens the way for a nonoriginal spirit of imitation. Gammon handles this paradox by following the historical course that the idea of exemplarity in Kant and additional thinkers of his time has undergone, thus exposing the variegated meaning that can be ascribed to exemplarity. This strategy, which may be described as the historical decomposing exemplarity from originality, enables Gammon to attribute exemplarity to various groups of "others" exhibiting different ways of utilizing the genius' originality. Through a typology of the modes of genial influence, and by an explication of the type of activity each one is engaged in, Gammon shows that not all exemplarity is a way of reworking an already existing rule,[28] and that the work of genius can become exemplary for others in ways that range from technical aping to the creation of another genius.[29]

The idea of historicizing the creation of genius in order to reconcile exemplarity with originality also is exemplified in an argument by Steinbrenner, who addresses, after Danto, the theme of the unimaginability of future art as owing to the originality of creation. Unlike Kant's idea of spontaneous creation, Steinbrenner notes that artists work under the pressure of constantly coming up with something new. This constant demand drives artists to produce original work and hinders our ability to imagine the particular new artwork to appear in the future. Steinbrenner links Danto's idea that we cannot imagine the art or artwork of the future,[30] to Kant's genius by arguing that, for Kant, exemplarity has an institutional streak, inasmuch as the artwork is exemplary in being a model for later schools or members of the art world.[31] Thus in addition to the rule-giving genius, the exemplary rests on the constitution of a school, and as such, the essence of the work as exemplary will first show itself only in future history. The exemplary characteristics of the work are not known to the genius, because they will only show their face in the future. The rule of the genius "cannot exist without a historical framework" and therefore remains incommunicable, until it can be communicated within a future domain of application. Exemplary originality is thus reconciled by postponing the exemplarity to the unimaginable art of the future.

Whether exemplary originality is solved by keeping the two ends apart or by reconciling them, it is clear that these strategies are fueled by the need to locate where the uniqueness of the genius is maintained, without compromising its potential consequence for the work of others. Both strategies account, then, for the shift from determinateness to indeterminateness (and vice versa) that the notion of genius requires. However, the attempt to reconcile the place of exemplarity and originality within the artist, which in a way considers the original standing of genius as already combining acquaintance with forms, with a drive to express or bring into art exceptional material and unique forms, necessarily compromises the uniqueness of genius. Genius is presented as never actually leaving, through the path of creation, the language of the Other; genius is presented as always already a locus of compromise. "Nature in the artist" or "the impulse to originality" in this context remains inaccessible.

The other philosophical solution seems to compromise the uniqueness of genius in another way, by making genius recognized as such only after the effect, once the work of genius has been codified into a communicable rule for art. It is in relation to an established rule of the school following genius that her creation can be truly appraised. Both strategies compromise the original uniqueness of the artist by bringing her creation into the realm of the communicable and the understandable. Nature in the artist cannot be appraised unless passing the press of determination.

GENIUS AND THE SUBJECT OF CREATION

The question of where to locate exemplarity vis-à-vis the originality of genius also implies different ways of addressing the *kind of entity genius is*: Should he or she be regarded as a person with an exceptional psychology? Is she a structural constituent or a logical, universal consequence of a theory of taste? Is she to be inferred from the nonlinear changes in the history of art, or is she the artist retroactively remembered from among the many artists of the past? This range of possibilities of dealing with the ontology of "genius" represents a variety of ways of dealing with the particularity and exceptional creation implied in the notion of "original genius."

Kant's aesthetics has suggested to commentators that genius designates the complex relations between artistic form and the audience's response to what goes above and beyond anything implied by the concept of form: "The audience . . . can respond both to the concepts the work embodies and to the freedom of the imagination that it represents and induces in themselves."[32] In other words, the genius, just as the object deemed beautiful or sublime, is not somebody, a person endowed with certain high mental capacities, but genius, like beauty, is a way to account for the enactment in the subject of a "quickening of cognitive powers." Hence, as the whole *Critique of Judgment* takes place within the subject, and thus can tell us very little, if anything, about the nature of the object, so the genius is not a kind of rare mentality to be psychologically explored but rather a constitutive requisite to be philosophically discussed as universal. Guyer opposes the idea that genius is a "rare talent" and locates genius as the point of harmony between nature and reason in a judgment of taste, that is, a point where the free play of imagination and understanding in the artist meets the free play of these faculties in the audience, in a way that is pleasing to the latter.[33]

Guyer here presents an approach to genius as *structurally necessitated* by Kant's overall view, a direction further explored by Gasché. Gasché refers to genius as a "paradoxical 'entity' " and claims that "the whole problematic of genius exclusively concerns 'a happy relation' of the faculties" and consequently has "a primarily transcendental thrust."[34] Gasché stresses Kant's claim that the product of genius is not accompanied by a conscious intent; the genius does not know how he came about producing the artwork in a certain way. He does not know his genius.

It is along these lines that Gasché's idea of the "denuding of the arts of determinateness" can be read. The determining judgment required by art as such has to be stripped of its determining power in order for the power of the product to be asserted. Pure aesthetic judgments upon the beautiful require the absence of all determinate concepts, and such an absence for objects of art must be actively engendered in order for them to be judged beautiful. Gasché thus calls for a "double denuding": a denuding of the concept behind the beautiful object design and a denuding of the determining character of the act of judgment. This denuding can only be the task of the genius.[35] The existence of genius is a necessary condition for producing beautiful art, just as a formula is required for solving an algebraic equation. However, in order that no rule shows through a beautiful work of art, the genius has to be an indeterminate logical requisite. Without the denuding function fulfilled by genius, the absence of rule will be interpreted as simply the skillful dissimulation of a rule actually present. But the indetermination required in order for beautiful art to exist must be more radical than dissimulation. In the beautiful arts, only an unknown rule is required, a rule that has not been known before it appears in an individual work of beautiful art, "a rule that has not yet been codified as a rule."[36] Although an artistic school can later take the mere form (and not a determining or cognitive form) and codify rules according to it, the unknown rule indicates that only an entity called "genius" can accomplish the logical function of denuding, of rendering the rule indeterminate.

Beauty can arise from indeterminacy because its source lies in the natural disposition of the subject producing it. "Thus the sole relevance of genius in Kant's aesthetics is to solve the paradox posed by the beautiful arts: namely, the idea that certain products of art can be conformed to a rule without a definite concept, and hence be beautiful."[37] The paradox of the exemplary genius is thus solved by assuming the genius' gift of nature to be a prerequisite for a beauty not determined by concept; genius is the missing link between the determining judgment of art and the indeterminate judgment of the beautiful in art. The rule eventually codified from the work of genius, hence, cannot be a given rule actually present in the creation of genius. It is rather something intuited (and abstracted) post facto from the products of genius by other talented individuals.[38] The genius acts freely, and it is through the genius as a paradoxical entity that "nature passes into freedom."[39] Hence, for Gasché, genius mediates what is impossible to mediate, unless an unsubjectified entity is assumed to serve in many respects, as the "black box" in which and through which the beautiful in art becomes a possibility.

Some of the commentary on Kant follows a different direction of stressing the unique cognitive disposition of a subject deserving the name of genius, as persona, as a personality. This direction is compatible with the idea that fine art, unlike nature, is a product of a conscious act and of specialized skill. In this direction, the psychology or empirical dimension of genius is explored in a way that can either be taken to diverge from Kant's naturally endowed genius or to follow the idea of an exceptionally skilled producer of art. Genius must be unique and not universal, hence, the genius as person must be endowed with cognitive or psychological uniqueness. Thus Allison, for instance, stresses the powerful imagination essential to artistic creation, an imagination that even when subjected to the confining forms of understanding is still powerful enough to supply the material for fine art.[40] Genius, Allison claims, creates what transcends conformity to taste. Genius is "someone who is blessed with the unteachable ability to produce coherent imaginative associations,"[41] hence, exemplary originality includes understanding and judgment, along with "an *inventive imagination*" as essential components.

The emphasis here on the genius' cognitive faculty of imagination points to the genius as someone exemplifying exceptional, unique, or extraordinary capacities.[42] Yet such philosophical discussions of genius reveal the difficulty in generalizing about this entity, whether in terms of universal psychological traits or in the transcendental terms of an epistemic, structural condition. Kant himself, in characterizing the genius of art in opposition to the genius of science, claims in §47 that "the artist's skill cannot be communicated but must be conferred directly on each person by the hand of nature. And so it dies with him."[43] That is, there is something about the genius that refuses to be generalized in terms of a universal "Genius." "The Genius" does not exist if we take Kant's words here to indicate that every genius is unique in his own way. The genius, as universal, is an impossible entity since, were he to exist, the very condition of indeterminacy and originality would have dissolved. At the same time, at the other end of a particularity that resists generalization, one can detect a tendency to departicularize genius. Considering genius to occupy a slot in a structure, or characterizing her in general cognitive terms of the unique harmony that she accomplishes between imagination and understanding (demonstrated in aesthetic ideas), indicates that genius, while a unique creator, is not taken to be a particularized subject. Genius can become a model for others neither through a generalized notion about creation nor by particularizing her specific act of creation into a communicable rule. It seems that Kant and his commentators insist on defining the unique creation of genius without this creation being understood or deciphered.

Philosophical discussions of genius waver regarding the degree of particularity or universality to be ascribed to the genius. Attempts to particularize the genius at the moment of her advent or through her unique creation are problematic, since her genius is noncommunicable and will remain so. Similarly, attempts to universalize genius in terms of cognitive or psychological attributes are problematic, because they miss the unique revelation of genius at the moment of creation, a moment that resists universalization. This philosophical wavering between the particularity and universality of genius, and the dialectic genius involved in terms of how the name of genius is to be understood within Kantian aesthetics, may find its explanation in the notion of "vanishing mediator,"[44] proposed by Slavoj Zizek, in order to come to terms with the "exasperating abstract reflections on 'dialectical method'" of Hegel and his later readers.[45] Extricating Zizek's argument regarding the notion of the vanishing mediator from his reading of Hegel, this notion appears as a surplus moment that indicates that the second moment of split (opposition) and the final reconciliation are tied through a dialectical necessity—the former creates the conditions for the emergence of the latter.[46] The vanishing mediator thus supplies a concrete content to a given structure whose constituents reveal an unavoidable discrepancy. Yet the concrete aspect of the vanishing mediator does not turn this factor into an empirical entity of any kind. The mediator is, however, "vanishing," that is, its disappearance is required to establish the terms of the opposition. The mediator is a particular repressed link that, as repressed, can never be said to exist. To account for this vanishing, one can use as an example the analogous terms of a "vanishing point" in visual art. Here again, the vanishing point disappears into the representation to enable the two-dimensional image to become a necessary condition for the representation of three dimensions. The vanishing point is, so to speak, the repressed, impossible point between the two dimensions of the converging lines (in the picture) and the three dimensions of parallelism (in the represented object), the relatedness of which is enabled by this impossible point, precisely at its moment of disappearance.

To think about the genius in similar terms would indicate why Gasché regards genius as the paradoxical entity that denudes concepts of their determinacy, thus presenting a radical solution that turns the genius into a condition for the emergence of beauty in art. This condition is neither abstract (a logical slot in a structure) nor empirical (a psychological persona). The vanishing mediator is the impossible point at which the particularity of absolute uniqueness converges with the Otherness of the art world.

In what follows I return to the case of Joyce, as analyzed by Lacan, to explore the idea of genius as a vanishing mediator. Genius is tantamount to the concrete core constituting the interrelatedness between the general rule, the forms and modes of imaging that come from the Other (culture, artistic tradition, the school of art), and the originality of the subject. Genius is hence capable of using these very forms to stir the cognitive faculties in ways that go beyond whatever can be determinately conceptualized. Genius is the concrete condition that enables the emergence of beauty in art by indicating the necessary yet concrete relatedness of the determinate and the indeterminate, of the purposive to the nonpurposive, of art to nature, and by enabling this emergence, the genius, as a case, vanishes.

LACAN WITH JOYCE

For Lacan, the case of Joyce, rather than bringing up a literary or an artistic question per se, touches on a psychoanalytic problem of "what it means to write."[47] When someone turns up asking in the name of some inhibition to be put in the position of writing, psychoanalysis should know it is worth looking long and hard into the question of what put this subject into the writing position. In this sense, the path of writing must be considered a symptom of the writing subject, and the turning to the territory of writing in the name of some inhibition means that "writing comes from somewhere other than the signifier."[48] This "somewhere other" is where the writing subject uses language for his or her own enjoyment. That is, in the seminar on Joyce, Lacan refers to writing as a mode of *jouissance.* Writing is a *sinthome* rather than a *symptom*, that is, "a kernel of enjoyment immune to the efficacy of the symbolic,"[49] resistant to analytic dissolution. This section will attempt to clarify the notion of writing as "a kernel of enjoyment" and to explain why, thus conceived, writing causes anxiety in the reader.

Writing is *a priori* taken to have a symptomatic core, which also implies that writing can only be writing if it occupies the place of *the* symptom of the subject who practices writing. Writing is taken to be a special symptom since, in general, identifying a given trait as the symptom with which the being of the subject is tied may involve considerable analytic effort. With writing, the symptom is already given as such. The works of Joyce, as a fact of writing, do not only constitute a symptom, but they can be described quite straightforwardly. But if writing manifests a core of enjoyment, then how can it be described in the symbolic terms of writing technique and practice, as a straightforward fact of writing? How can the symptom of writing both be symbolically recognized and articulated as such and yet be acknowledged as resistant to any signifying dissolution?

To answer this difficult question we can refer to Miller's description of the fact of Joycean writing, "*le dispositif Joycien*" (the Joycean apparatus).

Normally, Miller says, each word is susceptible to different significations of different degrees of possibility. Departing from the same sound, multiple senses are possible, and writing normally permits one to decide which sense is concerned, even when there is total homophony. With Joyce, multiple senses are treated differently:

> This marks the possibility of grinding the sound in order to make a juice of diverse meanings, a mixture. . . . This is what Joyce exploits. . . . But, at a second moment he makes the initial sound of the word bring back all the echoes of this word. . . .
>
> This is then the route: from a word, one obtains other words that are phonically kin-words and possible effects of sense, while returning to the first word to modify its sense by condensing words into it. The result is that of a signifier of pure neologism. Joyce writes through an after-effect . . . it is the whole swarm that reverts to the initial S_1.[50]

This account formalizes Joyce's inventive use of language resources. This formal diagnosis of writing is hence equivalent to the Kantian idea that genius must be trained in the forms of art and its traditions and must emerge from them. Yet Joyce opts for forms whose ultimate effect is that of dropping the support of meaning. As genius, his name stands for this mediation between the formal, unique use of signs and the resulting resistance to meaning.

Lacan's seminar is oriented in the direction of the far-reaching question of how such a mode of writing reveals the particular desire and the gist of enjoyment that writing constitutes for the subject—Joyce. In other words, how can we explain Joyce's choice of *this particular path of writing?* In what follows, the manner in which this path of writing reveals the originality of Joyce will be traced. A path of writing amounts to the way literary and language forms can only be motivated by the way they are tied to what makes writing necessary for Joyce as a writer.

To explain how writing, symbolically constituted by forms that are in the Other, can become the symptom necessary to withhold the subject's particular enjoyment, I examine how the Other functions in relation to writing in general and in relation to the writing of the genius in particular. To the same extent that the determinate purpose of art cannot anticipate the way the work of genius will articulate this purpose, so the forms of language and their purposive meanings as these come from the Other, cannot anticipate the purpose they serve for Joyce. The Other (with a capital "O") is defined as the locus of the word, of signs, a locus always evoked once there is a work, once there is writing. This third party, the Other, always exists in the relationship between the subject and the other (with a small "o") once there is signifying articulation. That is, in order to relate to others the writing subject has to place *his* or *her* writing in the Other of language as the locus of all signs and as the guarantor of signification. And yet the Other, as what guarantees the availability of words and forms and their signification, also is perpetually submitted to the question of *what* guarantees it: the Other as the locus of all signifiers is a function of the subject's use of language and is yet assumed as prior to the subject. There is therefore no guarantee that the subject will be authentically represented in the repertoire of signifiers, nor is the relation between the Other and the actual repertoire of signifiers known to the subject. In other words, the subject's position in language is always that of a questioning addressed to the Other in whom signs and significations allegedly reside. The Other is hence also "a perpetually vanishing Other and, by this very fact, one which puts us ourselves, as readers, in a perpetually vanishing position."[51] This Other, the origin of all forms and meanings of language, is not absolute, as the system of signifiers is always lacking with regard to the subject's demand for representation. In the case of Joyce, in order to guarantee that literary forms will exhibit the enjoyment-in-writing, Joyce circumvents the Other by occupying its place. Joyce's writing is such that while it "plays the game" of assuming the Other's guarantee of a "horizon of meaning," as evidenced in Joyce's certainty that readers and critics will toil over questions of meaning in his oeuvre, this Other has in fact vanished once writing forms have become part of the subject's own particular use of language, part of his or her invention.

So in the case of the creative artist, the notion of Other in a way already contains the unimaginable nature of the inventive forms to which it gives support, under the condition that this Other has already ceded its function to the writing subject himself or herself. The genius thus functions as a wedge between the Other's guarantee of artistic forms' address to others (the critics, the readers, and the school of artists) and the creative use made of these forms and materials in the genius' practice. It is the genius-as-Other that sponsors the unimaginable nature of the writing as what articulates the particular ends of enjoyment in writing that serves the subject of creation. Forms that are in the Other can thus become paths of enjoyment through writing, paths that originate in the universal treasure of signifiers (that is, in the Other), to be used as un-universalized symptoms of the genius' path of writing. Joyce has made use of forms whose origin is with the Other, yet by making these devoid of their supposed meaning, he has constituted himself in the place of the Other, as the Other supposed-to-know-everything-about-writing, as the locus of the law of writing not yet given to known experience.

Hence, Lacan's analysis of Joyce does not reveal, at the end, the genius as a particular subject given to analysis but sustains the genius in the vanishing zone of nonparticularity that cannot be universalized. Genius occupies the position of the Other vis-à-vis the judging subject more than the position of a subject (a position that we take the moot question of the ontology of genius to attest to). Genius brings together the two ends: that of particular enjoyment and that of the forms that are in the Other, but the genius is present in neither. It is this necessary nonparticularity of the vanishing genius in terms of which we can understand the way "nature through the subject" is exemplified in the case of Joyce. It is exemplified in this case because Lacan resists diagnosing Joyce as a case. The uniqueness of genius cannot be fully articulated by codifying the rule of nature in the genius, turning it into a communicable rule for the use of all. The genius as Other vanishes in the very act of articulating in writing his or her grasp of the purpose of art. Genius is an Other that cannot be semanticized; it cannot be reduced to the understandable language of an other (with a small "o") whose rules of writing are codified.

The genius is in between a subject and an Other. A genius like Joyce appears through facts of writing, which refer to the way he chooses a language to write in. Thus if the genius is a subject, then it is one who in fact creates a language and does not only use forms that come from the Other: "At each moment one gives the language which one speaks a little prod. . . . It is only living insofar as it creates itself at every instant. This is why there is no collective unconscious, only particular unconsciouses."[52] Hence, the fact of writing is never simply a way to use the language one speaks but rather a way to invent language so that it will give form to one's particular unconscious. Invention relates to something that is the particular real thing about the subject, the unique thing that cannot be universalized and thus lacks meaning. The genius is a particular subject in whom an indeterminate rule of language dwells.

What is the nature of the genius' creative originality if it takes place within the language of the Other? The order of the subject's particular being, the subject's uniqueness, is revealed when meaning is particularized as a hole, when meaning uniquely gives way to what cannot be formulated meaningfully. Accordingly, while the use of language assumes the Other as prior to the subject and as the locus from which signs originate (or, in other terms, it assumes the Name-of-the-Father as what is responsible for placing the subject in the social/linguistic order under the law of the father's interdiction), psychoanalysis finds the order of the subject's particular being, in the ways the subject oversteps the Other, where she or he bypasses the Name-of-the-Father. When the language of the Other is written by genius, its meaningfulness gives way to a particular lack in which the genius does not appear as concretely present but rather as concretely vanishing. The genius appears as particular at the moment/place where meaning (constrained by the Other) has collapsed. The genius is the one who knows how to occupy with her or his writing the place left vacant by the Name-of-the-Father, the place of the symbolic order.

In order to elucidate this point, I continue from the way each subject invents language while using it to the genius' way with language. The genius has the capacity of articulating the traumatic encounter with language by positioning herself or himself in relation to the rule of the Other. That is, when Kant refers to the genius' ignorance regarding the source of his or her unique ideas, he in fact ignores the genius' "other" knowledge, a knowledge the genius uses to seize his or her readers through the original invention that comes to him or her unknowingly. The genius always knows something. Every genius, in other words, has something of a God in him or her: he or she assumes the impossible position of *the Other of the Other*, as someone who knows what the Other wants, what the Other means, and what the Other enjoys. This position of the Other of the Other is nonhuman in many ways, as it assumes a subject, a genius, that takes a risk that humans usually do not. The genius bypasses the appeasing law of the Father in order to reveal something about the locus of a hole in the symbolic, a locus that resists signification.

A main direction in Lacan's seminar on Joyce has to do with the particular position Joyce takes in relation to the Other. Joyce, by naming in 1916 his first substantial and autobiographical novel *A Portrait of the Artist as a Young Man*, immediately raises this quandary regarding his definitive gesture. Why "the" artist, with a definite article? This, Lacan says, is due to the fact that Joyce considered himself *the artist*, one that will keep the pens of critics busy for the next 300 years at least. Why is it that Joyce attributed such a godly power to his literature? Why is it that in his writing, from "The Dubliners" to *Finnegans Wake*, he keeps referring to himself as redeemer? Was this a way of marking his enjoyment from writing? Lacan would claim that Joyce's writing indicates his being God the redeemer, precisely because without this writing he would have been reduced to nothing. Joyce's writing constitutes him as artist, enabling him to bear a name, to create a name, while cutting off the reader from any knowledge regarding the "true nature" of this writing. Joyce considered himself the redeemer of writing, the creator of a language, and as such no language can explain him. He is God-the-creator who knows something about the enjoyment of writing, and in his act of writing, he seals off this enjoyment from us. Joyce is the genius who knows something about the ways of language and uses them in order to transcend language. Through this act, he creates an unbridgeable gap between himself and his addressees.

To grasp something of Joyce's link to language, of his particular encounter with it, his writing should be examined through what it grants the writer. Joyce's writing locates him within the symbolic dimension that, as an "ordinary" subject, he defies. Thus writing occupies the place from which the symbolic rule has been foreclosed, constituting an image of his "ego," that is, creating the vase/containing vessel of his writing, specifically shaped and sized, around what is the originality of Joyce. Lacan read Joyce extensively, from his novels to his letters and daily notes; he read hundreds of books of criticism dedicated to Joyce's writing. He departed on a quest in which Joyce himself aimed to engage his readers in an attempt to name the unknown meaning of his writing. Joyce attributes much importance to the esteem that his writing gains in the eyes of others, because for him this esteem confirms something about him as Other, as the locus of the Word. The overestimation of the response of others, the need to have readers and critics as a constant, unchanging, and puzzled crowd before his writer's eyes, thus has to do with Joyce's position regarding the Name-of-the-Father, as the one who establishes the symbolic law for everyone else. But in this case, the symbolic law established by Joyce is not really one provided by a replacement father; rather, it is a law that defies the very foundations of the symbolic order.

One's father is always the one symbolizing castration vis-à-vis a natural, godly enjoyment that was only granted the primordial Father. Phallic, castrated enjoyment, inherited by son from father, generation after generation, symbolizes that the exceptional, primordial Father and the absolute limitless enjoyment lost with him will always remain outside of the communal, social structure. It is language, structured like the unconscious, that gives form to the relation between castrated enjoyment and lost enjoyment through the signifier, the signifier of castration that eclipses the mythology of a lost enjoyment. The castration spared from the primordial Father also is spared from God, as the enjoyment of God, the absolute Other, is limitless (within "God" as an absolute Other the knowledge of enjoyment lost for the subject resides). Yet Joyce is a unique subject, Lacan says, as he forecloses any knowledge of castration. He wants to use the symbolic language without subjecting himself to the law of the Father that would reduce his enjoyment to that of a castrated subject, of the son. Joyce's encounter with language begins where writing is not subjected to the law, to the law of castration. If we remember that anxiety has to do with what is prior to castration (discussed in chapter 4 here), with what is directed to an object-as-organ rather than to an object-as-signifier, then the *anxiety Joyce causes his readers and critics may show itself as inevitable.*

In his seminar on anxiety, Lacan connects the emergence of anxiety in psychosis to the position of the mother rather than to the father. How can we relate the case of Joyce and his foreclosure of the Father to psychotic anxiety? Lacan argues that anxiety has to do with the danger of *object a* not appearing in the field of the Other, as could be seen around the specular image constituted at the mirror stage. *Object a*, in order to emerge, requires that the ideal image of one's body be registered in the Other, thereby constituting that something which cannot be caught in the image and yet has its place in the alienated field of the Other. Thus, Lacan claims, outside of the field of the ego, outside of the domain of self, no image can serve as an ideal of identification, hence no image can give room to the emergence of *object a*. In neurotics, when the Other is recognized in the image, it is recognized as what stands for the subject's lack (which accounts for the subject's jubilation in front of the mirror image). Failing to see the Other in the image will elicit anxiety. With the neurotic, what conditions the appearance of the image in the field of the Other is a certain prior distance between mother and child, which will give to the subject "this distancing from himself that the dimension of the Other is designed to offer to him."[53] In the case of schizophrenics, though, the situation is different and indeed demands that we part ways with Freud, who was the first to insist that anxiety works as a signal in the field of the ego referring to the danger of separation. While in the case of neurosis anxiety indeed has to do with the relationship between the ideal ego (the ideal image of one's body) and the Other, psychosis refers to another cut, exemplified, somewhat metaphorically, by the separation Lacan identifies prior to birth. The cut relevant to the psychotic subject is prior to the constitution of the ego and holds between the fetus and the body on which it is a parasite, a separation introduced through the body's envelopes within the mother's body. It is in relation to the position of the Mother who avoids the symbolic dimension of the fetus' bodily presence and treats it as a real organ that the subject will be psychotic. Anxiety in the case of psychosis hence cannot be related to the ego and its imaging but to a real separation prior to any representation.

In the case of Joyce, as will be shown later, what Joyce lacks is a preliminary competence to image his own body, an imaginary knowledge of his self. This defect in the imaginary creates a particular symptom of writing, a writing that ignores the law of the father in all registers. With Joyce's creation, anxiety emerges due to the fact that "an object of art comes to compensate for the foreclosure of the Name-of-the-Father."[54] When the presence of the fetus within the foreign body of the mother is real rather than symbolically mediated, the subject to be constituted will lack the distancing effect of the Father and will thus elicit anxiety in others.

However, in what sense is the father absent from Joyce's writing? There is no denying that *Ulysses* is a novel extensively preoccupied with the father figure, with Bloom's father. Joyce is rooted in his father, even when he denies it, and this is exactly his symptom, his refusal to take on himself the Name-of-his-Father, through which his encounter with language would have been constituted. Joyce's language is a language from which the father is absent, as can be detected by the fact that Joyce writes without a master signifier. There is no S_1, a signifier that will determine the meaning and the location of all other signifiers. The absence of a master signifier is noticeable in the fact that Joyce, in his writing, assumes no definite knowledge. All frameworks of knowledge are equally posited—languages, histories, myths, sciences. Moreover, *epiphany*, the moment of revelation, a typical moment in the Joycean apparatus, especially in the early works, is linked to the most mundane, insignificant, spiritless moments rather than to a moment of knowledgeable insight. Epiphany is manifested "in the vulgarity of speech or gesture . . . in a dialogue of nothing."[55] Within this writing, with no spirit or knowledge from a "fatherly" source, it is Joyce's name that replaces the Name-of-the-Father, and it is this name that grants his writing a consistency required to make his writing an original work of genius.

Joyce's father was never a father to him, and Lacan provides evidence that Joyce chose writing as a way to relate to the father's giving up on him, delegating the responsibility for raising him to the Jesuits' institute. The "boozing, practically good-for-nothing father" appears in *Ulysses* as someone who changed his name, being incapable of holding to the name that should have symbolized what will pass on from father to son. The father cannot stand for the paternal law that will direct the son's subordination to the law of castration and will place him in regard to that law. In this place with no law, where the signifier obeys no imperative, where the body is located, severed from a body image (unlike the baby who sees an integrated image of his or her fragmented body in the mirror owing to the look of the Other, his or her m(O)ther), Joyce's writing situates itself. His gradual movement in his writing away from sense, his omission of meaning, is associated by Lacan with the idea that the subject, Joyce, is lacking a body image. Thus for Joyce writing becomes a critical matter—his writing cannot just register, echo the body through images of language, but it has to constitute a relation of his body to language in a way that will sustain his being. The path of writing, as we see, is a serious matter, supporting the very being of the writing subject, the creating genius.

This account of Joyce's writing also can be viewed as the psychoanalytic way of formulating the dilemma of genius in terms of a demand to bypass the law of the signifier, as Joyce's path of writing is that of transcending the unconscious (the signifying formation that exhibits what has been lost by repression). Psychoanalysis, since Freud, has been primarily psychoanalysis of the unconscious, which assumed the Name-of-the-Father and unconscious formations as the effects of castration. But later, psychoanalysis recognized that the Name-of-the-Father can be bypassed. Such is the writing of Joyce, defying the phallic signifier, bypassing the law of the Father.[56] While the enjoyment of "ordinary" people is castrated, the enjoyment of God is an absolute one, not split by language, driving people to try to decipher the nature of this enjoyment that has no limit. Joyce is a writer who enjoys his writing in this godly way; without it, he would have been reduced to nothing, to a psychotic, Lacan says. It is for this reason that the world of the artist must remain forever unknowable, unimaginable. It is a world that eludes us, going far beyond what our enjoyment can be from the artist's product of creation. The genius of producing beautiful art and the taste for judging beautiful art cannot involve the same position vis-à-vis the law of language. This faint enjoyment of ours, as appreciators of art, is called "aesthetic experience," and it predicates the spirited action of amassing meanings in order to decipher the work of genius. When language is devoid of meaning, when the loss is lost, when the language of the Other fails to constitute the object of lack, then anxiety emerges in the reader. And yet the genius has eluded this predicament by replacing the missing function with the real being of his or her own creation. The unimaginable enjoyment of Joyce is tied so intimately to writing that had the interpretive endeavor of appreciators of his work succeeded nothing of Joyce's genius would have remained in the lines he wrote.

Joyce is the name of a particular hole in language; it is not the name of a particular subject, which is why the genius is a paradoxical entity. When Lacan was asked during his seminar if Joyce was mad, Lacan retorted that Joyce had this desire to be an artist in order to preoccupy everyone, or at least as many as possible.[57] For Joyce, this overestimation of himself was supposed to compensate for what was lacking in his estimation for everyone else, for the esteem that did not return to him from his father's gaze. His name, Joyce, came in place of the Name-of-the-Father and aimed to be bigger than any master signifier. That is, if Joyce did not have writing to supplant the missing name of the castrating Father, who should have constituted his son as a subject with castrated sexuality, then he would have been psychotic.

This is surely not a diagnosis of a case—it only says what Joyce would have been like were he not a genius writer. *If Joyce was to be diagnosed determinately by Lacan, then he would no longer be a genius.* Diagnosing is tantamount to turning the genius into a subject, capturing him in the Oedipus structure, giving a name to his unconscious, to his enjoyment as subject not as genius, by using forms that are in the Other, and in which the particular originality of the genius would have vanished. Nature, Lacan claims in the beginning of his seminar on Joyce, is what disappears under its name; bearing a name makes nature risk being characterized by what lies outside of nature.[58]

As long as Joyce is not diagnosed, his genius is kept unarticulated but of real presence; it is nature not bearing a name. But as such, genius cannot be characterized; the hole he creates in the symbolic cannot be particularized. Genius as the vanishing mediator is a paradoxical entity that cannot be articulated as subject, and that vanishes as impossibility once the nature of his originality bears a name.

Joyce acts with language as if one could explicitly articulate all of its echoes. He provides the essence of language, thereby destroying the very possibility of assuming knowledge, or the very possibility of interpreting his writing knowledgeably. It is through this maneuver with language that Joyce turns himself into the subject supposed to know, so that all literary experts will struggle with his writing for generations to come. This taking over of the resources of language is Joyce's way of bypassing the Name-of-the-Father, the law of paternal castration. But with this bypassing, Joyce relinquishes something else. Lacan wishes to claim that Joyce lacks the fundamental imaginary competence, that competence that enables one to construct meanings, sequences, and consistent structures in language. In other words, Joyce has his own way of making use of the forms of language; he converts them into forms that are not in the Other.[59] His writing takes on itself a different status.

The work of genius cannot be simply described as transgressive; originality takes a rule that cannot be known, while only an existent rule can be transgressed. The role of consistency in Joyce's oeuvre can clarify this point. Consistency is, in principle, what holds things together; as such, it is a fictional thing to which one attributes a real presence. One depends, for instance, on the imaginary consistency of one's body, treating it as a container or a sack that holds the inside that one does not see. One is likewise trapped in the imaginary consistency of language, assuming that it can hold and convey determinate meanings in a systematic way. Joyce gave up, or gave up through a forced choice, this consistency, but he did not simply violate its imaginary function (if he did, his work would have amounted to original nonsense at most). For Joyce, Lacan claims, it is the language he actually writes that supplies the consistency that the body image he lacks should have provided him with.[60] Consistency is there, but it takes a *real* rather than an *imaginary* presence, a real rather than an imaginary or a symbolic one. Lacan demonstrates that Joyce lacks imaginary consistency through a story Joyce recounts in *The Portrait of the Artist* about an incident in which he was beaten up by his classmates.[61] Following the incident, Joyce wonders why he felt nothing against the boy who initiated this painful beating. Joyce expresses with a metaphor the way he felt toward his body at that point. He noticed, he says, that the whole event emptied him out, and he himself was like a fruit peeled off. Joyce divulges here a strange attitude toward his own body, considering the fact that the body is what gives one shape, protects one. The "I," the sense of self that one has, always depends on the image of one's body, while Joyce remains unaffected by what his body went through, and the incident slides off him like a peel off a fruit. The violence leaves no trace, because there is no body image to be affected by it. Joyce manifests something that generally structures one's being: that one does not *know* one's body, as one's body is always alien to oneself; one never fully identifies with it. What one has from one's body is the echo it leaves on one's images and forms of language. In Joyce, there is no body image: after being injured, the I, the ego responsible for the subject's imaginary consistency, does not pop up to sustain it.

This lack of imaginary consistency attests to the particular encounter of Joyce with language, the traumatic encounter he articulates in his writing. Joyce's language is particularized by a hole that marks the missing consistency, yet at the same time constitutes and locates the place of this consistency anew on real grounds. Joyce lacks the imaginary consistency that gives an image to one's body, but this lack also must take form, otherwise Joyce could not have become a writing subject, a genius. It is his genius that comes to occupy the vacancy of the lacking image.

Kant's vanishing mediation of the case of Joyce reveals a case in which genius invents language at every moment of using it. Joyce is a particular genius whose invention is that of going through language, while omitting its imaginary dimension, and bypassing the territory of meaning and sense. Joyce omitted this imaginary consistency and vacated the function of symbolic meaning, thereby sending a generation of critics to search after the meaning of his writing, just as Kant's genius, through whom the rule of nature appears in art, has sent many generations of commentators in search of the rule that will reconcile scholastic correctness with nature in this paradoxical entity.

NOTES

INTRODUCTION

1. Alain Badiou, "Lacan. Seminar Book X: Anxiety," *Lacanian Ink* 26 (2005): 70.

2. In the Introduction to the *Critique of Judgment*, Section IX, Kant presents an overview of all of the higher powers in their systematic unity; the mental powers that correspond to the power of judgment are both the feelings of pleasure *and* displeasure. See Immanuel Kant, *Critique of Judgment,* trans. Werner S. Pluhar (Indianapolis, IN: Hackett, 1987), 38.

3. Immanuel Kant, *Critique of Practical Reason,* trans. Mary Gregor (Cambridge: Cambridge University Press, 1997) §5, 24, remark I.

4. Martin Heidegger, *What Is Called Thinking?*, trans. J. Glenn Gray (New York: Perennial, 1976), 19.

5. This stipulation holds even if for Heidegger aesthetics constitutes the "bad" side of a philosophy of art, as for him "aesthetics" is the name of a philosophizing about art that severs the link between beauty and truth. *The Origin of the Work of Art,* 77.

6. See Rodolphe Gasché, *The Idea of Form: Rethinking Kant's Aesthetics* (Stanford, CA: Stanford University Press, 2003); Paul Guyer, *Kant and the Experience of Freedom* (Cambridge: Cambridge University Press, 1996); and Arthur Danto, *The Abuse of Beauty* (Chicago and LaSalle, IL: Open Court, 2003).

7. In this context, the work of Alenka Zupančič on Lacan and Kantian ethics should be mentioned, especially where she indicates the affinity between the affect of anxiety and the respect toward the moral law, which is the only purely *practical* feeling acknowledged by Kant. See Alenka Zupančič, *Ethics of the Real: Kant, Lacan* (London and New York: Verso, 2000), 141.

8. Alain Badiou, *Handbook of Inaesthetics* (Stanford, CA: Stanford University Press, 2005).

9. Guyer, 1997, pp. 71–72.

10. Jacques Lacan, *The Four Fundamental Concepts of Psychoanalysis: The Seminar of Jacques Lacan, Book XI,* trans. Alan Sheridan (New York and London: W. W. Norton and Company, 1964), 31. (Hereafter cited as *Seminar XI.*)

11. Freud, "The Uncanny," in *The Standard Edition* (hereafter *SE*), XVII, 217–56.

12. See Sigmund Freud, "The Uncanny," *SE*, XVII, 217–56; "Beyond the Pleasure Principle," *SE*, XVIII, 7–64; "Inhibitions, Symptoms, and Anxiety," *SE*, XX, 87–174.

13. Jacques Lacan, 1962–1963, *The Seminar of Jacques Lacan, Book X: Anxiety*, trans. Cormac Gallagher (Unpublished), 144 (6.3.63). (Hereafter cited as *Seminar X*.)

14. Ibid., 145.

15. The latter being one implication that can be drawn from Zupančič, "The Splendor of Creation: Kant, Nietzsche, Lacan," *Umbra: A Journal of the Unconscious* 1 (1999): 35–42.

16. Lacan, *Seminar X*, 75 (9.1.63).

17. Francois Leguil, "*Le Stade de L'angoisse*," *La Cause Freudienne: Nouvele Revue de Psychanalyse* 59 (2005): 27.

18. Freud, "Inhibitions, Symptoms, and Anxiety," *SE*, XX, 87–174.

CHAPTER 1

1. Two exemplary instances of the "institutional" objection to aesthetics can be found in Francis J. Coleman, "Is Aesthetic Pleasure a Myth?," *The Journal of Aesthetics and Art Criticism* 29:3 (1971): 319–32, and George Dickie, "The Myth of the Aesthetic Attitude," *American Philosophical Quarterly I* (1964): 56–65. While anti-aesthetic tendencies of this kind gained popularity in the late 60s and 70s, more recent trends actually divulge a revived interest in beauty, side by side with reflections on disgust and other aesthetic "displeasures."

2. See, for instance, Nick Zangwill, "The Beautiful, the Dainty, and the Dumpy," *British Journal of Aesthetics* 35:4 (1995): 317–29; Theodore A. Gracyk, "Sublimity, Ugliness, and Formlessness in Kant's Aesthetic Theory," *The Journal of Aesthetics and Art Criticism* 45:1 (1986): 49–56; Paul Mattick Jr., "Aesthetics and Anti-Aesthetics in the Visual Arts," *The Journal of Aesthetics and Art Criticism* 51:2 (1993): 253–59.

3. Kant, *Critique of Judgment*, §1, 44.

4. Freud, "Anxiety," *SE*, XVI, 403.

5. Freud, "Anxiety and Instinctual Life," *SE*, XXII, 81 ff.

6. Ibid., 93.

7. Beyond the pleasure principle, the subject orients himself or herself to a state of inertia, where neither stimulation nor discharge takes place, a fundamental state to which all existing beings strive to return. See Sigmund Freud, "Beyond the Pleasure Principle," *SE*, XVIII.

8. Kant, *Critique of Judgment*, §15, 228.

9. Rodolphe Gasché, *The Idea of Form: Rethinking Kant's Aesthetics* (Stanford, CA: Stanford University Press, 2003), 59.

10. An argument against this whole Kantian notion of "pure" aesthetic response can be found in Nick Zangwill, "Two Dogmas of Kantian Aesthetics," in *Selected Papers*, ed. Richard Woodfield, 233–38 (Nottingham: Nottingham Polytechnic Press, 1990).

11. Kant, *Critique of Judgment*, §9, 62.

12. Gasché, *The Idea of Form*, 50.

13. Ibid., 50–51.

14. Paul Guyer, *Kant and the Claims of Taste* (Cambridge: Cambridge University Press, 1979 [2d ed., 1997]), 103.

15. Henry E. Allison, *Kant's Theory of Taste: A Reading of the Critique of Aesthetic Judgment* (Cambridge: Cambridge University Press, 2001), 114–15.

16. Ibid., 189.

17. "But if cognitions are to be communicated then the mental state, i.e., the attunement of the cognitive powers that is required for cognition in general—namely, that proportion suitable for turning a presentation . . . into cognition—must also be universally communicable" (Kant, *Critique of Judgment*, §21, 88).

18. For commentaries on Kant with opposite conclusions, see Theodore Gracyk, "Sublimity, Ugliness, and Formlessness in Kant's Aesthetic Theory," *The Journal of Aesthetics and Art Criticism* 45:1 (1986), 49–56, and David Schier, "Why Kant Finds Nothing Ugly," *British Journal of Aesthetics* 38:4 (1998): 412–18.

19. Gasché, *The Idea of Form*, 49.

20. Ibid., 57.

21. Thus man is "not without a phallus," and anxiety is "not without an object."

22. For the relation between the "object" of Kantian judgments and the "not without an object" of Lacan, see my *Representing the Real* (Amsterdam and New York: Rodopi, 2002), 11–37.

23. Allison, *Kant's Theory of Taste*, 114.

24. David Shier, "Why Kant Finds Nothing Ugly," *British Journal of Aesthetics* 38:4 (1998): 412–18.

25. Ruth Lorand, "Beauty and Its Opposites," *The Journal of Aesthetics and Art Criticism* 52:4 (1994): 399–406.

26. Ibid., 405.

27. Matthew Kieran, "Aesthetic Value: Beauty, Ugliness, and Incoherence," *Philosophy* 72 (1997): 383–99.

28. Paul Guyer, *Kant and the Claims of Knowledge* (Cambridge: Cambridge University Press, 1987), 198, emphasis in original.

29. The relation of the sublime to displeasure, anxiety, and the object that elicits this experience is discussed in chapter 5 of this book.

30. Gasché, *The Idea of Form,* 145.

31. Ibid.

32. Ibid., 153.

33. In his earlier work on Kant's aesthetics, Guyer admits to having dismissed the topics of the sublime as "tied only loosely to the basic architectonic structure of the argument of the *Critique of Judgment*" (Paul Guyer, *Kant and the Experience of Freedom* [Cambridge: Cambridge University Press, 1996], 2), a conception typical of analytic approaches to Kant in the 70s.

34. As already mentioned in the Introduction, acknowledging the essential place granted to reason in pure aesthetic judgments in the Kantian scholarship of recent years marks a radical change of perspective.

35. Lacan, to be precise, refers to the subject's encounters with works of art as producing a judgment, even if not specifically an aesthetic judgment. This point will be discussed later.

36. Jacques Lacan, "The Mirror Stage as Formative of the I Function as Revealed in Psychoanalytic Experience." In *Écrits: A Selection*, trans. Bruce Fink (New York and London: Norton and Company, 2006), 75–81.

37. Lacan, *Seminar X*, 32 (28.11.62).

38. Jacques Lacan, *The Seminar of Jacques Lacan, Book V:* The Formations of the Unconscious (1957–1958), trans. Cormac Gallagher (Unpublished), 297. (Hereafter cited as *Seminar V.*)

39. Ibid., 33 (28.11.62).

40. Freud, "Inhibitions, Symptoms, and Anxiety," 164–65, emphasis in original.

41. Lacan, *Seminar X*, 29 (28.11.62).

42. Freud, "Mourning and Melancholia," *SE*, XIV, 243–58.

43. Lacan, *Seminar X*, 30 (28.11.62).

44. Martin Heidegger, *Being and Time,* trans. John Macquarrie and Edward Robinson (New York: HarperSan Francisco, 1962), 230, emphasis in original.

45. Miller, "*Introduction à la lecture de Séminaire de l'angoisse de Jacques Lacan,*" *La Cause Freudienne* 58 (2004): 64.

46. Gasché, *The Idea of Form*, 108.

CHAPTER 2

1. Lacan, *Seminar VII*, 238.

2. Kant, *Critique of Judgment*, §5, 51.

3. A judgment of taste relies on "reason's pure concept of the supersensible underlying the object as an object of sense and hence as appearance" (§57, 212).

4. Jacques Lacan, *The Seminar of Jacques Lacan, Book IX: Identification* (1961–1962), trans. Cormac Gallagher (Unpublished), 2 (15.11.61). (Hereafter cited as *Seminar IX.*)

5. Ibid.

6. Antigone's position combines the splendor and the transgressiveness (toward the social law) of the inaccessible Thing, which is why J. M. Rabaté defines Antigone as "both sublime and beautiful in her 'blinding way' precisely because she does not sublimate her own desire; rather, she heightens it and charges it with libidinal intensity, even when this desire is a desire for death." See Jean-Michel Rabaté, *Jacques Lacan: Psychoanalysis and the Subject of Literature* (New York: Palgrave, 2001), 79.

7. Lacan, *Seminar VII*, 271.

8. Lacan, *Seminar VII*, 238–39.

9. Thierry De Duve, *Kant after Duchamp* (Cambridge, MA and London: MIT Press, 1996).

10. Arthur Danto, *The Abuse of Beauty: Aesthetics and the Concept of Art* (Chicago and LaSalle, IL: Open Court Press, 2003), 6–8.

11. See the introduction of the catalogue editors of a Hirshorn exhibit: Benezra, Neal, and Viso, Olga, eds., *Regarding Beauty: A View of the Late Twentieth Century* (Washington, DC: Hirshhorn Museum, in association with Hatje Cantz, 1999).

12. The latter possibility is best represented by Danto, *The Abuse of Beauty*.

13. Kant, *Critique of Judgment*, §48, 180.

14. Lacan, *Seminar VII*, 261.

15. Ibid., 261.

16. Ibid.

17. Danto, *The Abuse of Beauty*, 8–9.

18. Ibid., 13.

19. This is to distinguish the current agenda from attempts to assert the death of aesthetics in the face of the possible ugliness of art and its potential disgusting effects ever since the avant-garde.

20. Kant, *Critique of Judgment*, §23, 98.

21. Sarah Kofman, *Freud and Fiction*, trans. Sarah Wykes (Boston, MA: Northeastern University Press, 1991), 122.

22. Freud, "The Uncanny," *SE*, XVII, 219–56.

23. Kofman, quoted earlier, rejects Freud's emphasis on the indeterminacy regarding the doll, an indeterminacy that reflects the character's point of view as either delusional or realistic. Freud's interpretation is inadequate for Hoffman's poetic project, because for Hoffman, so claims Kofman, all reality is equally visionary and results from fragments of "inner compulsion" that transform reality.

24. Freud, "The Uncanny," 237.

25. Jacques Lacan, "Position of the Unconscious," in *Reading Seminar XI: Lacan's Four Fundamental Concepts of Psychoanalysis*, ed. Richard Feldstein, Bruce Fink, and Maire Jaanus, 275 (Albany: State University of New York Press, 1995).

26. Dylan Evans, *An Introductory Dictionary of Lacanian Psychoanalysis* (London and New York: Routledge, 1996), 33.

27. Lacan, *Seminar X*, 34 (28.11.62).

28. Ibid., 40 (5.12.62).

29. Ibid., 32 (28.11.62).

30. Freud, "Beyond the Pleasure Principle," *SE*, XVIII.

31. Freud, "Inhibitions," 169.

32. Jacques Lacan, "The Subversion of the Subject and the Dialectic of Desire," in *Écrits: A Selection*, trans. Bruce Fink (New York and London: W. W. Norton & Company, 1977), 289–90.

33. The latter, for instance, is the case of Freud's sitting in a train compartment "when a more than usually violent jolt of the train swung back the door of the adjoining washing-cabinet and an elderly gentleman in a dressing-gown and a travelling cap came in. I assumed that in leaving the washing-cabinet, which lay between the two compartments, he had taken the wrong direction and come into my compartment by mistake. Jumping up with the intention of putting him right, I at once realized to my dismay that the intruder was nothing but my own reflection in the looking-glass on the open door." See Freud, "The Uncanny," 248.

34. Paul Guyer, *Values of Beauty: Historical Essays in Aesthetics* (Cambridge: Cambridge University Press, 2005), 183–84, 196.

35. The proximity of the ideal of beauty to the notion of "aesthetic idea" here becomes evident. An "aesthetic idea" refers to the power of the imagination that makes, through a strike of genius, "a rational or moral idea on the one side palpable through a sensible form and a wealth of imagery on the other" (Guyer, *Values of Beauty*, 184).

36. Gasché, *The Idea of Form*, 107.

37. Ibid., 103.

38. Kant, *Critique of Judgment*, §17, 79.

39. Ibid., §49, 181–82.

40. Gasché, *The Idea of Form*, 113.

41. Jennifer Mundy, *Surrealism: Desire Unlimited* (London: Tate, 2001).

42. Foster himself dedicated a book-length study to surrealist aesthetics, see Hal Foster, *Compulsive Beauty* (Cambridge, MA, and London: MIT Press, 1993).

43. Hal Foster, "Violation and Veiling in Surrealist Photography: Woman as Fetish, as Shattered, as Phallus," in *Surrealism: Desire Unlimited*, 208.

44. Lacan, *Seminar VII*, 279.

45. Ibid., 239.

46. Foster, *Compulsive Beauty*.

47. Foster, "Violation and Veiling in Surrealist Photography," 215.

48. Lacan, *Seminar VII*, 71.

49. Freud, "The Uncanny," 232.

50. The original work was a holographic photograph of a virtual figure of a pop star, with a headshot of the artist herself wearing pink contact lenses. The later work, here presented, is a photograph with, again, a three-dimensional effect but with a doll-head. Both images are accompanied by a pop song composed and sung by the artist.

51. Lacan, *Seminar XI*, 103.

52. Hal Foster, *The Return of the Real* (Cambridge and London: MIT Press, 1996), 132, emphasis in original.

53. Freud, "Anxiety and Instinctual Life," *SE*, XXII, 85.

54. Kant, *Critique of Judgment*, §17, 80.

CHAPTER 3

1. Kant, *Critique of Judgment*, §23, 98.

2. Guyer, *Kant and the Claims of Taste*, 105.

3. Ibid., 25.

4. "Affects" because, as explained in the first chapter, after Kant the only possibility to think about aesthetic experience as distinct from psychological sentiments is by the structure (cognitive for Kant, psychic for Freud and Lacan) within which the logic of aesthetic experience can be articulated, hence "affect" and not "effect." We refer to anxiety and not to an "anxiety state," to aesthetic displeasure and not to displeasing sentiments or pain.

5. Jacques-Alain Miller, "Introduction à la lecture de Séminaire de l'angoisse de Jacques Lacan," *La Cause Freudienne* 58 (2004): 62.

6. Kant, *Critique of Judgment*, §25, 106.

7. Lacan, *Seminar VII*, 321.

8. Freud, "On Psychotherapy," *SE*, VII, 261.

9. Freud, "Freud's Psycho-analytic Procedure," *SE*, VII, 249.

10. Lacan, *Seminar VII*, 134.

11. Aristotle, *Poetics* (London: Everyman's Library, 1963), 12.

12. Aristotle, *Politics* (New York: The Modern Library, Random House, 1943), book VIII, part 5.

13. Aristotle, *Politics,* book VIII, part VII.

14. Lacan, *Seminar VII,* 246.

15. "*Jouissance*" is distinguished by Lacan from pleasure. While the pleasure principle limits enjoyment, the prohibition on it is constantly transgressed by the subject. Beyond the pleasure principle reached through transgression, the subject touches the possibility of limitless excessive pleasure that is unbearable and hence painful for the subject. Beyond the pleasure principle is hence a satisfaction derived through suffering (see Evans, *An Introductory Dictionary of Lacanian Psychoanalysis,* 91–92).

16. Lacan, *Seminar VII,* 246.

17. Ibid., 321–22.

18. "*Vous saississez à quoi sert la tragédie: À nous raeler ą nous, sujets de la science voués au service des biens, quel franchissement de la limite suose l'expérience de notre désir*" (François Regnault, *Conférences d'Esthétique Lacanienne* [Paris: Agalma Diffusion Seuil, 1997], 93).

19. Lacan, *Seminar VII,* 247.

20. ". . . through pity and fear effecting the proper purgation of these emotions." (Aristotle, *Poetics,* footnote 9).

21. Juan-David Nasio, *The Book of Love and Pain: Thinking at the Limit with Freud and Lacan,* trans. David Pettigrew and Francois Raffoul (Albany: State University of New York Press, 2004), 96.

22. Freud, "Civilization and Its Discontents," *SE,* XXI, 79.

23. Lacan, *Seminar VII,* 247.

24. Ibid., 247–48.

25. Stephen Halliwell, "Pleasure, Understanding, and Emotion in Aristotle's *Poetics,*" in *Essays on Aristotles's Poetics,* ed. Amélie Oksenberg Rorty, 241–60 (Princeton, NJ: Princeton University Press, 1992).

26. Martha Nussbaum, "Tragedy and Self-Sufficiency: Plato and Aristotle on Fear and Pity," in *Essays on Aristotles's Poetics,* ed. Amélie Oksenberg Rorty, 272 (Princeton, NJ: Princeton University Press, 1992).

27. Ibid., 281.

28. Ibid., 282–83.

29. Jonathan Lear, "Katharsis," in *Essays on Aristotles's Poetics,* ed. Amélie Oksenberg Rorty, 315–40 (Princeton, NJ: Princeton University Press, 1992).

30. Ibid., 317.

31. Ibid., 318.

32. Ibid., 333.

33. Ibid.

34. Ibid., 334.

35. See Regnault, *Conférences d'esthétique lacanienne.*

36. Lacan, *Seminar VII,* 221.

37. Kant, *Critique of Judgment,* §28, 120, emphasis added.

38. Ibid.

39. Nasio, *Book of Love and Pain,* 78.

CHAPTER 4

1. This notion of anxiety as a cause is not incompatible with Alenka Zupančič's apparently opposite claim that anxiety has no cause, a claim she raises in the context of her treatment of the similarity between anxiety and the Kantian respect for the moral law (140 ff.). Situating respect for the moral law in the same register as anxiety is based for her on the fact that both *do not have a cause*, but they have an object. In both the lack of a cause correlates with the emergence of the object. Yet the cause that anxiety and respect lack is the cause that makes part of a chain of causality, and lack in the chain is where the object-as-cause emerges. I refer to this place of the object as signaling the cause of desire.

2. See Jacques-Alain Miller, "Sept rémarques de Jacques-Alain Miller sur la création," *La lettere mensualle*, publishd by *Ecole de la cause Freudienne* 68 (1988): 9–13.

3. Freud, "Inhibitions," 134, emphasis in original.

4. Ibid., 138.

5. Miller, *Introduction à la lecture de Séminaire de l'angoisse de Jacques Lacan*, 62.

6. Freud, "Inhibitions," 144.

7. Ibid., 166.

8. Leguil, "*Le Stade de L'angoisse*," 23–32.

9. The first phase of the phantasm relates the memory or account of the subject/patient, staging the scene as if the subject is not part of it: a child is being beaten. During analysis, further modifications of the initial formulation take place, usually replacing the impersonal form with concrete agents: my father is beating my brother, my uncle is beating another child. Since the structure of the phantasm stages an unconscious desire, the core of the phantasm cannot become known to the subject and is only the product of the analyst's work of reconstruction: my father is beating me. This latter, intermediate phase is never brought to consciousness and is, in fact, eternally omitted from the subject's memory.

10. Freud, "Inhibitions," 135.

11. Leguil, "*Le Stade de L'angoisse*," 25 ff.

12. Freud, "Inhibitions," 132.

13. Ibid., 166.

14. I refer from now on to "drives" whenever possible, although in Stratchey's canonical translation of Freud the drives are referred to as "instincts," thus making it difficult to discern Freud's notion of "*Trieb*" from "*Instinkt*." See Evans, "Drive," *An Introductory Dictionary of Lacanian Psychoanalysis*, 46–49.

15. Freud, "Inhibitions," 145.

16. Lacan, *Seminar X*, 107 (23.1.63).

17. Lacan, *Seminar X*, 293.

18. Lacan, "Introduction to the Names-of-the-Father Seminar," in *Television*, ed. Joan Copjec, 81–95 (New York and London: W. W. Norton & Company, 1990), 82.

19. Nasio, *Book of Love and Pain*, 96.

20. Lacan, *Seminar X*, 142 (6.3.63).

21. Roberto Harari, *Lacan's Seminar on "Anxiety": An Introduction* (New York: Other Press, 2001), 227.

22. Lacan, *Seminar X*, 3 (14.11.62).

23. Arthur C. Danto. "Play/Things," in *Peter Fischli and David Weiss: In a Restless World*, ed. Elizabeth Armstrong, 111 (Minneapolis: Walker Art Center, 1996), emphasis in original.

24. Freud, "Anxiety and Instinctual Life," 93–95.

25. Harari, *Lacan's Seminar on "Anxiety,"* 264.

26. Kant, *Critique of Judgment*, §8, 59–60.

27. Heidegger, *Being and Time*, §40, 228–35.

28. Lacan, *Seminar X*, 5 (14.11.62).

29. Lacan, "Introduction to the Names-of-the-Father Seminar," 82.

30. Freud, "Anxiety," 393–94; "Inhibitions," 144 ff.

31. Leguil, "*Le Stade de L'angoisse*," 27.

32. Kant, *Critique of Judgment*, §8, 60.

33. Lacan, *Seminar XI*, 29–41.

34. Freud, "Anxiety," 395.

35. Ibid., 396.

36. Lacan, *Seminar XI*, 224–27.

37. Freud, "The Unconscious," *SE*, XIV, 166–204.

38. Leguil, "*Le Stade de L'angoisse*," 29.

39. Ibid., 31.

40. Lacan, *Seminar X*, 196 (8.5.63).

41. Ibid., 197 (8.5.63).

42. Ibid., 197–98 (8.5.63).

43. Lacan, *Seminar XI*, 67–78; Evans, *An Introductory Dictionary of Lacanian Psychoanalysis*, 190.

44. Freud, "Inhibitions," 143.

45. See my *Representing the Real*, 119; Miller, "Reflections on the Formal Envelope of the Symptom," *Lacanian Ink* 4 (1991): 13–21.

46. Lacan refers to Kierkegaard in his seminar and rejects his idea of anxiety as concept. See Lacan, *Seminar X*, 14 (21.11.62).

47. Miller, *Introduction*, 77.

48. Lacan, *Seminar X*, 294 (3.7.63).

49. Ibid., 297 (3.7.63).

50. Ibid., 296 (3.7.63).

51. Ibid.

52. Ibid., 302 (3.7.63).

53. Ibid.

54. Miller, *Introduction*, 70.

55. Ibid., 72, 90.

56. Jacques Lacan, *Le Seminaire, Livre IV. La relation d'objet* (Paris: Seuil, 1994).

57. Miller, *Introduction*, 82–84.

58. Ibid., 81

59. Lacan, *Seminar X*, 300 (3.7.63).

60. Lacan, *Seminar VII*, 121.

61. Miller, "*Sept rémarques de Jacques-Alain Miller sur la création*," 9–13.

62. Freud, "Leonardo da Vinci and the Memory of His Childhood," *SE*, XI, 63–137.

63. Miller, "*Sept rémarques de Jacques-Alain Miller sur la création*," 10.

64. Willy Apollon refers to *the sexual division* in similar terms when he describes the sexual positions as ones toward the procreating father. Procreation is a singular act that happens once, without any possibility of repetition, and it is to be distinguished from mechanical, biological reproduction that scientific discourse can represent. The procreative paternal act hence exhibits a *jouissance* "that comes from beyond need and satisfaction." The speaking subject, being the product of the father's act of procreation, encounters the Other's *jouissance* in the paternal procreative *jouissance*, an encounter that can lead to various ethical solutions in the sexual position. This idea that the sexual position requires a mode of creation by way of response to recreation also bridges the distance between the modernist doctrine: "everyone is an artist" and Kant's genius. See Willy Apollon, "The Jouissance of the Other and the Sexual Division in Psychoanalysis," in *After Lacan: Clinical Practice and the Subject of the Unconscious*, ed. W. Apollon, D. Bergeron, and L. Cantin, 53 (Albany: State University of New York Press, 2002).

CHAPTER 5

1. Charles Shepherdson, "Lacan and Philosophy," in *The Cambridge Companion to Lacan*, ed. J-M. Rabaté, 125 (Cambridge: Cambridge University Press, 2003).
2. Kant, *Critique of Judgment*, §23, 98.
3. Ibid., §23, 99–100.
4. Ibid., §26, 113.
5. Ibid.
6. Martin Heidegger, "The Origin of the Work of Art," in *Poetry, Language, Thought*, trans. Albert Hofstadter (New York: HarperCollins, Perennial Classics, 1971), 40–41.
7. Kant, *Critique of Judgment*, §27, 114–15.
8. Ibid., §27, 115.
9. Harari, *Lacan's Seminar on "Anxiety*," 33–35.
10. Kant distinguishes between two kinds of sublime: the mathematical sublime is when we call something large beyond all comparison (it has to do with absolute magnitude); the dynamical sublime is when we see something as having inscrutable might and dominance.
11. Gasché, *The Idea of Form*, 111.
12. It obviously could be claimed that Friedrich misinterpreted Kant, as many have done after him, taking the sublime to be a feature of the object observed, yet we refer to this artistic gesture of introducing the observing subject as symptomatic of something crucial regarding the sublime and its object.
13. Guyer, for instance, justifies his limited interest (to say the least) in the sublime in his earlier book *Kant and the Claims of Taste* (1979) with his then-decisive opinion that the relations between aesthetics and morality lie outside of the main concerns of the third critique.

14. Jean-François Lyotard, *The Postmodern Condition: A Report on Knowledge*, trans. Geoff Bennington and Brian Massumi (Minneapolis: University of Minnesota Press, 1984).

15. For Lyotard, the postmodern is part of the modern, that is, it also has to do with the sublime relation between the presentable and the conceivable; yet while the modern emphasizes the powerlessness of the faculty of presentation (a nostalgia for presence), the postmodern emphasizes "the increase of being and the jubilation which results from the invention of new rules of the game" (79–80).

16. David Martyn argues in relation to the sublime, that critique of the sublime as a feigned failure of the imagination giving rise to the dominance of reason is a critique whose history runs from romanticism, through Horkheimer and Adorno and up to Paul de Man, and is part of a more general critique of such Enlightenment concepts as selfhood and reason, and a critique of Enlightenment's ideology. See David Martyn, *Sublime Failures* (Detroit, MI: Wayne State University Press, 2002), 135 ff.

17. Jacques Derrida, *The Truth in Painting*, trans. Geoff Bennington and Ian McLeod (Chicago and London: University of Chicago Press, 1987), 139.

18. Ibid.

19. Ibid., 143.

20. Kant, *Critique of Judgment*, §26, 109.

21. Alenka Zupančič, "The Splendor of Creation," *Umbra: A Journal of the Unconscious* (1999) 35–42.

22. Freud, "Inhibitions," 165.

23. Lacan, *Seminar X*, 140–41 (6.3.63).

24. Ibid., 286 ff. (26.6.63).

25. Ibid.

26. Lacan refers to the question regarding the object at the origin of desire with Winnicott's "transitional object" ("the shred of blanket or beloved shard the child's lips or hands never stop touching"), an emblem by which he describes the relations between desire and the absolute Other. Desire can alleviate anxiety in the subject because it reverses the demand for love instated in the Other so the Other is constituted as absolute (in its ability to satisfy) but also as detached. This detachment necessary to mediate overwhelming need is exemplified in the early phase of adopting a transitional object. Although this notion of transitional object is "representation's representative in the absolute condition," it clarifies the way separation is enacted through an odd object, thereby alleviating anxiety. See Lacan, "The Subversion of the Subject and the Dialectic of Desire," 689, and Philippe van Haute, *Against Adaptation: Lacan's "Subversion" of the Subject* (New York: Other Press, 2002), 119 ff.

27. James Joyce, "The Dead," in *Dubliners*, 199–255 (London: Jonathan Cape [1954], 1914).

28. Ibid., 239–40.

29. A branch of mathematics, nonquantitative geometry dealing with geometric configurations (shapes and spaces) that remain unchanged by stretching, bending, or twisting and with properties retained under deformation. "Lacan has widely and increasingly used topology as providing a non-intuitive purely intellectual means of

expressing the concept of structure beyond any imaginary capture. With topology there is no occultation of the symbolic." See Evans, *An Introductory Dictionary of Lacanian Psychoanalysis*; Ellie Ragland and Dragan Milovanovic, *Lacan: Topologically Speaking* (New York: Other Press, 2004).

30. It is significant to quote in this context J-A. Miller, who in an address to American academics at Yale reminds them that unlike literary analysts who wish to master the finite totality of their corpus (for which reason, in France, a thesis cannot be written on a living author), psychoanalysts interpret with the intention of changing something for the living subject. See Miller, "The Analytic Experience: Means, Ends, and Results," in *Lacan and the Subject of Language,* ed. Ellie Ragland-Sullivan and Mark Bracher, 83–99 (New York and London: Routledge, 1991).

31. Jacques Lacan, "Notes on the Work of François Rouan," in *As Painting: Division and Displacement,* ed. Philip Armstrong, Laura Lisbon, and Stephen Melville, 233–42 (Cambridge, MA and London: MIT Press, 2001).

32. Kant, *Critique of Judgment,* §49, 183.

33. Ibid., §57, 215.

34. Ibid.

35. Ibid., §49 182.

36. De Duve, *Kant after Duchamp.*

37. Ibid., 321.

38. Gasché, *The Idea of Form.*

39. Paul Guyer, *Kant and the Experience of Freedom* (Cambridge: Cambridge University Press, 1996).

40. Ibid.

41. Ibid., 216 ff.

42. Ibid., 220–21.

43. Gasché, *The Idea of Form,* 123–24.

44. Gasché, *The Idea of Form,* 124, emphasis added.

45. Ibid., 125.

46. Ibid., 126.

47. Ibid.

48. Gasché, *The Idea of Form,* 145.

49. Kant, *Critique of Judgment,* §23, 98.

50. A suggestion along similar lines was made by Zupančič with regard to the object of creation in general. See Zupančič, "The Splendor of Creation: Kant, Nietzsche, Lacan," *Umbra: A Journal of the Unconscious* 1 (1999): 35–42.

51. Let us be reminded that while Freud's *Trieb* was translated as "instinct" in the standard edition (thus conflating drive and instinct), I use "drive" here, unless quoting directly from Freud.

52. Freud, "Instincts and their Vicissitudes," *SE,* XIV, 122–23.

53. Ibid., 132.

54. Freud, "On Narcissism: An Introduction," *SE,* XIV, 94.

55. "With Kant the sublime designates the relation of an inner-worldly, empirical, sensuous object to *Ding an sich,* to the transcendent, trans-phenomenal, unattainable Thing-in-itself." See Slavoj Zizek, *The Sublime Object of Ideology* (London and New York: Verso, 1989), 202–203.

56. Gasché, *The Idea of Form*, 141–42.
57. Ibid., 153.
58. Lacan, *Seminar VII*, 91.
59. Ibid., 91–92.
60. Ibid., 110.
61. Freud, "Three Essays on Sexuality," *SE*, VII, 135–243.
62. Ibid., 178.
63. Ibid., 238.
64. Ibid., 156.
65. Lacan, *Seminar VII*, 98.
66. Freud, "Three Essays on Sexuality," 161.
67. Lacan, *Seminar VII*, 112.

CHAPTER 6

1. Jacques Lacan, *The Seminar of Jacques Lacan Book XXIII*: *Le Sinthome*, 20 (13.1.76).
2. James Joyce, *Finnegans Wake* (London: Penguin Classics [1992] 1939).
3. Kant, *Critique of Judgment*, §49, 183.
4. Lacan, *Seminar XXIII*, 62 (11.5.76).
5. Kant, *Critique of Judgment*, 178.
6. Gasché, *The Idea of Form*, 189.
7. De Duve, *Kant after Duchamp*, 352 ff.
8. Jacques-Alan Miller, "Joyce avec Lacan," *La Cause Freudienne* 38 (1998).
9. Ibid., 11, my translation.
10. Lacan, *Seminar XI*, 198–99.
11. "Awaken" here is a play on *Finnegans Wake*.
12. "However, I sometimes wonder about the affinity between the formation of a corporeal pain and the genesis of a psychotic symptom." See Nasio, *Book of Love and Pain*, 75.
13. Kant, *Critique of Judgment*, §46, 174–75.
14. In a gallery talk of Maya Cohen-Levi, in Alon-Segev Gallery, June 2004.
15. Kant, *Critique of Judgment*, §49, 183.
16. Ibid., §47, 176–77.
17. Ibid., §49, 186.
18. Paul Guyer, "Exemplary Originality: Genius, Universality, and Individuality," in *The Creation of Art: New Essays in Philosophical Aesthetics*, ed. Berys Gaut and Paisley Livingston, 125 (Cambridge: Cambridge University Press, 2003).
19. Kant, *Critique of Judgment*, §47, 178.
20. Ibid., §47, 177–78.
21. Ibid., §46, 175.
22. Martin Gammon, " 'Exemplary Originality': Kant on Genius and Imitation," *Journal of the History of Philosophy* 35:4 (1997): 563–92.
23. Guyer, "Exemplary Originality."
24. Guyer, *Kant and the Experience of Freedom*, 301.

25. Kant, *Critique of Judgment*, §50, 188.

26. Guyer, "Exemplary Originality," 128.

27. See Gammon, "Exemplary Originality," 563–92.

28. Ibid., 592.

29. "Historical," in the context of Kant, has a specific status. Although Kant raises in the context of genius some historical considerations (such as his thesis regarding the "end of art," §47, 177), "exemplary originality" for Kant must refer to the epistemology of the subject and not to actual historical circumstances, unless we are already exceeding the confines of the Kantian mode of thought. Guyer, for instance, refers to historical facts about the stimulating effects that genius has on art, as motivated by Kant's very conception of genius, whose implication is that the history of art will be one of "constant upheaval in forms of artistic success" (Guyer, "Exemplary Originality," 132). History is hence relevant inasmuch as it is a logical consequence of epistemology.

30. An idea Danto expresses or an instance in "The End of Art," in *The Philosophical Disenfranchisement of Art*, ed. Arthur Danto, 81–116 (New York: Columbia University Press, 1986), and in *After the End of Art: Contemporary Art and the Pale of History* (Princeton, NJ: Princeton University Press, 1997).

31. Jakob Steinbrenner, "The Unimaginable," *History and Theory* 37:4 (1998): 122–23.

32. Guyer, *Kant and the Experience of Freedom*, 157.

33. Ibid.

34. Gasché, *The Idea of Form*, 187.

35. Ibid., 185.

36. Ibid., 186.

37. Ibid.

38. Ibid., 188.

39. Ibid., 187.

40. Allison, *Kant's Theory of Taste*.

41. Ibid., 286.

42. To this branch of interpretations of genius also belongs Denis Dutton's review "What Is Genius?," which after the work (of Keith Simonton) on the origins of genius explores the common personality and mental dispositions of geniuses in terms such as "inventive," "introverted," "unconventional," and the like. See Denis Dutton, "What Is Genius?," *Philosophy and Literature* 25 (2001): 181–96.

43. Kant, *Critique of Judgment*, §47, 177.

44. "Vanishing mediator" is a necessary kernel that must be repressed so understanding can take place. This vanishing mediator, at least the concept, can be found in Schelling and is outlined in more detail in the work of Jameson and Zizek (when they talk about the quadratic structure of Hegel).

45. Slavoj Zizek, *For They Know Not What They Say: Enjoyment as a Political Factor* (London and New York: Verso, 1991), 182.

46. Slavoj Zizek, *The Indivisible Remainder* (London and New York: Verso, 1996), 92.

47. Lacan, *Seminar XXIII*, 58 (11.5.76).

48. Ibid.

49. Evans, *An Introductory Dictionary of Lacanian Psychoanalysis*, 189.

50. Miller, "Joyce avec Lacan," 13–14.

51. Lacan, *Seminar VIII*, 95 (1.3.61).

52. Lacan, *Seminar XXIII*, 52 (13.4.76).

53. Lacan, *Seminar X*, 105 (23.1.63).

54. Miller, *Sept remarques de Jacques-Alain Miller sur la création*, 10, my translation.

55. Ibid., 29–30, 20.1.76.

56. See Roberto Harari, *How James Joyce Made His Name: A Reading of the Final Lacan* (New York: Other Press, 2002), 63, 137 ff.

57. Lacan, *Seminar XXIII*, 3–4 (18.11.75).

58. Ibid., 1.

59. Which is the way Miller defines the work of the poet in his article "Reflections on the Formal Envelope of the Symptom," *Lacanian Ink* 4 (1991): 13–21.

60. Lacan, *Seminar XXIII*, 60 (11.5.76).

61. Ibid., 59 (11.5.76).

BIBLIOGRAPHY

Allison, Henry E. *Kant's Theory of Taste: A Reading of the Critique of Aesthetic Judgment.* Cambridge: Cambridge University Press, 2001.

Apollon, Willy. "The Jouissance of the Other and the Sexual Division in Psychoanalysis." In *After Lacan: Clinical Practice and the Subject of the Unconscious,* edited by W. Apollon, D. Bergeron, and L. Cantin, 49–58. Albany: State University of New York Press, 2002.

Aristotle. *Poetics.* Translated by John Warrington. London: Everyman's Library, 1963.

———. *Politics.* Translated by Benjamin Jowett. New York: The Modern Library, Random House, 1943.

Badiou, Alain. *Handbook of Inaesthetics.* Stanford, CA: Stanford University Press, 2005.

———. "Lacan. Seminar. Book X: Anxiety." *Lacanian Ink* 26 (2005): 70–71.

Benezra, Neal, and Viso, Olga M. *Regarding Beauty.* Washington, DC: Hirshorn Museum, 1999.

Coleman, Francis, J. "Is Aesthetic Pleasure a Myth?" *The Journal of Aesthetics and Art Criticism* 29:3 (1971): 319–32.

Danto, Arthur C. *The Abuse of Beauty: Aesthetics and the Concept of Art.* Chicago and LaSalle, IL: Open Court Press, 2003.

———. *The Philosophical Disenfranchisement of Art.* New York: Columbia University Press, 1986.

———. *After the End of Art: Contemporary Art and the Pale of History.* Princeton, NJ: Princeton University Press, 1997.

———. "Play/Things." In *Peter Fischli and David Weiss: In a Restless World.* edited by Elizabeth Armstrong, 95–113. Minneapolis, MN: Walker Art Center, 1996.

De Duve, Thierry. *Kant after Duchamp.* Cambridge, MA, and London: MIT Press, 1996.

Derrida, Jacques. *The Truth in Painting.* Translated by Geoff Bennington and Ian McLeod. Chicago and London: University of Chicago Press, 1987.

Dickie, George. "The Myth of the Aesthetic Attitude." *American Philosophical Quarterly* 1 (1964): 56–65.

Dutton, Denis. "What Is Genius?" *Philosophy and Literature* 25 (2001): 181–96.

Evans, Dylan. *An Introductory Dictionary of Lacanian Psychoanalysis.* London and New York: Routledge, 1996.

Foster, Hal. *Compulsive Beauty*. Cambridge, MA, and London: MIT Press, 1993.

———. *The Return of the Real*. Cambridge, MA, and London: MIT Press, 1996.

———. "Violation and Veiling in Surrealist Photography: Woman as Fetish, as Shattered, as Phallus." In *Surrealism: Desire Unbound*, edited by Mundy Jennifer, 203–26. London: Tate, 2001.

Freud, Sigmund. "Anxiety." In *Introductory Lectures on Psycho-Analysis* 1916–1917. *SE*, XVI, 392–411, 1963.

———. "Anxiety and Instinctual Life." In *New Introductory Lectures on Psycho-Analysis*. 1932. *SE*, XXII, 81–111, 1960.

———. "A Child Is Being Beaten." 1919. *SE*, XVII, 179–204, 1955.

———. "Beyond the Pleasure Principle." 1920. *SE*, XVIII, 7–64, 1955.

———. "Civilization and Its Discontents." 1930. *SE* XXI, 64–145, 1961.

———. "Freud's Psycho-analytic Procedure," 1904. *SE*, VII, 249–54, 1953.

———. "Inhibitions, Symptoms, and Anxiety." 1926. *SE*, XX, 75–172, 1959.

———. "Instincts and Their Vicissitudes." 1915. *SE*, XIV, 117–40, 1957.

———. "Leonardo da Vinci and the Memory of His Childhood." 1910. *SE*, XI, 63–137, 1957.

———. "Mourning and Melancholia." 1917. *SE*, XIV, 243–58, 1957.

———. "On Narcissism: An Introduction." 1914. *SE*, XIV, 73–102, 1957.

———. "On Psychotherapy." 1904. *SE*, VII, 257–68, 1953.

———. *The Standard Edition of the Complete Psychological Works of Sigmund Freud*. Edited by James Strachey. London: Hogarth Press and the Institute of Psycho Analysis, 1953. (Cited in text as *SE*).

———. "Three Essays on Sexuality." 1905. *SE*, VII, 135–243, 1953.

———. "The Uncanny." 1919. *SE*, XVII, 219–56, 955.

———. "The Unconscious." 1915. *SE*, XIV, 166–204, 1957.

Gammon, Martin. "Exemplary Originality": Kant on Genius and Imitation. *Journal of the History of Philosophy* 35:4 (1997): 563–92.

Gasché, Rodolphe. *The Idea of Form: Rethinking Kant's Aesthetics*. Stanford, CA: Stanford University Press, 2003.

Gracyk, Theodore A. "Sublimity, Ugliness, and Formlessness in Kant's Aesthetic Theory." *The Journal of Aesthetics and Art Criticism* 45:1 (1986): 49–56.

Guyer, Paul. "Exemplary Originality: Genius, Universality, and Individuality." In *The Creation of Art: New Essays in Philosophical Aesthetics*, edited by Berys Gaut and Paisley Livingston, 116–37. Cambridge: Cambridge University Press, 2003.

———. *Kant and the Claims of Knowledge*. Cambridge: Cambridge University Press, 1987.

———. *Kant and the Claims of Taste*. Cambridge: Cambridge University Press, 1979. (2d ed. 1997).

———. *Kant and the Experience of Freedom*. Cambridge: Cambridge University Press, 1996.

———. *Values of Beauty: Historical Essays in Aesthetics*. Cambridge: Cambridge University Press, 2005.

Halliwell, Stephen. "Pleasure, Understanding, and Emotion in Aristotle's *Poetics*." In *Essays on Aristotles's Poetics*, edited by Amélie Oksenberg Rorty, 241–60. Princeton, NJ: Princeton University Press, 1992.

Harari, Roberto. *How James Joyce Made His Name: A Reading of the Final Lacan*. New York: Other Press, 2002.

———. *Lacan's Seminar on "Anxiety": An Introduction*. New York: Other Press, 2001.

Heidegger, Martin. *Being and Time*. 1926. Translated by John Macquarrie and Edward Robinson. New York, HarperCollins Books: HarperSan Francisco, 1962.

———. "The Origin of the Work of Art." 1935–1936. In *Poetry, Language, Thought*, 15–86. New York: HarperCollins Books, Perennial Classics, 1971.

———. *What Is Called Thinking?* 1954. Translated by J. Glenn Gray. New York: Perennial, 1976.

Joyce, James. "The Dead." In *Dubliners*. London: Jonathan Cape [1954], 1914.

———. *Finnegans Wake*. London: Penguin Classics, (1992), 1939.

Kant, Immanuel. *Critique of Judgment*. 1790. Translated by Werner S. Pluhar. Indianapolis, IN: Hackett, 1987.

———. *Critique of Practical Reason*. 1788. Translated by Mary Gregor. Cambridge: Cambridge University Press, 1997.

Kieran, Matthew. "Aesthetic Value: Beauty, Ugliness, and Incoherence." *Philosophy* 72 (1997): 383–99.

Kofman, Sarah. *Freud and Fiction*. Translated by Sarah Wykes. Boston, MA: Northeastern University Press, 1991.

Lacan, Jacques. *The Ethics of Psychoanalysis: The Seminar of Jacques Lacan, Book VII*. 1959–1960. Translated by Dennis Porter. New York and London: W. W. Norton and Company, 1986.

———. *The Four Fundamental Concepts of Psychoanalysis: The Seminar of Jacques Lacan, Book XI*. 1964. Translated by Alan Sheridan. New York and London: W. W. Norton and Company, 1998.

———. "Introduction to the Names-of-the-Father Seminar. In *Television*. 1963. Edited by Joan Copjec. Translated by Denis Hollier, Rosalind Krauss, and Annette Michelson. New York and London: Norton, 1990.

———. "The Mirror Stage as Formative of the *I* Function as Revealed in Psychoanalytic Experience." 1949. In *Écrits: A Selection*. Translated by Bruce Fink. New York and London: Norton and Company, 2006, 75–81.

———. "Notes on the Work of François Rouan." In *As Painting: Division and Displacement*. 1978. Edited by Philip Armstrong, Laura Lisbon, and Stephen Melville. Cambridge, MA, and London: MIT Press, 2001.

———. "Position of the Unconscious." In *Reading Seminar XI: Lacan's Four Fundamental Concepts of Psychoanalysis*. 1964. Edited by Richard Feldstein, Bruce Fink, and Maire Jaanus. Albany: State University of New York Press, 1995.

———. *Le Seminaire, Livre IV. La relation d'objet*. 1956–1957. Edited by J-A Miller. Paris: Seuil, 1994.

———. *The Seminar of Jacques Lacan, Book IX: Identification*. 1961–1962. Translated by Cormac Gallagher. Unpublished.

———. *The Seminar of Jacques Lacan, Book V:* The Formations of the Unconscious. 1957–1958. Translated by Cormac Gallagher. Unpublished.

———. *The Seminar of Jacques Lacan, Book VIII: The Transference*. 1960–1961. Translated by Cormac Gallagher. Unpublished.

———. *The Seminar of Jacques Lacan, Book X: Anxiety*. 1962–1963. Translated by Cormac Gallagher, from unedited French manuscript. Unpublished.

———. *The Seminar of Jacques Lacan Book XXIII: Le Sinthome*. 1975–1976. Translated by Luke Thurston. Unpublished.

———. "The Subversion of the Subject and the Dialectic of Desire." 1966. In *Écrits: A Selection*. Translated by Bruce Fink. New York and London: W. W. Norton & Company, 2006, 671–702.

Lear, Jonathan. "Katharsis." In *Essays on Aristotles's Poetics*, edited by Amélie Oksenberg Rorty, 315–40. Princeton, NJ: Princeton University Press, 1992.

Leguil, Francois. "Le Stade de L'angoisse." In *La Cause Freudienne: Nouvele Revue de Psychanalyse* 59 (2005): 23–32.

Lorand, Ruth. "Beauty and Its Opposites." *The Journal of Aesthetics and Art Criticism* 52:4 (1994): 399–406.

Lyotard, Jean-François. *The Postmodern Condition: A Report on Knowledge.* Translated by Geoff Bennington and Brian Massumi. Minneapolis: University of Minnesota Press, 1984.

Martyn, David. *Sublime Failures.* Detroit, MI: Wayne State University Press, 2002.

Mattick Jr., Paul. "Aesthetics and Anti-Aesthetics in the Visual Arts." *The Journal of Aesthetics and Art Criticism* 51:2 (1993): 253–59.

Miller, Jacques-Alain. "The Analytic Experience: Means, Ends, and Results." In *Lacan and the Subject of Language,* edited by Ellie Ragland-Sullivan and Mark Bracher, 83–99. New York and London: Routledge, 1991.

———. "Introduction à la lecture de Séminaire de l'angoisse de Jacques Lacan." *La Cause Freudienne* 58 (2004): 61–100.

———. "Introduction à la lecture de Séminaire de l'angoisse de Jacques Lacan." *La Cause Freudienne* 59 (2004): 67–103.

———. "Joyce avec Lacan." *La Cause Freudienne: Revue de Psychanalyse* 38 (1998): 7–20.

———. "Reflections on the Formal Envelope of the Symptom." *Lacanian Ink* 4 (1991): 13–21.

———. "*Sept rémarques de Jacques-Alain Miller sur la création.*" *La lettere mensualle, Ecole de la cause Freudienne* 68 (1988): 9–13.

Mundry, Jennifer, ed. *Surrealism: Desire Unbound*. London: Tate, 2001.

Nasio, Juan-David. *The Book of Love and Pain: Thinking at the Limit with Freud and Lacan.* Translated by David Pettigrew and Francois Raffoul. Albany: State University of New York Press, 2004.

Nussbaum, Martha. "Tragedy and Self-Sufficiency: Plato and Aristotle on Fear and Pity." In *Essays on Aristotle's Poetics,* edited by Amélie Oksenberg Rorty, 261–90. Princeton, NJ: Princeton University Press, 1992.

Rabaté, Jean-Michel. *Jacques Lacan: Psychoanalysis and the Subject of Literature.* New York: Palgrave, 2001.

Ragland, Ellie, and Dragan Milovanovic. "Introduction: Topologically Speaking." In *Lacan: Topologically Speaking,* edited by E. Ragland and D. Milovanovic, xiii–xl. New York: Other Press, 2004.

Regnault, François. *Conférences d'Esthétique Lacanienne.* Paris: Éditions Agalma, Diffusion Seuil, 1997.

Reinhardt, Kenneth. "Kant with Sade, Lacan with Levinas." *MLN* 110:4 (1995): 785–808.

Ronen, Ruth. *Representing the Real.* Amsterdam and New York: Rodopi, 2002.

Shepherdson, Charles. "Lacan and Philosophy." In *The Cambridge Companion to Lacan,* edited by J-M.Rabaté, 125–52. Cambridge: Cambridge University Press, 2003.

Shier, David. "Why Kant Finds Nothing Ugly." *British Journal of Aesthetics* 38:4 (1998): 412–18.

Steinbrenner, Jakob. "The Unimaginable." *History and Theory* 37:4 (1998): 115–26.

Van Haute, Philippe. *Against Adaptation: Lacan's "Subversion" of the Subject.* New York: Other Press, 2002.

Zangwill, Nick. "The Beautiful, the Dainty, and the Dumpy." *British Journal of Aesthetics* 35:4 (1995): 317–29.

———. "Two Dogmas of Kantian Aesthetics." In *Selected Papers,* edited by Richard Woodfield, 233–38. Nottingham: Nottingham Polytechnic Press, 1990.

Zizek, Slavoj. *For They Know Not What They Say: Enjoyment as a Political Factor.* London and New York: Verso, 1991.

———. *The Indivisible Remainder.* London and New York: Verso, 1996.

———. *The Sublime Object of Ideology.* London and New York: Verso, 1989.

Zupančič, Alenka. *Ethics of the Real: Kant, Lacan.* London and New York: Verso, 2000.

———. "The Splendor of Creation: Kant, Nietzsche, Lacan." *Umbra: A Journal of the Unconscious,* 1 (1999): 35–42.

INDEX